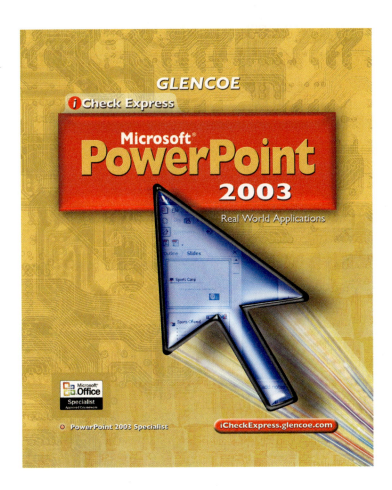

Lead Consultants

C. Jacqueline Schultz, Ph.D.
Career and Business Education Instructor
Warrensville Heights High School
Warrensville Heights, Ohio

Linda Wooldridge, M.B.A.
School of Information Technology Instructor
Santa Susana High School
Simi Valley, California

New York, New York   Columbus, Ohio   Chicago, Illinois   Peoria, Illinois   Woodland Hills, California

Copyright © 2006 by the McGraw-Hill Companies, Inc. All rights reserved. Except as permitted under the United States Copyright Act, no part of this publication may be reproduced or distributed in any form or by any means, or stored in a database or retrieval system, without prior written permission of the publisher.

Microsoft, Microsoft Office, Microsoft Word, Microsoft Excel, Microsoft Access, Microsoft PowerPoint, Internet Explorer, and Windows and all other Microsoft names and logos are trademarks or registered trademarks of Microsoft Corporation in the United States and/or other countries.

All other brand names are trademarks or registered trademarks of their respective companies.

Glencoe/McGraw-Hill is independent from Microsoft Corporation, and not affiliated with Microsoft in any manner. This publication may be used in assisting students to prepare for a Microsoft Office Specialist Exam. Neither Microsoft, its designated program administrator or courseware reviewer, nor Glencoe/McGraw-Hill warrants that use of this publication will ensure passing.

Between the time that Web site information is gathered and published, it is not unusual for some sites to have changed URLs or closed. URLs will be updated in reprints or on the Online Resource Center when possible.

Printed in the United States of America

Send all inquiries to:

Glencoe/McGraw-Hill
21600 Oxnard Street, Suite 500
Woodland Hills, CA 91367

ISBN 0-07-869037-4 (Student Edition)
ISBN 0-07-872881-9 (Teacher Annotated Edition)

1 2 3 4 5 6 7 8 9 027 10 09 08 07 06 05

Advisory Review Board

Elisa Bunn
East Coweta High School
Sharpsburg, Georgia

Gordon S. DeFacis
Mifflinburg Area High School
Mifflinburg, Pennsylvania

Dawn Johnston
Northwestern High School
Kokomo, Indiana

Judie Reasons
Peabody High School
Trenton, Tennessee

David Salem
John Dewey High School
Brooklyn, New York

Dan Shuster
Royal High School
Simi Valley, California

Kelley Todd
Van Buren High School
Van Buren, Arkansas

Reviewers

Juana Benson
Guthrie High School
Guthrie, Oklahoma

Doug Bergman
Porter-Gaud School
Charleston, South Carolina

Robert Bloom
Chaparral High School
Las Vegas, Nevada

Scott Ciarlone
Cohoes High School
Cohoes, New York

Earl W. Cobb
Hilldale High School
Muskogee, Oklahoma

Suzi Cotton
Pea Ridge High School
Pea Ridge, Arkansas

Daryl Daniels
New Milford High School
New Milford, Connecticut

Carol Evans
Adolfo Camarillo High School
Camarillo, California

Leah Franco
Comanche High School
Comanche, Texas

Lori C. Houck
Anderson County High
Clinton, Tennessee

Margaret Irby
Permian High School
Odessa, Texas

Regina W. Johnson
McBee High School
McBee, South Carolina

Robert Kane
Newton North High School
Newtonville, Massachusetts

Dorothy Lewis
Dougherty Comprehensive
   High School
Albany, Georgia

Angie Marquart
Clear Fork High School
Bellville, Ohio

Linda Robinson
Winter Haven High School
Winter Haven, Florida

Ann Rosborough
Decatur Middle School
Indianapolis, Indiana

Joan Staley
Grayslake High School
Grayslake, Illinois

Gwin D. Wyatt
Murrah High School
Jackson, Mississippi

Table of Contents

Why Study Computer Applications?	xvi
Be an Active Reader	ix
Take the iCheck Office 2003 Cyberhunt	xi
Operating Your Computer	xiv
Using Student Data Files	xiv
Student Online Learning Center	xv
Technology Standards Overview	xvii
Technology Handbook	H1
Part 1: Hardware	H2
Part 2: Software	H13
Part 3: Ready, Set, Process	H18
Part 4: Living Online	H31
Part 5: Outlook and Productivity Tools	H41

Unit 1 PowerPoint 2003: The Power of Presentations — 1

Career Facts	2
Before You Begin	3

LESSON 1 PowerPoint Basics — 4

EXERCISES

1-1	Identify Parts of the PowerPoint Screen	7
1-2	Use Toolbars and Menus	8
1-3	Use the Task Pane	9
1-4	View a Presentation in Normal View	10
1-5	Create a New Folder	11
1-6	Name and Save a Presentation	12
1-7	Switch Between Slides Pane and Outline Pane	13
1-8	Use Slide Sorter View	14
1-9	Move Among Slides	15
1-10	Add Text to a Slide	16
1-11	Edit Text on a Slide	17
1-12	Set Up and Run a Slide Show	18
1-13	Select Slides for a Show	19
1-14	Use the Help Feature	20
1-15	Preview a Presentation	21
1-16	Print Slides	22
1-17	Print a Presentation Handout	23
1-18	Close a Presentation	24

● Quick Reference	26
● Concept Review	27
● Practice It Activities	28
● You Try It Activities	31
● Critical Thinking Activities	33
● Challenge Yourself Projects	34

LESSON 2 Create Content and Collaborate — 35

EXERCISES

2-1	Create a Presentation Using a Template	38
2-2	Add Text to Slides	39
2-3	Delete Text from Slides	40
2-4	Import Text from Other Sources	41
2-5	Promote and Demote Text	42
2-6	Create a Diagram	43
2-7	Create a Table	45
2-8	Add Clip Art to a Slide	46

Table of Contents

2-9	Create a Chart	48
2-10	Add a Picture to a Slide	50
2-11	Add Shapes to Slides	51
2-12	Add WordArt to a Slide	52
2-13	Insert an Object into a Presentation	53
2-14	Use the Thesaurus	55
2-15	Use the Spelling Checker	56
2-16	Add, Edit, and Delete Comments	57
2-17	Compare and Merge Presentations	58
2-18	Track, Accept, and Reject Changes	59
2-19	Create a Presentation with the AutoContent Wizard	60

- Quick Reference — 63
- Concept Review — 64
- Practice It Activities — 65
- You Try It Activities — 68
- Critical Thinking Activities — 70
- Challenge Yourself Projects — 71

LESSON 3 Formatting Content — 72

EXERCISES

3-1	Apply Design Templates	75
3-2	Customize Slide Backgrounds	76
3-3	Modify Slide Layout	77
3-4	Modify Fonts and Font Styles	78
3-5	Modify Font Size and Color	79
3-6	Align Text	80
3-7	Modify Bulleted Lists	81
3-8	Change the Size and Color of a Graphic	82
3-9	Add an Effect to a Graphic	83
3-10	Format and Add an Effect to a Shape	84
3-11	Rotate, Resize, and Recolor a Picture	86
3-12	Align and Connect Pictures	87
3-13	Add Effects to Connectors and Pictures	89
3-14	Rotate and Align Shapes and Other Graphics	90
3-15	Apply an Animation Scheme	91
3-16	Apply Transition Effects and Run the Slide Show	92
3-17	Modify Page Setup	93
3-18	Customize a Template	94
3-19	Use a Title Master	95
3-20	Use a Slide Master	96
3-21	Add, Delete, and Modify Placeholders	97
3-22	Use Footers and Headers	98

- Quick Reference — 100
- Concept Review — 101
- Practice It Activities — 102
- You Try It Activities — 105
- Critical Thinking Activities — 107
- Challenge Yourself Projects — 108

LESSON 4 Managing Presentations — 109

EXERCISES

4-1	Add, Delete, and Rearrange Slides	112
4-2	Copy Slides Between Presentations	113
4-3	Add Hyperlinks to Slides	114
4-4	Create and Modify an Action Button	116
4-5	Display Grids and Guides	117
4-6	Use Notes Pages and Zoom Views	118
4-7	Print Outlines and Speaker Notes	119

Table of Contents

4-8	Change Preview Options	120
4-9	Modify Printing Options	121
4-10	Hide Slides	122
4-11	Create and Edit a Custom Show	123
4-12	Navigate in Slide Show View	125
4-13	Use Pens, Highlighters, and Arrows	126
4-14	Rehearse and Save Timings	127
4-15	Package Presentations for Storage on a CD	128
4-16	Save Slides with Different Names and Formats in Different Folders	130
4-17	Save Presentations as Web Pages	131
4-18	Publish Presentations as Web Pages	132
4-19	Export a Presentation to Microsoft Word	133

- **Quick Reference** — 135
- **Concept Review** — 136
- **Practice It Activities** — 137
- **You Try It Activities** — 140
- **Critical Thinking Activities** — 142
- **Challenge Yourself Projects** — 143

Unit Review

Making Connections	144
Ethics in Action	145
Portfolio Project	146
Appendix A: Quick Reference Summary	151
Appendix B: Microsoft Office Specialist Certification	156
Glossary	158
Glosario	161
Index	164
Image Credits	169

Features

Writing Matters

| Know Your Audience | 25 |
| Understanding Copyrights | 99 |

21st Century Learner

| Develop Media Literacy | 62 |
| Communicate Effectively | 134 |

To The Student

Why Study Computer Applications?

When you master the computer skills used in Microsoft Office 2003, you will benefit in both your business and academic careers. There is no business today that is untouched by computers. Whether you plan to become a mechanic, an architect, a photographer, or the CEO of a corporation, you will be expected to know some basic computer applications. In any business, time is money. People who can use the computer to save time gives themselves a competitive advantage in the job market.

A book report that is free of misspelled words or a research paper that includes citations and footnotes will result in better grades. The student who knows how to import tables or graphics into a report will be able to make a stronger case for a particular point of view.

The architectural firm described below illustrates how Microsoft Office is used in every aspect of a typical business.

- **Microsoft Word** is used to generate detailed drawing notes that are inserted into computer-aided-drafting. Large projects require specification books that are thousands of pages long to make sure builders meet critical safety codes. Careful documentation is required in memo form to communicate with every member of a design team.

- **Microsoft Excel** is used to calculate costs for code requirements. Excel files are inserted into computer-drafted drawings for door schedules, window schedules, and finish schedules. Area calculations for large buildings use Excel spreadsheets to calculate that the required space is provided to exit a building in the case of an emergency.

To The Student

Why Study Computer Applications? (Continued)

- **Microsoft Access** databases are used to track the use of building materials on a project. Databases are also used to track documentation and to manage the contact information for the many members of design and construction teams.

- **Microsoft PowerPoint** is used by the initial architect to communicate his or her ideas to clients and to the community. PowerPoint is the tool used to create presentations in many industries and professions.

- **Microsoft Outlook** extends beyond sending and receiving e-mail. It is an organizational tool that allows team members to schedule meetings with design team members, check their schedules, and organize communication to groups within the team.

The managers in an architecture firm require all staff members from architects to accountants to administrative personnel to know these software applications well. In today's competitive job market, the person with the greatest computer abilities is often placed at the top of the hiring list.

Throughout the book, you will notice this logo. This logo indicates that the exercise or activity meets one of the **Microsoft Office Specialist** standards. These standards cover topics from the Microsoft Office Specialist certification exam.

The Microsoft Office Specialist logo means that this book has been approved by the Microsoft Office Specialist Program to help you master Microsoft Office desktop applications. This book can also help you prepare for the Microsoft Office Specialist certification exam. For more information about Microsoft Office Specialist certification, see page 156.

To The Student

Be an Active Reader!

When you read this textbook, you are gaining insights into technology and how it is used in the world around you. This textbook is an example of non-fiction writing—it describes real-world ideas and facts. It is also an example of technical writing because it explains and demonstrates in detail how to use technology.

Here are some reading strategies that will help you become an active textbook reader. Choose the strategies that work best for you. If you have trouble as you read your textbook, look back at these strategies for help.

Before You Read

Set a Purpose
- Why are you reading the textbook?
- How might you be able to use what you learn in your own life?

Preview
- Read the lesson title to find out what the topic will be.
- Read the subtitles to see what you will learn about the topic.
- Skim the screen captures, photos, charts, or graphs.
- Look for vocabulary words that are boldfaced and highlighted. How are they defined?

Draw From
- What do you already know about the topic?
- How is the new information different from what you already know?

Image Credits

Courtesy of Adesso Inc. H4(tc); Scott Barrow 143(tl); Vincent Besnault/Getty Images H2(tr); Bettmann/CORBIS H31; Mark Burnett H7(bl), H8(cl); Cooperphoto/CORBIS H7(br); Images 71(bl); Bob Daemmerich/PhotoEdit 147; Dex Images/CORBIS H2(b); Hunter Freeman Photography 2002/Courtesy Apple Computer, Inc. H3(cr); Tony Freeman/PhotoEdit H9(tl), 134; Tim Fuller Photography 109; Richard G./StockImage/Age Fotostock 34(bl); Glencoe/McGraw-Hill H9(tr); Charles Gupton/CORBIS 4; Aaron Haupt H3(br); Hewlett Packard H8(tr); Courtesy of International Business Machines Corporation. Unauthorized use not permitted. H2(c), H4(c), H5(tcl), H5(tl), H32(br); Intel Corporation ©2002 H6(br); Courtesy of Iomega Corporation H7(bc); Lou Jones/Getty Images 148; Ken Karp 108; Lars Klove/Getty Images H5(c); Lawrence Manning/Royalty Free/CORBIS H3(tc), H8(cr); Mug Shots/ Corbis H2(cl); Dwayne Newton/PhotoEdit 62; Michael Newman/PhotoEdit H2(tr), H9(bl), H9(br), 149; Nikon USA H4(br); Richard T. Nowitz/Phototake Inc./Alamy Images H33(l); Gabe Palmer/CORBIS 72; Jose L. Pelaez/CORBIS xv; Mark Richards/PhotoEdit H39; Bill Ross/CORBIS 71(tl); Charles E. Rotkin/CORBIS H32(tr); Royalty-Free H33(c); Royalty-free/BananaStock/Alamy Images H34; Royalty Free/CORBIS H3(cl), H4(cr), H5(tr), H33(r); Royalty-free/Digital Vision/Getty Images vi; Royalty-free/Masterfile H2(tl); Royalty-free/Photodisc/Getty Images H9(cl), ix, xvii, 35; Royalty-free/Stockbyte/Getty Images 108(tl); Royalty-free/Stockbyte/SuperStock 25; RyanStock/Getty Images vii; Seagate H7(tl), H7(tr); Juan Manuel Silva/Age Fotostock 1; Phillip and Karen Smith/SuperStock H2(cr); Courtesy of Sony H4(bcr), H5(b), H8(bl); David Stoecklein/CORBIS 144; Superstock 37(r); Stephen Swintek/Getty Images H3(bl); William Whitehurst/CORBIS H4(cl); David Young-Wolff/PhotoEdit H16(r), 34(tl), 143(bl); Vaughn Youtz/Zuma/CORBIS H4(bcl).

Abbreviation Key: MS = Screen shots used by permission from Microsoft Corporation.

© 1981-2001 MS Windows XP, H13, H15–H16, H19–H28; © 1983-2003 MS Explorer, H37; National Park Service, H37, H38; © 2005 Google, H38; ©1983-2003 MS Outlook, H41-H44; © 2004 Microsoft Corporation. All rights reserved., H43; © 1983-2001 MS PowerPoint, 3, 7-24, 28-32, 38-61, 65-69, 75-98, 102-106, 112-132, 137-141, 146; © Fender Musical Instruments Corporation. All rights reserved. 99.

To The Student

As You Read

Question
- What is the main idea?
- How well do the details support the main idea?
- How do the photos, charts, graphs, and maps support the main idea?

Connect
- Think about people, places, and events in your own life. Are there any similarities with those in your textbook?

Predict
- Predict events or outcomes by using clues and information that you already know.
- Change your predictions as you read and gather new information.

Visualize
- Use your imagination to picture the settings, actions, and people that are described.
- Create graphic organizers to help you see relationships found in the information.

IF YOU DON'T KNOW WHAT A WORD MEANS...

- think about the setting, or context, in which the word is used.
- check if prefixes such as *un-*, *non-*, or *pre-* can help you break down the word.
- look up the word's definition in a dictionary or glossary.

READING DOs
Do...
- ✓ establish a purpose for reading.
- ✓ think about how your own experiences relate to the topic.
- ✓ try different reading strategies.

READING DON'Ts
Don't...
- ⊘ ignore how the textbook is organized.
- ⊘ allow yourself to be easily distracted.
- ⊘ hurry to finish the material.

After You Read

Summarize
- Describe the main idea and how the details support it.
- Use your own words to explain what you have read.

Assess
- What was the main idea?
- Did the text clearly support the main idea?
- Did you learn anything new from the material?
- Can you use this new information in other school subjects or at home?

Index

package for CD, 135
run, 26, 30
Slide Show button, 19
Slide Show toolbar, 125–126, 138
Slide Show View, 125
Slide Sorter toolbar, 122
Slide Sorter View, 14, 26, 29, 31, 91, 112
Slides
    add, 123
    arrange, 112
    change order, 29, 31, 33
    copy between presentations, 113, 142
    format with Design Template, 75–76
    from Word outline, 65
    hide, 122
    import text, 41
    insert from other presentations, 135
    insert from Word outline, 63
    move, 123
    navigate among, 15, 125
    per page, 121
    print, 22, 26, 30–31, 34, 57, 59, 135, 147
    print hidden, 122
    rearrange, 29, 31, 33, 112, 123, 137
    save in various formats, 130, 139
    select, 19
    store in folders, 130
Slides pane, 5, 13, 28, 115
Slides tab, 13
Snap to grid or guide, 110, 117
Source
    formatting, 113
Spacebar, 17–18, 29
Speaker notes, 119
Spelling checker, 56, 63, 67, 69–70
Standard toolbar, 3, 7
Status bar, 3, 5, 7
Sticky notes, 57
Study breaks, 72
Studying with friends, 35
Subordinate box, 44
Subtitle, 32, 39, 97
Switch
    panes in PowerPoint, 13
Synonyms, finding 63

T

Table
    create, 45
    defined, 36
    insert, 45, 63, 68, 71
Task pane
    Clip Art, 46–47, 65
    Custom Animation, 83, 106
    defined, 5
    Getting Started, 9
    Revisions, 36, 59, 69
    Search Results, 20
    Slide Design, 75, 91, 105
    Slide Layout, 9, 77, 102, 112

Thesaurus, 55
    use of, 9
Template, 60
Template
    customize, 94
    defined, 36
    design, 70–71, 75–76, 144, 148
    for presentation, 38, 70–71
Text
    add to slide, 16, 39
    align, 80
    bulleted, 39
    delete from slide, 40
    demote, 42, 63
    edit on slide, 17, 29, 31
    format, 103
    import to slides, 41
    keying, 17, 34
    placeholder for, 98
    promote, 42, 63, 65
    title, 94, 105
Text box, 16, 39, 80, 112
Thesaurus, 36, 55, 63, 70–71
Timings
    rehearse, 110, 127, 135, 141–142, 149
Title
    master, 95
    slide, 16
    text, 105
Title bar, 3, 5, 7
Title box, 112
Title master
    defined, 73
Title slide, 103
Title slide
    create, 32
    defined, 3
    new, 32
Title text, 94
Title text box, 40
Title-and-text slide
    defined, 3
Toolbar
    defined, 5
    Drawing, 51–52, 84, 86
    Formatting, 3, 7, 79, 112
    Organization Chart, 43, 66
    Outlining, 42, 119
    Rehearsal, 127
    Reviewing, 59
    Slide Master View, 95–97
    Slide Show, 125–126, 138
    Slide Sorter, 122
    Standard, 3, 7
    use of, 8
Toolbars
    displaying, 63
Track changes, 59
Tracking, 36, 59
Transition, 92, 100, 102, 107–108, 127, 135, 144, 148
Transition
    defined, 73

Transparency, 84–85
TrueType fonts, 129, 140
Typeface, 73, 78

U

Unapply button, 59, 67
Underline, 100
Understanding audiences, 4, 19, 25, 31, 33, 75, 107–108, 134
Ungroup objects, 100
United States Department of Labor, 2

V

View
    Normal, 10, 14, 29, 91, 97, 104, 112
    Notes Page, 118
    Outline, 119
    Slide Master, 95–96, 100
    Slide Show, 125
    Slide Sorter, 14, 26, 29, 31, 91, 112, 122, 137–138, 147
Volunteering, 14

W

Web page
    convert presentation to 131–132, 135, 139, 141
    preview, 131
Web server, 110, 132
Window
    Help, 20
Wipe effect, 89
Wizard
    AutoContent, 36, 60–61, 70, 147, 149
Word
    delete, 17
    import outline into PowerPoint, 41
    select, 17
WordArt, 69–70, 148
WordArt
    add to slide, 52
    defined, 36
    format, 82, 100
    insert, 63, 66
    insert on slide, 52
    modify, 106
    rotate, 90

Z

Zoom, 21, 93, 98, 118–119, 135, 140
Zoom, faded, 91

To The Student

Take the iCheck Microsoft Office 2003

Cyberhunt!

Did you know that your text contains many features that can **make learning easier for you?** Explore how to get the most out of your textbook by following the clues on pages xi–xii to discover useful features, activities, tips and tools that are integrated into the lessons in this text. Then use these elements to help reach your computer applications learning goals.

Clue #1

It is easier to learn a new skill if you understand how this knowledge will help you get ahead and stay ahead. How could learning PowerPoint help you share information? (Hint: See **Why It Matters** on page 1.)

Clue #2

You will move through the lessons more quickly if you know the basics before you begin. What should you already know about creating presentations to help you succeed with the lessons? (Hint: See **Before You Begin** on page 3.)

Clue #3

Improving interpersonal ("soft") skills, such as communicating and goal setting, help you achieve in all your school classes and in work and daily life. What feature on page 133 discusses the importance of communicating effectively? (Hint: Interpersonal skills are even more important **today and going forward** than ever!)

Clue #4

Learning new skills is made easier by breaking them into small steps, so any one task or exercise does not seem too hard or time consuming. How many **steps** does it take to complete the exercise Use Footers and Headers? (Hint: See page 98.)

Index

merge, 58, 67
Presentations, uses for, 4
Preview
    Design Template, 38
    graphic effect, 83
    options, 120
    outlines, 119
    presentation, 21, 26
    presentation as Web page, 131
    speaker notes, 119
Print
    comments, 138
    handouts, 30, 33–34, 135, 139, 148
    hidden slides, 122
    multiple slides per page, 23
    notes, 134, 142
    options, 121
    outline, 142
    outlines, 119
    presentation, 22, 26, 34, 57, 59, 143
    presentation handouts, 23
    range, 121
    slides, 22, 26, 30–31, 34, 57, 59, 135, 147
    speaker notes, 119
Print Preview, 21, 26, 120, 140
Print Preview
    defined, 110
Print range, 22
Print What, 120
Promote
    defined, 36
    text, 65
Promote text, 42, 63
Proofreading, 147–148
Publish
    defined, 110
Publish presentation as Web page, 132

R

Rearrange
    slides, 29, 31, 33, 112, 123, 137
Recolor
    Clip Art, 86
    picture, 106
Rehearsal toolbar, 127
Rehearse timings, 127, 135, 141–142, 149
Reject changes, 59, 63
Remove
    hyperlink from slide, 115
    slide transition, 92
Rename
    presentation, 130
Research task pane, 55
Resize
    chart, 49
    Clip Art, 47, 65, 77, 86, 93
    graphic, 82, 103
    picture, 50, 68, 86
    placeholder, 97
    shape, 84
Reviewing toolbar, 59

Revisions task pane, 36, 59, 69
Rich Text Format, 130, 139
Right
    align, 80, 100
Right-click, 11
Rotate
    Clip Art, 86
    defined, 73
    graphic, 106
    picture, 86
    shape, 90
    WordArt, 90
Run slide show, 18–19, 26, 30

S

Save
    presentation, 12, 26, 31
    slides in different formats, 130
    slides in various formats, 139
Save As, 26
Save as Web page, 135, 139, 141
Scanner, 50
Screen
    PowerPoint, 7, 28
ScreenTip, 3, 5, 8, 114–115
Scroll bar, 5, 15
Search
    for synonyms, 63
    PowerPoint Help, 20
Search Results task pane, 20
Select
    word, 17
Select All button, 49
Set
    transition times, 135
Set Up Show, 18–19, 30
Shadow, 94, 95–96, 100
Shadow style, 89
Shape
    create, 63
    effect, 84
    format, 84, 100
    insert, 63
    insert onto slide, 84
    modify, 106
    rotate, 90
    size, 84
Shapes
    add to slide, 51
    align, 90
    center, 90
    insert on slide, 51
Sharing information, 1
Shortcut menu, 125
Shortcuts
    for slide show, 135
    for slides, 125
    for slide–show navigation, 143
    keyboard, 55
    slide, 135
Size
    chart, 49

Clip Art, 86
    graphic, 82
    of bullets, 81
    of font, 79
    picture, 50, 86
    shape, 84
Sizing handles, 47, 49–50, 77, 97
Slide
    add, 112, 135
    add Clip Art, 46–47
    add content, 68
    add hyperlink, 114
    add picture, 50
    add shapes, 51
    add text, 16, 39
    add WordArt, 52
    background, 76, 149
    bulleted list, 16, 33–34, 39
    change order, 20
    create, 34, 39, 65
    defined, 3
    delete, 112, 135
    delete text, 40
    design, 100, 102
    edit, 17
    edit text, 29, 31
    format, 102, 105, 107–108
    format text, 103
    hide, 135, 138
    insert picture, 50
    insert shapes, 51, 84
    insert WordArt, 52
    layout, 77, 100
    master, 95–96, 103, 108
    new, 34, 39, 66, 135
    shortcut menu, 125
    show, 3, 92
    subtitle, 3
    title, 3, 16, 103
    title and text, 3
    transition, 92, 100, 102, 107–108, 127, 144, 148
Slide button, 125
Slide Design task pane, 75, 91, 105
Slide Finder, 110, 113
Slide icon, 5, 13
Slide layout
    defined, 73
Slide Layout task pane, 9, 77, 102
Slide master
    defined, 73
Slide Master View, 95–96, 100
Slide Master View toolbar, 95–97
Slide pane, 7, 17
Slide pane
    defined, 5
    location, 3
Slide shortcut menu, 135
Slide show, 18–29, 123–124, 127
Slide show
    customize, 135, 141–143
    defined, 3
    exit, 26
    keyboard shortcuts, 135

To The Student

Clue #5
All people learn and progress at different rates. What feature in the Step-by-Step helps you move at your own pace by letting **you check** the way your screens should look at critical points throughout the Exercise? (Hint: See Exercise 2-17 on page 58.)

Clue #6
It takes many repetitions of a skill or action to become proficient. How many opportunities do you have **to practice** the computer application skill sets? (Hint: See pages 65–67.)

Clue #7
Summarizing key terms and concepts is a very useful tool for reviewing and reinforcing what you have learned. What two charts in each lesson summarize important information for you? (Hint: These charts provide a **quick reference** for **key terms** and **commands**.)

Clue #8
Reading, writing, and arithmetic are foundation skills for lifelong learning. In any career you choose, you will need to read competently and perform basic calculations. How can knowing your audience help you communicate more effectively? (Hint: See **Writing Matters** on page 25.)

Clue #9
Before an assessment, it can be helpful to know whether you have really learned the lessons. Where can you find a **self check** quiz on each lesson that will help you test yourself? (Hint: The quizzes are not in the text. See page 33.)

Clue #10
The real importance of learning new skills is to be able to **apply** this knowledge to create something of your own. What original **projects** do you create after completing the unit on PowerPoint? (Hint: Work that you create and collect together is called a **portfolio**.)

Index

L

Landscape orientation, 73, 93
Launch
    PowerPoint, 7, 28, 32, 68
Layout
    of slides, 100, 102, 112
    slide master, 97
Left
    align, 80, 100
Line color, 73, 82
List
    bulleted, 16, 84–85

M

Markups, 36, 58–59, 63
Master Layout, 97
Master slide, 103, 108
Master View, 103
Media literacy, 62
Menu, 5, 8
Menu bar, 3, 5, 7
Menu command, 5, 8
Merge
    presentations, 58, 67
Mnemonics, 109
Modify
    action button, 116
    background, 100
    bulleted list, 81
    bullets, 100
    Clip Art, 106
    font, 100
    graphic, 103
    placeholder, 97
    shape, 106
    slide layout, 77
    slide transition, 92
    WordArt, 106
Move
    among folders, 12
    among slides, 15
    slides, 123
Multiple
    slides, print on page, 23

N

Name
    folder, 11
    presentation, 12
Navigate
    among folders, 12
    among slides, 15, 125, 143
    among slides in browser, 132
Navigation
    keys, 15
New
    folder, 11, 32, 130–132, 139
    presentation from AutoContent Wizard, 60–61
    presentation, 26, 32, 34, 144
    presentation from template, 38
    slide, 34, 39, 66, 112, 135
    title slide, 32
Normal View, 10, 14, 29, 91, 97, 104
Notes
    print, 119, 135
Notes and Handouts, 104
Notes page, 98, 104, 135
Notes Page View, 118
Notes pane, 137, 140, 142
Number of copies, 121

O

Object
    defined, 36
    insert, 53–54, 63
Objects
    group, 100
    ungroup, 100
Occupational groups, 2
Open
    presentation, 26
Oral presentations, 33
Organization, 4, 32
Organization chart, 43–44, 63, 66, 71
Organizing thoughts, 4
Orientation
    landscape, 93
    portrait, 93, 146
Outline
    import from Word, 41
    insert in PowerPoint, 63
    preview, 119
    print, 119
Outline pane, 5, 13, 28, 31, 115, 119
Outline tab, 13, 40
Outline View, 119
Outlining toolbar, 42, 119

P

Package for CD, 110, 128, 135, 140, 143, 149
Page
    setup, 93, 100
Pane
    Notes, 137, 140, 142
    Outline, 13, 28, 31, 115, 119
    Presentation, 93
    slide, 7, 17
    Slides, 13, 28, 115
    Slides and Outline, 7
Panes
    switch between, 13
Peer teaching, 31
Pen tool, 126, 134, 138
Permissions, obtaining, 99
Picture
    add to slide, 50
    format, 86, 100, 103, 106
    insert, 63, 68, 70, 144
    insert on slide, 50
    recolor, 86, 106
    resize, 50, 68, 86
    rotate, 86, 106
    sources, 50
Pictures
    align, 87–88
    connect, 87–88
Pie chart, 48–49, 136, 142
Placeholder, 3, 38, 66, 73, 95, 97, 100
Pointer, 5, 7–8
Portrait orientation, 73, 93, 146
PowerPoint
    close, 24
    exit, 24, 26
    Help, 20, 26
    import Excel worksheet, 53–54
    import text, 41
    insert other applications, 53–54
    interface, 7, 28
    launch, 7, 28, 32, 68
    screen, 7, 28
    uses for, 34
    Viewer, 110, 128
Presentation, 10
Presentation
    accept changes, 59
    close, 26
    create, 26, 32, 34, 107–108, 142, 144, 146, 148
    create from AutoContent Wizard, 60–61
    create from template, 38
    customize, 141–143
    defined, 3
    edit, 33–34, 69–70, 140
    from template, 70–71
    handouts, 23
    insert object, 53–54
    insert other applications, 53–54
    name, 12
    new, 26, 32, 34, 144
    new from AutoContent Wizard, 60–61
    new from template, 38
    open, 26
    package for CD, 128, 140, 143, 149
    preview, 21, 26
    print, 22, 26, 57, 59, 143
    print handouts, 30, 33–34
    print slides, 34
    publish as Web page, 132
    reject changes, 59
    rename, 130
    save, 12, 26, 31
    save as Web page, 131, 141
    save in different formats, 130
    title, 61
    tools, 134
    track changes, 59
    type, 60
    uses for, 34
Presentation pane, 93
Presentations
    compare and merge, 58, 63, 67
    copy slides between, 113

To The Student

What Is Your Cyberhunt Skill Rating?

POINTS	CYBERHUNT RATING
90 to 100	You really know how to let your text work for you!
70 to 89	You know how to find your way around a text book!
Less than 70	Consider working with your teacher or a classmate to learn how to use your book more effectively—you will gain skills you can use your whole life.

Give yourself 10 points for each correct answer.

1. Many schools and businesses use PowerPoint to share information. Knowing Powerpoint can help you now and in business.

2. You should know the meanings of the following terms: presentation, slide show, slide, title slide, title and text slide, placeholder text, format, and edit.

3. 21st Century Learner

4. Eleven

5. iCheck

6. Three

7. Key Terms and Quick Reference

8. When you know your audience, you can better meet their needs.

9. Student Online Learning Center

10. Portfolio Project—Planning a Town Recreation Center: Part 1: Create a Slide, Part 2: Create a Certificate of Excellence, Part 3: Create a Presentation, Part 4: Create a Proposal

Index

word, 17
Demote text, 36, 42, 63
Design
    of slide, 100, 102
Design template, 38, 70–71, 75–76, 144, 148
Diagram
    create, 43–44
    defined, 36
    insert, 43–44, 63, 66
Dialog box, 5, 11
Digital camera, 50
Display
    grid and drawing guides, 117
    toolbars, 63
Double-click, 17
Drag
    slides, 29
    to draw AutoShapes, 51
Drawing toolbar, 51–52, 84, 86

E

Edit
    color scheme, 94
    comment, 57
    defined, 3
    presentation, 33–34, 69–70, 140
    slide show, 124
    slide text, 29, 31
    slide, 17
Effects
    animation, 105
    connectors, 89
    fill, 85
    graphic, 83, 106
    shape, 84
    transition, 92, 102, 107–108
Empathy, 4, 33
Enlarge
    Clip Art, 77
    picture, 50
Eraser tool, 126
Ethical behavior, 72, 107
Evaluate
    class officers, 145
    media messages, 62
Excel
    import into PowerPoint, 53–54
Exit
    PowerPoint, 24, 26
    slide show, 26

F

Fade, 102, 105
Faded zoom, 91
Felt tip pen, 126, 138, 142–143
Fill
    color, 73, 82, 89, 106
    effects, 85
Fit on page, 139
Fit on paper, 120–121
Fit on slide, 77, 93

Fit text, 43, 66
Fly In effect, 89
Folder
    create, 11, 32, 130–132, 139
    name, 11
    new, 11, 32, 130–132, 139
Folders
    navigate among, 12
Font
    color, 79, 100, 103, 105
    defined, 73
    modify, 78, 100
    size, 79, 95, 100
    style, 78, 95
Font style
    defined, 73
Footer, 73, 98, 100, 104, 108
Format
    defined, 3
    picture, 86, 100, 103, 106
    placeholder, 97
    shape, 84, 100
    slide, 102, 105, 107–108
    slide text, 103
    WordArt, 82, 100
Formats
    convert slides to, 139
Formatting
    defined, 73
    keeping source, 113
    toolbar, 7
    with design templates, 75–76
Formatting toolbar, 79, 112
Formatting toolbar
    location, 3

G

Getting involved, 35, 70, 145
Getting Started task pane, 9
Gradient, 73, 84–85
Graphics
    add effects, 106
    align, 90, 106
    center, 90
    color, 82
    effect, 83
    insert, 143, 148
    modify, 103
    resize, 103
    rotate, 106
    size, 82
Grayscale, 120
Grid and guides, 11, 110, 117, 135, 142–143
Group objects, 100
Guides, 110, 117, 141

H

Handouts, 23, 30, 33–34, 93, 98, 120–121, 134–135, 139, 148
Header, 73, 98, 100, 104, 120
Help

PowerPoint, 20, 26
Highlighter tool, 126, 134, 142–143
HTML, 110, 131–132
Hyperlink, 94, 116, 131, 135, 137–138, 143
Hyperlink
    add ScreenTip, 114
    add to slide, 114
    defined, 110
    edit, 116
    insert on slide, 114
    remove from slide, 115

I

Icon
    for animation, 83
    slide, 13
Import
    text to slides, 41
    Word outline, 41
Increase Font Size, 100
Initiative, taking, 109, 142
Ink, 126, 139
Insert
    AutoShape, 148
    chart, 48–49, 63
    Clip Art, 46–47, 63, 65, 70
    comment, 57, 63, 70
    diagram, 43–44, 63, 66
    graphic, 148
    hyperlink, 114, 135, 137, 143
    object, 63
    object into presentation, 53–54
    picture, 63, 68, 70, 144
    picture on slide, 50
    shape, 63, 84
    shapes on slide, 51
    slides from other presentations, 135
    slides from Word outline, 63
    table, 45, 63, 68, 71
    WordArt, 63, 66, 147
    WordArt on slide, 52
Insertion point, 5, 17
Interface
    PowerPoint, 7, 28
Internet access, 2
Internet research, 34, 107
Italic, 78, 100

J

Jobs,
    computer, 2
Justify, 80, 100

K

Key
    defined, 5
Keyboard, use for navigation, 15
Keyboard shortcuts, 55, 135, 143
Keying text, 17, 34

To The Student

Operating Your Computer

The following tips should be used to operate your computer correctly. Your teacher may provide you with additional instructions.

Turning the computer on
- ✓ Make sure there are no diskettes in the computer's diskette drive.
- ✓ Power on the computer and monitor.
- ✓ Wait for the start-up process to finish before starting any programs; you may be required to enter a network user ID and password at this time.
- ✓ Insert diskettes and/or CD-ROMs if necessary.

Turning the computer off
- ✓ Save data and files if necessary and close all windows.
- ✓ Remove any diskettes and CD-ROMs from the drives.
- ✓ Use the desktop shut-down procedure; click Start on the taskbar, click Shut Down, choose the Shut down option, and click OK.
- ✓ Power off the computer and monitor (if necessary).

Diskettes and CD-ROMs
- ✓ Handle diskettes and CD-ROMs carefully, holding them by the edges.
- ✓ Protect diskettes and CD-ROMs from dirt, scratches, moisture, extremes in temperature, and magnetic fields.
- ✓ Insert and remove diskettes and CD-ROMs gently.
- ✓ Do not attempt to remove a diskette or CD-ROM when the drive indicator light is on.

Work area
- ✓ Keep the area around your computer neat and free from dust and dirt.
- ✓ Do not eat or drink near your computer, as spilled food and drinks can cause damage to the computer.

Using Student Data Files

To complete some Exercises in this book, Data Files are required.

- When you see the Data File icon, locate the needed files before beginning the exercise.
- Data Files are available at the Student Online Learning Center at iCheck.glencoe.com and on the Teacher Resource CD. Your teacher will tell you where to find these files.
- Some exercises require you to continue working on a file you created in an earlier exercise. If you were absent and could not complete the previous exercise, your teacher may choose to provide you with the Solution File for the missed exercise.

Index

A

Accent, 94
Accept
   changes, 59, 63, 69
Action button, 110, 116, 135, 138, 142–143, 149
Add
   action button, 142–143
   Clip Art to slide, 46–47
   comment, 57
   effect to graphic, 83
   effect to shape, 84
   hyperlink to slide, 114
   picture to slide, 50
   placeholder, 97
   shapes to slide, 51
   slide, 112, 123, 135
   slide content, 68
   slide transition, 144
   text to slide, 16, 39
   WordArt to slide, 52
Alignment
   center, 80, 90, 100
   defined, 73
   graphics, 90, 106
   justify, 80
   left, 80, 100
   middle, 106
   pictures, 87–88
   right, 80, 100
   shapes, 90
   text, 80
Animation
   custom, 106
   icon, 83
   scheme, 73, 91, 100, 105
Annotation, 110, 138, 143, 149
Annotation pen, 135
Aly button, 59, 63, 67
Arrange
   slides, 112
Arrow tool, 126
Audiences, understanding, 4, 19, 25, 31, 33, 75, 107–108, 134
AutoContent Wizard, 36, 60–61, 70, 146, 148
AutoShapes, 51, 63, 69, 70, 84, 87–88, 100, 148

B

Background, 100, 102, 105
Background
   color, 94–95
   defined, 73
   of slides, 149
   slide, 76
Bold, 78, 100
Browser, 131–132
Bullet
   style, 95
Bulleted list, 84–85
Bulleted list
   modify, 81
   on slide, 16, 33–34, 39
Bullets
   color, 81
   modify, 100
   size, 81
Bullets and Numbering, 81, 103
Buttons, 5, 8

C

Careers, 2
CD
   package presentation for, 128, 135, 140, 143, 149
CD-ROM, 50
Cell, 45
Center, 80, 100
Center
   graphics, 90
   shapes, 90
Change
   color, 94
   slide order, 20, 29, 31, 33
Changes
   accept, 59, 63, 69
   reject, 59, 63
   track in PowerPoint, 59
Chart
   create, 48–49, 68
   defined, 36
   insert, 48–49, 63
   options, 49
   organization, 43–44, 63, 66, 71
   pie, 48–49, 137, 143
   resize, 49
Check
   spelling, 56, 63, 67, 69–70
Citizenship, 145
Clip Art
   add to slide, 46–47
   defined, 36
   insert, 63, 65, 70
   modify, 106
   recolor, 86
   resize, 47, 65, 77, 86, 93
   rotate, 86
Clip Art task pane, 46–47, 65
Close
   PowerPoint, 24
   presentation, 24, 26
Close Window, 9, 24, 28–29
Color
   background, 94–95
   change, 94
   fill, 89
   of bullets, 81
   of Clip Art, 86
   of font, 79
   of graphic, 82
   of lines, 73, 82
   of shape fills, 73, 82
   scheme, 73, 76, 94–95, 105
Color scheme
   defined, 73
Comment box, 57
Comments
   add, 57
   defined, 36
   delete, 57
   edit, 57
   insert, 57, 63, 70
   markup, 63
   print, 139
Compare and merge presentations, 36, 58, 63, 67
Computer jobs, 51
Connect pictures, 87–88
Connectors, 87–89, 106
Content
   defined, 36
   for slides, 36, 38, 60, 68
Copies, number of, 121
Copy
   slides between presentations, 113, 142
Copyright, 99
Create
   action button, 116, 135, 138
   chart, 48–49, 68
   company logo, 108
   diagram, 43–44
   employee orientation, 70
   flyer, 146
   folder, 11, 32, 130–132, 139
   hyperlink, 137
   organization chart, 43–44
   presentation, 26, 32, 34, 107–108, 142, 144, 146, 148
   presentation from AutoContent Wizard, 60–61
   presentation from template, 38
   shape, 63
   slide, 34, 39, 65
   slide show, 123–124, 141–142
   table, 45
   title slide, 32
Cursor, 17
Cursor
   defined, 5
Custom
   slide show, 123–124
Custom Animation task pane, 83, 106
Custom Show, 135, 141–143
Customize
   presentation, 141–143
   template, 94

D

Datasheet, 48–49
Datasheet
   defined, 36
Decrease Font Size, 100
Delete
   comment, 57
   placeholder, 97, 100
   slide, 112, 135
   text from slides, 40

To The Student

Student Online Learning Center

The Student Online Learning Center is an exciting Web site developed especially for students using *iCheck Express Microsoft PowerPoint 2003: Real World Applications*. The Student Online Learning Center offers you opportunities to review the material you have learned in the text so you will be prepared for quizzes and tests. It also offers additional information and copies of the data files you will use to complete the activities in the text.

Here is what you will find online:

- **Self Checks** These Self Checks provide you with ten multiple choice questions to help you review the material presented in the lesson. There is also a question called Troubleshooter where you will have to decide what is wrong and how to fix it.

- **Review** This is another opportunity to review the material presented in the lessons. You will review the material by playing one of the following games: Matching, Tic Tac Toe, Crossword Puzzle, Flying Answers, or Drag and Drop.

- **Keyboarding** The Student Online Learning Center provides a link to an optional Keyboarding program where you can brush up on your keyboarding skills.

iCheckExpress.glencoe.com

Glosario

Rotate/Rotar Dar vuelta a un objeto, generalmente 90 grados, a la derecha o a la izquierda. (p. 86)

S

ScreenTip/ScreenTip Descripción de un botón que aparece cuando apuntas hacia ese botón. (p. 8)

Scroll bar/Barra de desplazamienton Barra que se encuentra a la derecha o en la parte inferior de la pantalla y que te permite moverte hacia arriba o hacia abajo o a la izquierda o derecha de un documento. (p. 15)

Slide/Diapositiva Una página de una presentación. (p. 3)

Slide Finder/Buscador de diapositivas Despliega una miniatura de cada diapositiva en una presentación que tú puedes seleccionar e insertar en la presentación en uso actual. (p. 113)

Slide icon/Icono de diapositiva En el panel de Esquema, es la pequeña imagen de diapositiva localizada a un lado del contenido de la diapositiva. Haz clic en la imagen para moverte de una diapositiva a otra. (p. 13)

Slide layout/Diseño de la diapositiva Arreglo del texto y gráficos en una diapositiva. (p. 77)

Slide master/Master de diapositiva Diapositiva que sirve de modelo para las demás diapositivas en una presentación, excepto para la diapositiva del título. (p. 96)

Slide pane/Panel de diapositivas Parte de la pantalla de PowerPoint donde tú tecleas el texto. (p. 17)

Slide Show/Presentación de diapositivas Presentación que se muestra una diapositiva a la vez por medio del monitor de una computadora o un proyector. (p. 3)

Slides pane/Clasificador de diapositivas Panel que despliega miniaturas de las diapositivas en una presentación. (p. 13)

Slide Sorter View/Vista Ordenar Diapositivas Vista que puedes usar para agregar más diapositivas, borrar diapositivas o cambiar el orden de las diapositivas. (p. 14)

Snap/Alinear Ajustar algo a una cuadrícula o guía cuando se arrastra cerca de ella. (p. 117)

Status bar/Barra de estado Barra en la parte inferior de la pantalla que muestra información como el número de diapositiva actual y el número total de diapositivas en la presentación. (p. 7)

T

Table/Tabla Conjunto de filas y columnas en que se organiza la información. (p. 45)

Task pane/Panel de tareas Parte opcional de la pantalla de PowerPoint que ofrece un acceso fácil a tareas comunes. (p. 9)

Template/Plantilla Guía que contiene el formato de un documento específico. (p. 38)

Thesaurus/Diccionario de sinónimos (Tesoro) Colección de palabras con sus sinónimos, semejante a un diccionario. (p. 55)

Timing/Tiempo de transición Característica de PowerPoint que determina el tiempo que dura visible una diapositiva durante una presentación antes de moverse automáticamente a la siguiente. (p. 127)

Title bar/Barra de título La barra en la parte superior de la pantalla que muestra el nombre de la presentación en uso. (p. 7)

Title master/Master de título Diapositiva que sirve de modelo para la diapositiva del Título. (p. 95)

Title slide/Diapositiva de título Diapositiva que contiene el título de una presentación. Normalmente es la primera diapositiva de una presentación. (p. 3)

Title and text slide/Diapositiva de título y texto Diapositiva que contiene un título con texto abajo. Con frecuencia el texto tiene el formato de una lista con viñetas. (p. 3)

Toolbar/Barra de herramientas La barra que contiene botones que se pueden pulsar para ejecutar diferentes tareas. (p. 8)

Tracking/Control de cambios Característica que muestra todos los cambios hechos en una presentación por un revisor. Los cambios que hacen varias personas se distinguen por usar colores diferentes. (p. 59)

Transition/Transición Efecto que ocurre entre diapositivas en una presentación visual. (p. 92)

Typeface/Tipo de letra El diseño de un conjunto de caracteres. (También llamado fuente.) (p. 78)

W

Web server/Servidor de web Computadora en la Internet que almacena páginas web. (p. 132)

WordArt/WordArt Texto decorativo que se sombra, se rota, se extiende o se ajusta a formas predefinidas. (p. 52)

To The Student

Student Online Learning Center (Continued)

- **Activities and Answers** Additional activities and answers to the PowerUp Activities, which appear at the beginning of each unit, are provided in this section of the Student Online Learning Center.

- **Data Files** The data files you will need to complete the exercises in *iCheck Express Microsoft PowerPoint 2003: Real World Applications* are provided at the Student Online Learning Center for your convenience.

- **TechSIM™ Interactive Tutorials** Three simulation tutorials are provided to help you learn more about electronic mail, file management, and how to use the control panel. These interactive, animated tutorials will walk you through basic information in these three areas.

- **Resource Links** This part of the Student Online Learning Center will provide you with links you will need to complete the Internet research activities located throughout the text.

iCheckExpress.glencoe.com

Glosario

Grid/Cuadrícula Serie de líneas verticales y horizontales puesta sobre una diapositiva para ayudarte a alinear objetos. (p. 117)

Guide/Guía Línea vertical u horizontal que se coloca en una diapositiva para alinear los objetos. (p. 117)

Header/Encabezado Texto que aparece en la parte superior de cada página de notas o página impresa de la presentación. (p. 98)

HTML Ve *Hypertext Markup Language/Lenguaje de Marcado de Hipertexto.*

Hyperlink/Hiperenlace (Hipervínculo) Texto o botón que al hacer clic te dirige a otra diapositva de la presentación, abre otro archivo o abre una página web. (p. 114)

Hypertext Markup Language (HTML)/ Lenguaje de Marcado de Hipertexto (HTML) Lenguaje de programación que usan los navegantes de Internet para leer y desplegar páginas web. (p. 131)

Insertion point/Punto de inserción Barra vertical parpadeante que indica el punto en que aparecerá el texto que se ha ingresado. También se llama cursor. (p. 17)

Key/Teclear Teclear texto en un documento. (p. 17)

Landscape/Orientación horizontal Orientación de una diapositiva que se muestra más ancha que alta. (p. 93)

Line color/Color de línea Color aplicado a una línea o al borde de una forma. (p. 82)

Markups/Marcas Cuadros de leyendas que contienen el nombre del revisor, la fecha y detalles de los comentarios y cambios que se hicieron. (p. 58)

Menu/Menú Una lista de commandos relacionados. (p. 8)

Menu bar/Barra de menús Una barra que muestra los nombres de los menús disponibles. (p. 7)

Menu command/Comando de menú Una opción individual de un menú. (p. 8)

Object/Objeto Documento, figura, hoja de trabajo, presentación o cualquier otro objeto que pueda ser insertado en un archivo abierto en otra aplicación. (p. 53)

Outline pane/Panel de esquema Panel que despliega la vista de esquema o el texto de la presentación. (p. 13)

Package for CD/Empaquetar para CD Modo rápido de agrupar una presentación de PowerPoint y todos los archivos relacionados (tales como archivos vinculados y el Visor de PowerPoint) dentro de una sola carpeta. (p. 128)

Placeholder text/Marcador de posición Texto que te dice qué tipo de contenido debe ir en las diferentes áreas de una diapositiva. (p. 3)

Pointer/Apuntador (Puntero) Flecha que se usa para seleccionar objetos en pantalla como menús y botones. (p. 7)

Portrait/Orientación vertical Orientación de una diapositiva que es más alta que ancha. (p. 93)

PowerPoint Viewer/Visor de PowerPoint Aplicación de computadora que te permite ver una diapositiva sin usar PowerPoint. (p. 128)

Presentation/Presentación Archivo de PowerPoint. Una presentación puede incluir texto, fotos, gráficas, vínculos a otras páginas y otros objetos. (p. 3)

Print Preview/Vista Preliminar Vista preliminar de las diapositivas que se imprimirán. (p. 120)

Promote/Aumentar nivel En esquemas, cambia el texto seleccionado al siguiente nivel superior de encabezado (subir un nivel, mover a la izquierda). (p. 42)

Publish/Publicar Copiar los archivos necesarios HTML en un servidor de la web para que puedan verse por Internet. (p. 132)

Revisions task pane/Panel de revisiones Te permite ver fácil y rápidamente una lista de sugerencias de cambios para una presentación. (p. 59)

Technology Standards

ISTE and NETS

The International Society for Technology in Education (ISTE) has developed National Educational Technology Standards to define educational technology standards for students (NETS-S). The activities in this book are designed to meet ISTE standards. The Standards box on each lesson opening page indicates which standards and performance indicators are covered in the lesson.

NETS-S Standards

To live, learn, and work successfully in an increasingly complex and information-rich society, students must be able to use technology effectively. The ISTE standards identify skills that students can practice and master in school, but the skills are also used outside of school, at home, and at work. For more information about ISTE and the NETS, please visit www.iste.org.

Glosario

A

Action Button/Botón de acción Botón que cuando se pulsa ejecuta una acción en una presentación de diapositivas, como avanzar a otra diapositiva. (p. 116)

Alignment/Alineación Posición del texto y de gráficos en relación con los márgenes de un cuadro de texto y con otro texto y otros gráficos de una diapositiva. (p. 80)

Animation scheme/Esquema de animación Efecto que cuando se aplica hace que el texto y los gráficos se muevan y se desplieguen de manera específica. (p. 91)

Annotation/Anotación Marca o nota que se hace con una herramienta de pluma cuando se ve una diapositiva. (p. 126)

AutoContent wizard/Asistente para Autocontenido Herramienta que te ayuda a hacer una presentación profesional. (p. 60)

B

Background/Fondo (Segundo plano) Colores, estampados o figuras que llenan toda la diapositiva y aparecen detrás del contenido de la diapositiva. (p. 76)

Button/Botón Icono gráfico en el que se hace clic para efectuar una tarea específica. (p. 8)

C

Chart/Gráfica (Gráfico) Presentación gráfica de información. (p. 48)

Clip Art/Imágenes prediseñadas Gráficos que se han hecho previamente y que pueden insertarse en una presentación. (p. 46)

Color scheme/Esquema de color Los ocho colores usados en el diseño de una diapositiva. Cada plantilla de diseño tiene un esquema de color que se usa para el fondo de la presentación, el texto y las líneas, el sombreado, texto del título, llenados, acentos e hipervínculos. (p. 76)

Comments/Comentarios Notas que pueden agregarse a una presentación sin que aparezcan como cambios reales en la presentación. (p. 57)

Compare and Merge/Comparar y combinar Herramienta para combinar los comentarios y las revisiones que se han hecho a múltiples copias de la misma presentación en una sola presentación. (p. 58)

Content/Contenido Texto y gráficos que se incluyen en una diapositiva. (p. 74)

Cursor/Cursor Marca parpadeante que te indica en qué parte de la pantalla aparecerá el texto que tecleaste. También se llama punto de inserción. (p. 17)

D

Datasheet/Hoja de datos Contiene información en las celdas. Semejante a la hoja de cálculo. (p. 48)

Demote/Disminuir nivel En esquemas, cambia el texto seleccionado al siguiente nivel inferior de encabezado (bajar un nivel, mover a la derecha). (p. 42)

Diagram/Diagrama Gráfico que te dice cómo organizar y presentar visualmente la información en una diapositiva. (p. 43)

Dialog box/Cuadro de diálogo Cuadro que se usa para ingresar información específica para realizar una tarea particular así como nombrar y guardar un documento. (p. 11)

E

Edit/Editar Hacer cambios al contenido de una presentación. (p. 3)

F

Fill color/Color de relleno Color que se aplica al interior de una forma. (p. 82)

Folder/Carpeta Un objeto que le ayuda al usuario a organizar los archivos. (p. 11)

Font/Fuente Diseño general de un conjunto de caracteres. (También llamado tipo de letra.) (p. 78)

Font style/Estilo de fuente Efecto que puede aplicarse a una fuente, tal como negritas, cursivas y subrayado. (p. 78)

Footer/Pie de la diapositiva Uno o más cuadros de texto al fondo de cada diapositiva, documento impreso o página de notas. Puede incluir la fecha, el título de la presentación o el número de diapositiva. (p. 98)

Format/Modificar formato Cambiar la apariencia de una presentación. (p. 3)

Formatting/Formato Aspecto del contenido en una diapositiva. (p. 75)

G

Gradient/Gradiente El sombreado gradual de un gráfico de un lado al otro. (p. 84)

Technology Standards

Technology Foundation Standards for All Students

The NETS are divided into the six broad categories that are listed below. Activities in the book meet the standards within each category.

1 Basic operations and concepts
- Students demonstrate a sound understanding of the nature and operation of technology systems.
- Students are proficient in the use of technology.

2 Social, ethical, and human issues
- Students understand the ethical, cultural, and societal issues related to technology.
- Students practice responsible use of technology systems, information, and software.
- Students develop positive attitudes toward technology uses that support lifelong learning, collaboration, personal pursuits, and productivity.

3 Technology productivity tools
- Students use technology tools to enhance learning, increase productivity, and promote creativity.
- Students use productivity tools to collaborate in constructing technology-enhanced models, prepare publications, and produce other creative works.

4 Technology communications tools
- Students use telecommunications to collaborate, publish, and interact with peers, experts, and other audiences.
- Students use a variety of media and formats to communicate information and ideas effectively to multiple audiences.

5 Technology research tools
- Students use technology to locate, evaluate, and collect information from a variety of sources.
- Students use technology tools to process data and report results.
- Students evaluate and select new information resources and technological innovations based on the appropriateness for specific tasks.

6 Technology problem-solving and decision-making tools
- Students use technology resources for solving problems and making informed decisions.
- Students employ technology in the development of strategies for solving problems in the real world.

Glossary

Slide pane The part of the PowerPoint screen where you key in text. (p. 17)

Slide Show A presentation that is shown one slide at a time using a computer monitor or projector. (p. 3)

Slides pane The pane that displays miniatures of the slides in a presentation. (p. 13)

Slide Sorter View View you can use to add more slides, to delete slides, or to rearrange the order of slides. (p. 14)

Snap To line up with a grid or guide when something is dragged close to it. (p. 117)

Status bar The bar at the bottom of the screen that displays information such as the current slide number and the total number of slides in the presentation. (p. 7)

T

Table A device used to organize information into rows and columns. (p. 45)

Task pane An optional part of the PowerPoint screen that provides easy access to common tasks. (p. 9)

Template A guide that contains the formatting for a particular type of document or presentation. (p. 38)

Thesaurus A research tool that allows you to find synonyms for words and replace them in the text. (p. 55)

Timing A PowerPoint feature that determines how long a slide should remain visible during a slide show before automatically moving to the next slide. (p. 127)

Title bar The bar at the top of the screen that displays the name of the current presentation. (p. 7)

Title master A slide that serves as a model for the Title slide. (p. 95)

Title slide Slide that contains a presentation's title. Usually the first slide in a presentation. (p. 3)

Title and text slide Slide that contains a title with text underneath. Text is often formatted as a bulleted list. (p. 3)

Toolbar The bar that contains buttons that can be clicked to perform different tasks. (p. 8)

Tracking A feature that shows all changes made to a presentation by a reviewer. Changes by different people are indicated by different colors. (p. 59)

Transition An effect that occurs between slides during a slide show. (p. 92)

Typeface The unique design of a set of characters. Also referred to as font. (p. 78)

W

Web server A computer on the Internet that stores Web pages. (p. 132)

WordArt Decorative text that is shadowed, rotated, stretched, or fitted to predefined shapes. (p. 52)

Technology Standards

Educational Technology Performance Indicators for Students

In this text, students will have opportunities to demonstrate the following performance indicators for technological literacy. Each performance indicator refers to the NETS Foundations Standards category or categories (listed on previous page) to which the performance is linked.

1. Identify capabilities and limitations of contemporary and emerging technology resources and assess the potential of these systems and services to address personal, lifelong learning and workplace needs. (2)

2. Make informed choices among technology systems, resources, and services. (1, 2)

3. Analyze advantages and disadvantages of widespread use and reliance on technology in the workplace and in society as a whole. (2)

4. Demonstrate and advocate for legal and ethical behaviors among peers, family, and community regarding the use of technology and information. (2)

5. Use technology tools and resources for managing and communicating personal/professional information (e.g., finances, schedules, addresses, purchases, correspondence). (3, 4)

6. Evaluate technology-based options, including distance and distributed education, for lifelong learning. (5)

7. Routinely and efficiently use online information resources to meet needs for collaboration, research, publications, communications, and productivity. (4, 5, 6)

8. Select and apply technology tools for research, information analysis, problem-solving, and decision-making in content learning. (4, 5)

9. Investigate and apply expert systems, intelligent agents, and simulations in real-world situations. (3, 5, 6)

10. Collaborate with peers, experts, and others to contribute to content-related knowledge base by using technology to compile, synthesize, produce, and disseminate information, models, and other creative works. (4, 5, 6)

Reprinted with permissions from *National Education Technology Standards for Students—Connecting Curriculum and Technology*, ©2000, ISTE (International Society for Technology in Education), 800.336.5191 (U.S. & Canada) or 541.302.3777 (Int'l). iste@iste.org. All Rights Reserved. Permission does not constitute an endorsement by ISTE.

Glossary

Hyperlink Text or button that, when clicked, takes you to another slide within your presentation, opens another file, or opens a Web page. (p. 114)

Hypertext Markup Language (HTML) A programming language used by Internet browsers to read and display Web pages. (p. 131)

Insertion point A blinking mark that indicates where the text you key will appear on the screen. Also known as a cursor. (p. 17)

Key To type text. (p. 17)

Landscape The orientation of a slide that is wider than it is tall. (p. 93)

Line color The color applied to a line or to the border of a shape. (p. 82)

M

Markups Call-out boxes containing a reviewer's name, date, and details of the comments and changes made. (p. 58)

Menu A list of related commands. (p. 8)

Menu bar A bar that displays the names of available menus. (p. 7)

Menu command An individual option on a menu. (p. 8)

O

Object A document, picture, worksheet, presentation, or other item that can be inserted into an open file in another application. (p. 53)

Outline pane The pane that displays the outline view, or text, of the presentation. (p. 13)

Package for CD A fast way to group a PowerPoint presentation and all related files (such as linked files and PowerPoint Viewer) into one folder. (p. 128)

Placeholder text Text that tells you what type of content should be placed in different areas of a slide. (p. 3)

Pointer The arrow used to select on-screen items, such as menus and buttons. (p. 7)

Portrait The orientation of a slide that is taller than it is wide. (p. 93)

PowerPoint Viewer A computer application that allows people to view a slide show without using PowerPoint. (p. 128)

Presentation A PowerPoint file. A presentation can contain text, pictures, charts, links to other pages, and other objects. (p. 3)

Print Preview A preview of slides to be printed. (p. 120)

Promote In outlines, changes selected text to the next-higher heading level (up one level, to the left). (p. 42)

Publish To copy necessary HTML files to a Web server so that they can be seen over the Internet. (p. 132)

R

Revisions task pane Allows you to quickly and easily view a list of suggested changes to a presentation. (p. 59)

Rotate To turn an object, usually 90° to the left or right. (p. 86)

ScreenTip The description of an object such as a button that appears when you point to the object. (p. 8)

Scroll bar A bar at the right side or bottom of the screen that allows you to move up and down or left and right in a document. (p. 15)

Slide One page in a presentation. (p. 3)

Slide Finder Displays a miniature of each slide in a presentation that you can select and insert into the current presentation. (p. 113)

Slide icon In the Outline pane, the small slide image that is located next to the slide content. Click the image to move among slides. (p. 13)

Slide layout The arrangement of text and graphics on a slide. (p. 77)

Slide master A slide that serves as a model for every slide in a presentation except the Title slide. (p. 96)

Technology Handbook

Computers are everywhere—in businesses, schools, and homes, in ATMs, drive-up windows, and cars. Learning about how computers work can help make your life a little easier. The information in this *Technology Handbook* will help you better understand how to make computers work for you!

Contents

PART 1
Computers and Computer Hardware — H2

- How Have Computers Changed the World? — H2
- Types of Computers and Computer Systems — H3
- Input Devices — H4
- Output Devices — H5
- Processing Components — H6
- Storage Devices — H7
- Networks — H10
- Part 1 Assessment — H12

PART 2
Software — H13

- Operating System Software — H13
- Application Software — H14
- Utility Programs — H15
- Part 2 Assessment — H17

PART 3
Ready, Set, Process — H18

- Getting Ready — H18
- Getting Set: Working with Files and Folders — H22
- Processing: Working with Windows — H28
- Part 3 Assessment — H30

PART 4
Living Online — H31

- Impact of Computers on Society: Fun, Work, Shopping — H31
- Staying Safe Online — H34
- Ethics and Technology — H36
- Using the Internet — H37
- Emerging Technology — H39
- Part 4 Assessment — H40

PART 5
Outlook and Productivity Tools — H41

- Outlook — H41
- Online Communication — H42
- Using Help and Other Productivity Tools — H43
- Part 5 Assessment — H44

Glossary

A

Action Button A button that, when clicked, performs an action during a slide show, such as advancing to another slide. (p. 116)

Alignment The position of text and graphics in relation to a text box's margins and to other text and graphics on a slide. (p. 80)

Animation scheme An effect that, when applied, causes text and graphics to move and display on screen in specific ways. Animation Schemes can be Subtle, Moderate, or Exciting. (p. 91)

Annotation A mark or note made with a pen tool when viewing a slide show. (p. 126)

AutoContent wizard A tool that helps you put content together into a professional presentation. (p. 60)

B

Background Solid colors, patterns, or pictures that fill the entire slide and appear behind the slide's content. (p. 76)

Button A graphic item that can be clicked to perform a specific task. (p. 8)

C

Chart A graph created from the data entered into a datasheet. (p. 48)

Clip Art Pre-made graphics that can be inserted into a presentation. (p. 46)

Color scheme The eight colors used in a slide's design. Each design template has a specific color scheme that is used for the presentation's background, text and lines, shadows, title text, fills, accents, and hyperlinks. (p. 76)

Comments Notes that can be added to a presentation without appearing as actual changes to the presentation. (p. 57)

Compare and Merge A tool for combining the comments and edits made to multiple copies of the same presentation into one presentation. (p. 58)

Content The text and graphics included on a slide. (p. 74)

Cursor A blinking mark that indicates where the text you key will appear on the screen. Also known as an insertion point. (p. 17)

D

Datasheet Holds information in cells. Similar to a worksheet. (p. 48)

Demote In outlines, changes selected text to the next-lower heading level (down one level, to the right). (p. 42)

Diagram A graphic that you use to organize and present information visually in a slide. (p. 43)

Dialog box A box that is used to enter specific information to perform a particular task, such as naming and saving a document. (p. 11)

E

Edit To make changes to the content of a presentation. (p. 3)

F

Fill color The color applied to the interior of a shape. (p. 82)

Folder An item that helps the user organize files. (p. 11)

Font The unique design of a set of characters. Also referred to as typeface. (p. 78)

Font style Effects such as bold, italic, underline, and shadow that are applied to text. (p. 78)

Footer One or more text boxes at the bottom of every slide, handout, or Notes Page. May contain the date, presentation title, or slide number. (p. 98)

Format To change the look of a presentation. (p. 3)

Formatting The appearance of content on a slide. (p. 75)

G

Gradient The gradual shading of a graphic from one side or corner to the other. (p. 84)

Grid A series of horizontal and vertical lines laid over a slide to help align items on a slide. (p. 117)

Guide A horizontal or vertical line you place on a slide to help align objects. (p. 117)

H

HTML See Hypertext Markup Language

PART 1 Computers and Computer Hardware

How Have Computers Changed the World?

Key Terms
- Computer
- Technology

A **computer** is an electronic device that processes data and converts it into information that people can use. Chances are you cannot imagine a world without computers!

Common conveniences such as fast food restaurants and ATMs use computers to provide quick, easy service to customers.

Some computer-created games are so realistic that it seems as if you can see, hear, and sometimes even feel the action around you!

Doctors and medical technicians depend on heart monitors, full-body scanners, and other computer-based devices.

The term **technology** refers to the practical application of an art or skill. Nearly every part of the globe has been touched by technology.

E-mail and cell phones make it easy to contact friends and family—even if they live on the other side of the world!

TECH CHECK

1. **Identify** What aspects of your life do not involve computers?
2. **Make Predictions** What would life be like without computers? How would your life change if computers suddenly disappeared from the world?
3. **Interview** Talk to someone who is older than you, such as a parent or a grandparent. Did they use computers when they were young? How was their life different from the way you live now?

APPENDIX B: Microsoft Office Specialist Certification

Microsoft Office Specialist Standards

iCheck Express Microsoft PowerPoint 2003 covers the Microsoft Office Specialist standards for PowerPoint. This chart provides an overview of the coverage of the Microsoft Office Specialist standards in *iCheck Express Microsoft PowerPoint 2003*.

Microsoft PowerPoint 2003 Specialist Standards

Standard	Skill Sets and Skills	Text Correlation
PP03S-1	**Creating Content**	
PP03S-1-1	Create new presentations from templates	38, 65, 70
PP03S-1-2	Insert and edit text-based content	39, 40, 65, 70
PP03S-1-3	Insert tables, charts, and diagrams	43, 66, 71
PP03S-1-4	Insert pictures, shapes, and graphics	50, 66, 71
PP03S-1-5	Insert objects	53
PP03S-2	**Formatting Content**	
PP03S-2-1	Format text-based content	78, 79, 103, 107
PP03S-2-2	Format pictures, shapes, and graphics	82–84, 103, 107
PP03S-2-3	Format slides	77, 102, 107
PP03S-2-4	Apply animation schemes	91, 105, 108
PP03S-2-5	Apply slide transitions	92, 102, 108
PP03S-2-6	Customize slide templates	94, 105, 108
PP03S-2-7	Work with masters	96, 97, 103, 108
PP03S-3	**Collaborating**	
PP03S-3-1	Track, accept, and reject changes in a presentation	59, 70
PP03S-3-2	Add, edit, and delete comments in a presentation	57, 69, 71
PP03S-3-3	Compare and merge presentations	58, 67, 69, 71
PP03S-4	**Managing and Delivering Presentations**	
PP03S-4-1	Organize a presentation	112, 136, 141
PP03S-4-2	Set up slide shows for delivery	18, 30, 34
PP03S-4-3	Rehearse timing	127, 140, 141
PP03S-4-4	Deliver presentations	18, 30, 33
PP03S-4-5	Prepare presentations for remote delivery	128, 139, 142
PP03S-4-6	Save and publish presentations	131, 132, 140
PP03S-4-7	Print slides, outlines, handouts, and speaker notes	119, 138, 141
PP03S-4-8	Export a presentation to another Microsoft Office program	115, 123–125

Types of Computers and Computer Systems

Key Terms
Desktop
Laptop
Macintosh
Mainframe
Personal computer (PC)
Personal digital assistant (PDA)

In today's world, computers are everywhere. They come in different shapes and sizes and they serve vastly different purposes.

Windows PC

A **desktop** computer is designed to remain in one location. The **personal computer (PC)** and the **Macintosh** support one user at a time. A company called Apple makes Macintosh computers. Several different companies make PCs.

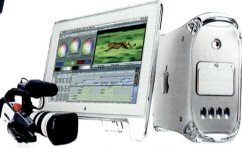

Macintosh PC

A **laptop** computer is designed to be carried from place to place.

Mainframes are very powerful computers that can do many things at once. While only one person at a time can use a PC or Macintosh, hundreds of people can use a mainframe at once.

A **personal digital assistant (PDA)** is a computer that is small enough to hold in one's hand.

TECH CHECK

1. **Describe** What is the difference between a laptop and a desktop?
2. **Predict** Would a laptop or a desktop be more useful for someone who travels a lot?
3. **Explain** How are PCs and a mainframe different? Which type of computer might be used by a large company? Why?

Visit the **Student Online Learning Center** to learn more about this topic.
iCheckExpress.glencoe.com

Part 1: Computers and Computer Hardware

Technology Handbook H3

APPENDIX B: Microsoft Office Specialist Certification

What does this logo mean?

It means that this courseware has been approved by the Microsoft® Office Specialist Program to be among the finest available for learning Microsoft Office 2003, Microsoft Word 2003, Microsoft Excel 2003, Microsoft PowerPoint® 2003, and Microsoft Access 2003. It also means that upon completion of this courseware, you may be prepared to take an exam for Microsoft Office Specialist qualification.

What is a Microsoft Office Specialist?

A Microsoft Office Specialist is an individual who has passed exams for certifying his or her skills in one or more of the Microsoft Office desktop applications such as Microsoft Word, Microsoft Excel, Microsoft PowerPoint, Microsoft Outlook, Microsoft Access, or Microsoft Project. The Microsoft Office Specialist Program typically offers certification exams at the "Specialist" and "Expert" skill levels.* The Microsoft Office Specialist Program is the only program in the world approved by Microsoft for testing proficiency in Microsoft Office desktop applications and Microsoft Project. This testing program can be a valuable asset in any job search or career advancement.

More Information:

To learn more about becoming a Microsoft Office Specialist, visit www.microsoft.com/officespecialist

To learn about other Microsoft Office Specialist approved courseware from Glencoe/McGraw-Hill, visit www.glencoe.com

*The availability of Microsoft Specialist certification exams varies by application, application version and language. Visit www.microsoft.com/officespecialist for exam availability.

Microsoft, the Microsoft Logo, PowerPoint, and Outlook are trademarks or registered trademarks of Microsoft Corporation in the United States and/or other countries, and the Microsoft Office Specialist Logo is under license from owner.

Input Devices

Key Terms
Input device
Joystick
Keyboard
Microphone
Mouse
Peripheral
Port
Scanner

Anything connected to your computer is considered a **peripheral**. In order for a computer to work, it must first have data. You can use peripherals called **input devices** to put information into a computer.

A **keyboard** is used to enter information in the form of words, numbers, and punctuation. You can also use a keyboard to give commands to some programs.

A **scanner** collects information in the form of pictures and sends the information to the computer.

A **mouse** is used to control objects seen on a computer screen. A mouse allows you to give information to a computer in a variety of ways.

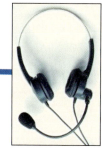

A **microphone** can be used to input audio such as music into a computer.

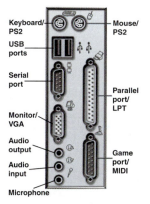

A **port** allows users to connect external input devices to the computer system.

A **joystick** is an input device that usually has buttons that can be pressed to send instructions to the computer.

A digital camera captures photographs as digital files that can be uploaded directly to a computer. A digital camcorder is used to create original video files.

TECH CHECK

1. **Differentiate** What type of information would you enter into a computer using a keyboard?
2. **Relate** In this topic, you learned about keyboards, mice, and scanners. Name three other devices that can be used as input devices.

Part 1: Computers and Computer Hardware — Technology Handbook H4

APPENDIX A: Quick Reference Summary

Function	Button	Menu	Keyboard Shortcuts	Speech
Promote text to Heading 1	✦		ALT + SHIFT + ←	✓
Record Macro		Tools>Macro>Record New Macro	ALT + F8	✓
Redo	↻	Edit>Repeat	CTRL + Y	✓
Reject suggested revision				✓
Replace		Edit>Replace	CTRL + H	✓
Run slide show		Slide Show>View Show	F5	✓
Save file	💾	File>Save	CTRL + S	✓
Save As		File>Save As	F12	✓
Save as Web page		File>Save as Web Page		✓
Slide Sorter View		View>Slide Sorter		
Spell check File	ABC	Tools>Spelling	F7	✓
Underline	U	Format>Font	CTRL + U	✓
Undo	↺	Edit>Undo	CTRL + Z	✓
Ungroup objects		Draw>Ungroup	CTRL + SHIFT + H	✓
Open the Research task pane		Tools>Research		✓
View markup comments		View>Markup		✓
View Slide Master	SHIFT +	View>Master>Slide Master		✓
Web Page Preview		File>Web Page Preview		✓
Zoom in or out	100%	View>Zoom		✓

Output Devices

Key Terms
Monitor
Output device
Printer
Speaker

You have learned that input devices put information *into* a computer. **Output devices** carry information *out* of a computer. First, the computer changes the information into a useable format. Then, the output devices present the information to the computer user.

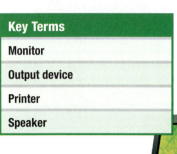

You use a **printer** to transfer images from a monitor to paper. For instance, when you key an essay on a computer, you can then print it out to turn in for class. You can also use a printer to print pictures.

A **monitor**, which is also called a computer screen, displays information visually, just like a television set. An LCD (liquid crystal display) monitor is much thinner than a CRT (cathode ray tube) monitor.

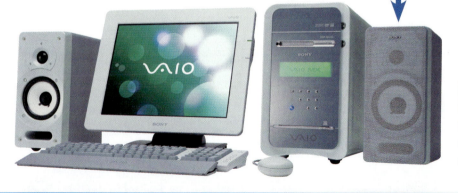

Speakers carry information in the form of sound. They can output music, speech, and noises.

TECH CHECK

Activity Information flows out of a computer through output devices. Create a diagram that shows information flowing from a computer to three different output devices. Write a brief explanation next to each output device that explains what sort of information the device outputs.

Part 1: Computers and Computer Hardware

APPENDIX A: Quick Reference Summary

Function	Button	Menu	Keyboard Shortcuts	Speech
Insert picture	🖼	Insert>Picture>From File		✓
Insert Symbol or Special Character		Insert>Symbol		✓
Insert table	▦	Insert>Table		✓
Insert Text Box		Insert>Text Box		✓
Insert WordArt		Insert>Picture>WordArt		✓
Italic	*I*	Format>Font	CTRL + I	✓
Modify Background		Format>Background		✓
Modify bullets		Format>Bullets and Numbering		✓
Modify font	Times New Roman	Format>Font	CTRL + SHIFT + F	✓
Modify Font Color	A	Format>Font		✓
Modify font size	10	Format>Font	CTRL + SHIFT + P	✓
Open a file	📂	File>Open	CTRL + O	✓
Open a presentation	📂	File>Open	CTRL + O	✓
Open Office Clipboard		Edit>Office Clipboard		✓
Page Setup		File>Page Setup		✓
Paste		Edit>Paste	CTRL + V	✓
Paste Options		Edit>Paste	CTRL + V	✓
Paste Special		Edit>Paste Special		✓
Print	🖨	File>Print	CTRL + P	✓
Print Preview		File>Print Preview	CTRL + ALT + I	✓

Appendix A: Quick Reference Summary

Processing Components

Key Terms
Clock speed
CPU
Memory
Microprocessor
Motherboard
RAM
Process
Storage devices

A computer uses hardware to **process** data into useful information. The part of the computer that processes information has many parts that work together. The **microprocessor** is the brain of a computer. A computer makes almost all of its calculations in the microprocessor. Not all microprocessors are the same. Some can perform more calculations per second than others. A processor's **clock speed** is the number of calculations the processor can do each second. Today's handheld PDAs process data many times faster than the early mainframe computers.

The **CPU**, or central processing unit, is made of one microprocessor in small computers. In larger machines, the CPU can be made of several microprocessors working together.

Memory, where computers keep their information, comes in the form of computer chips.

RAM, or random access memory, holds information temporarily.

Storage devices, also called secondary storage devices, are another place where information is kept in a computer. Unlike memory, however, storage devices hold information permanently. Storage comes in the form of hard disks, floppy disks, CDs, and DVDs.

The **motherboard** is the main circuit board in a computer. All of the other circuit boards connect to the motherboard. In many computers, the microprocessor and memory can be found on the motherboard.

TECH CHECK

1. **Describe** List three pieces of hardware in a computer and explain what each does.
2. **Compare** How are memory and storage alike? How are they different?
3. **Classify** What makes some microprocessors different from others?

Part 1: Computers and Computer Hardware

Technology Handbook   H6

APPENDIX A: Quick Reference Summary

Function	Button	Menu	Keyboard Shortcuts	Speech
Font Size	12	Format>Font	CTRL + SHIFT + < CTRL + SHIFT + >	☑
Format Painter	🖌			☑
Format Picture	🖼	Format>Picture		☑
Format Shapes		Format>AutoShape		☑
Format WordArt		Format>WordArt		☑
Group objects		Draw>Group	CTRL + SHIFT + G	☑
Header and footer		View>Header and Footer		☑
Help	🖼	Help>Microsoft Office PowerPoint Help	F1	☑
Insert AutoShape	AutoShapes▼	Insert>Picture>AutoShapes		☑
Insert Chart	📊	Insert>Chart		☑
Insert Clip Art	🖼	Insert>Picture>Clip Art		☑
Insert comment	🗨	Insert>Comment		☑
Insert Date and Time		Insert>Date and Time	ALT + SHIFT + D	☑
Insert Diagram	🖼	Insert>Diagram		☑
Insert embedded object		Insert>Object		☑
Insert Hyperlink	🌐	Insert>Hyperlink	CTRL + K	☑
Insert linked object		Insert>Object, check Link to File		☑
Insert object		Insert>Object		☑

Appendix A: Quick Reference Summary

Storage Devices

Key Terms
CD-R
CD-ROM
CD-RW
DVD-ROM
Flash memory
Floppy disk
Hard drive
Optical disk
ZIP disk

As you have already learned, computers change data into useful information. Computers are also useful for storing information. In this section, you will learn about some of the devices that are used to store information.

A **hard drive**, also called a hard disk, is the most widely used secondary storage device. They can be internal or external. Hard drives today can usually hold 10 to 100 gigabytes of data. One gigabyte is equal to 1000 megabytes. A hard drive with 100 gigabytes could hold an entire library floor of journals and magazines!

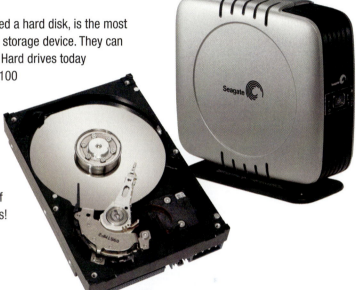

A **floppy disk** contains a small portable disk inside a plastic cover. Floppy disks can hold up to 1.4 megabytes of information, which is about enough space to store the words in a small book.

A **ZIP disk**, like a floppy disk, has a portable disk inside a plastic case. A ZIP disk can hold 100 to 250 megabytes. Two hundred fifty megabytes is roughly equal to five volumes of an encyclopedia!

Flash memory, used in digital cameras and other devices, uses chips to hold information. You can add information to flash memory in large chunks rather than piece by piece, making storage faster and easier than with other types of memory.

APPENDIX A: Quick Reference Summary

Function	Button	Menu	Keyboard Shortcuts	Speech
Close window	X	File>Close	CTRL+W	✓
Compare and Merge multiple presentations		Tools>Compare and Merge Presentations		✓
Copy	📋	Edit>Copy	CTRL+C	✓
Create new file	📄	File>New	CTRL+N	✓
Create a new presentation	📄	File>New	CTRL+N	✓
Create slides based on an outline		Insert>Slides from Outlines		✓
Cut	✂	Edit>Cut	CTRL+X	✓
Decrease Font Size		Format>Font	CTRL+SHIFT+<	✓
Delete placeholder		Edit>Clear	DELETE	✓
Demote text to lower level	→		ALT+SHIFT+→	✓
E-mail Attachment		File>Send To>Mail Recipient (as Attachment)		✓
E-mail for Review		File>Send To>Mail Recipient (for Review)		✓
Exit PowerPoint	X	File>Exit	ALT+F4	✓
Exit slide show			ESC	
Find	🔍	Edit>Find	CTRL+F	✓
Find a synonym	📖	Tools>Thesaurus		✓
Find and Replace		Edit>Replace	CTRL+H	✓

Appendix A: Quick Reference Summary

Storage Devices (Continued)

All of the storage devices you have read about so far use electric charges to store information. **Optical disks**, another type of storage device, use lasers to read and write information. Four types of optical disks are explained below.

Information can only be put on CD-ROM and CD-R disk once. A **CD-RW** is an optical disk that can record information many times. CD-RW disks are useful for making copies of important information for backup.

A **CD-R**, which stands for **C**ompact **D**isk-**R**ecordable, is a CD-ROM disk that does not yet contain any information. A CD-R drive writes information onto the CD-R disk. A CD-R can hold about the same amount of information that the CD-ROM can hold.

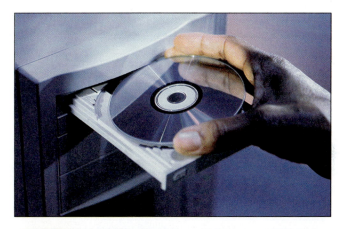

A **CD-ROM** is an optical disk that can hold up to 1 gigabyte of information. One gigabyte of information is equal to 700 floppy disks or 300,000 pages of text. CD-ROM drives are very common in PCs because the CD-ROM is a cheap way to store lots of information.

Like the CD-ROM, a **DVD-ROM** is an optical disk. However, the DVD-ROM can hold up to 17 gigabytes of information. It would take 17 CD-ROMs to hold the information in one DVD-ROM. DVD-ROM disks are commonly used to store movies.

APPENDIX A: Quick Reference Summary

The following commands were covered in this book.

Function	Button	Menu	Keyboard Shortcuts	Speech
Accept suggested revision	✓			☑
Align Center	≡	Format>Alignment>Center	CTRL + E	☑
Align Justified		Format>Alignment>Justify	CTRL + J	☑
Align Left	≡	Format>Alignment>Align Left	CTRL + L	☑
Align Right	≡	Format>Alignment>Align Right	CTRL + R	☑
Apply Italic	*I*	Format>Font	CTRL + I	☑
Apply Shadow	▨	Format>Font		☑
Apply Underline	U	Format>Font	CTRL + U	☑
Bold	**B**	Format>Font	CTRL + B	☑
Bullets	≔	Format>Bullets and Numbering		☑
Change chart options		Chart>Chart Options		☑
Change chart type		Chart>Chart Type		☑
Choose Animation Schemes		Slide Show>Animation Schemes		☑
Choose print options		File>Print	CTRL + P	☑
Choose Slide Design	Design	Format>Slide Design	ALT + S	☑
Choose Slide Layout		Format>Slide Layout		☑
Choose Slide Transition		Slide Show>Slide Transition		☑
Close a presentation	X	File>Close	CTRL + F4	☑

Appendix A: Quick Reference Summary

Storage Devices (Continued)

If you have problems using a storage device, try the basic troubleshooting procedures below.

For Floppy Disks:

Make sure the write-protect tab is in the locked position. Look at the bottom right and bottom left corners of the disk. If there is a hole in both corners, turn the disk over. Then move the tab in the bottom right corner to cover the hole.

Make sure there is not a disk in the drive already.

Make sure the disk is right side up and the metal side is facing the drive. The disk being inserted in this photo is not facing the correct way. The bottom disk is facing the correct way.

Put a different floppy disk into the drive. If neither floppy works, the disk drive may be broken.

For Optical Disks:

Make sure the CD or DVD is seated right side up in the disk tray. The shiny side should be on the bottom. Make sure there is not more than one CD or DVD in the tray.

If a CD will not work, as a last resort, wipe it with a very soft cloth. Wipe the shiny side gently from the center of the disk outward. Ask your teacher or a parent before attempting this.

TECH CHECK

1. **Distinguish** Describe two ways that flash memory is different than other storage devices that were discussed in this section.

2. **Identify** What are the storage capacities of floppy disks, ZIP disks, and hard drives?

3. **Describe** Describe three things you can do if your CD-ROM is not working.

Visit the **Student Online Learning Center** to learn more about this topic.
iCheckExpress.glencoe.com

Contents

Appendix A: Quick Reference Summary   **151**

Appendix B: Microsoft Office Specialist Certification   **156**

Glossary   **158**

Glosario   **161**

Index   **164**

Image Credits   **169**

Networks

Key Terms
Ethernet cable
LAN
Network
Network hardware
Network interface card (NIC)
Network operating system (NOS)
Network topology
Router
Server
WAN

A **network** is a group of computers that are connected to each other. There are two basic types of networks.

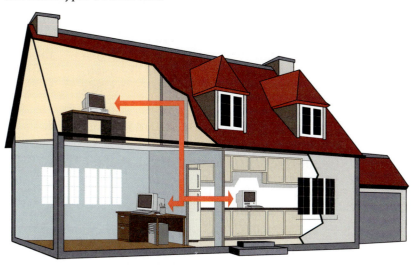

A **LAN,** or **L**ocal **A**rea **N**etwork, is a connected group of computers that are close to each other. For example, a connected group of computers in a home or in an office is a LAN.

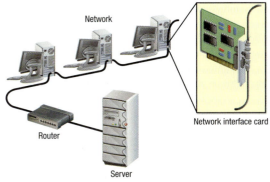

All computers on a network need a **network interface card (NIC)** so that the computers can communicate over the network. One way to connect computers is by **Ethernet cable**. A **router** connects multiple computers to each other as well as to a WAN (like the Internet). A **server** manages the flow of information on a network. This allows network resources, like files and printers, to run smoothly.

A **WAN**, or **W**ide **A**rea **N**etwork, is a connected group of computers that are not close to each other. For example, the Internet is a WAN. A WAN provides users with access to large amounts of information.

UNIT 1 Portfolio Project

Part 4: Create a Proposal

Goal Based on the meeting's results, the town planner is going to propose the construction of a multi-use recreation center. She would like you to help create the presentation that promotes this proposal.

Create Use the AutoContent Wizard to create the presentation.

- For the type of presentation, choose **Project Overview**. Key content for the proposal on the slides. Include a minimum of six slides in your presentation and a Title Slide.
- Change the background to a lighter color.
- Add graphics such as Clip Art, WordArt, charts, or diagrams as needed.
- Add an Action Button.
- Add transitions between the slides.

Self Assess Use the Have You...? checklist to review your presentation. Carefully preview your presentation and make corrections. With your teacher's permission, print the presentation so the annotations appear. Follow your teacher's instructions for naming the presentation and saving it in your Portfolio Folder.

Have You...?

- ✓ Included a minimum of six slides
- ✓ Changed the slides' background color
- ✓ Added graphics as needed
- ✓ Added an Action Button
- ✓ Added slide transitions
- ✓ Rehearsed timings
- ✓ Added annotations
- ✓ Packaged the presentation for a CD
- ✓ Printed the presentation so the annotations appear

Networks (Continued)

Connecting computers properly so that they can communicate is challenging. Devices called **network hardware** and software called **network operating systems (NOS)** help computers share information.

A **network topology** is the actual arrangement of computers in a network. Three network topologies are shown below.

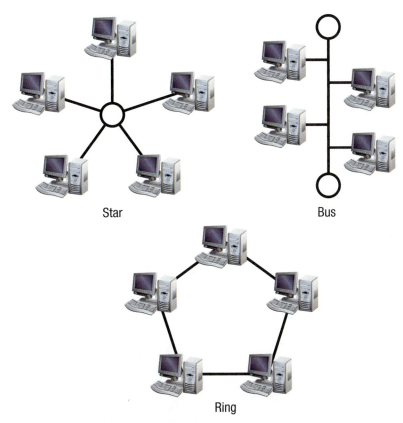

Star

Bus

Ring

Networks can also have combinations of these topologies, such as a star-bus network or a star-ring network.

TECH CHECK

1. **Differentiate** What is the difference between a LAN and a WAN? Describe one use for a LAN and one for a WAN.
2. **Construct** Draw a diagram of a star-ring network.

Part 1: Computers and Computer Hardware

UNIT 1 Portfolio Project

Part 3: Create a Presentation

Goal You are a teenager who lives in the town. You read the flyer about the town meeting and have an idea you want to present. You decide to create a short presentation about your idea.

Create Think of businesses that might attract you to your town's business district. For example, you may think the town needs a movie theater, a skating rink, a recreation center, or an arcade.

Use a Design Template to create a presentation proposing your idea. In your presentation, include the following items:
- A Title slide with a title.
- A slide that describes the business you would like to see in your town.
- A bulleted slide with information about your selected business.
- A piece of WordArt, an AutoShape, and another graphic such as a chart or diagram.
- Transitions between slides.

Self Assess Use the Have You...? checklist to review your presentation. View the slide show. With your teacher's permission, print a handout of your presentation. Follow your teacher's instructions for naming the presentation and saving it in your Portfolio Folder.

When finished, proceed to Part 4.

Have You...?

✓	Included a Title slide
✓	Included a slide describing your business
✓	Included a slide with a bulleted list
✓	Included WordArt
✓	Included an AutoShape
✓	Included a graphic
✓	Added slide transitions
✓	Printed a handout of your presentation

PART 1 Assessment

Key Term Review

Answer the following questions on a separate piece of paper.

1. _____ refers to the practical application of an art or skill. (p. H2)
2. A computer designed to remain in one location is a(n) _____. (p. H3)
3. A computer designed to be carried from place to place is a(n) _____. (p. H3)
4. _____ are powerful computers that can do many things at once. (p. H3)
5. Keyboards and printers are examples of _____. (p. H4)
6. An input device that has buttons to push and a control stick is called a(n) _____. (p. H4)
7. You must connect peripheral devices to the computer through a(n) _____. (p. H4)
8. A(n) _____ displays visual information similar to a television set. (p. H5)
9. The brain of a computer is called the _____. (p. H6)
10. All circuit boards in a computer connect to the _____, or main circuit board. (p. H6)
11. Three types of optical storage disks are _____, _____ and _____. (p. H8)
12. A group of computers that are connected to each other is called a(n) _____. (p. H10)
13. A(n) _____ allows network resources to run smoothly by managing the flow of information on a network. (p. H10)
14. A connected group of computers that are close to each other is called a(n) _____. (p. H10)
15. The actual arrangement of computers in a network is called a(n) _____. (p. H11)

Concept Review

Answer the following questions on a separate piece of paper.

16. Information goes into a computer through _____ and comes out through _____. (pp. H4, H5)
17. Most of the calculations done in a computer take place in the _____. (p. H6)
18. Tapes or disks that are used to store information for a long time are called _____. (p. H7)
19. A mainframe is the best type of computer for _____ users. (p. H3)
20. A group of connected computers that are far apart is called a _____. (p. H10)

Critical Thinking

Complete the following exercises to reinforce your understanding of the lesson.

21. **Organize** Create a diagram that shows how a basic microcomputer system handles information. The diagram should show the flow of information, where information is stored, and where it is processed. Locate and label the following items:
    - at least three input devices
    - at least three output devices
    - memory
    - storage devices
    - processing locations

22. **Compile** Create a table that you can use to evaluate or compare microcomputer systems.
    - On the left side of your paper, create a column that contains at least seven categories (such as "Amount of Memory" and "Cost") that you can use to evaluate a computer system.
    - Find an online computer store or look at an advertising flyer.
    - Look up two different computer systems and fill in the categories you have created.
    - Compare your results. Which system seems the better bargain?

ISTE Standards

The following ISTE standards are covered in Part 1. Refer to pages xvii to xix for a description of the standards listed here.

NETS•S	Performance Indicator
1, 3	2, 5

Part 1: Computers and Computer Hardware

UNIT 1 Portfolio Project

Part 2: Create a Certificate of Excellence

Goal At the start of the town meeting, the president of the Town Council will recognize students who volunteered their time in town.

Create Pretend three of your classmates will be given Certificates of Excellence. Use the AutoContent Wizard to create the certificates:

- For the type of presentation, choose **Certificate**. Leave the Presentation title box and Footer box blank.
- Delete the first and last slides in the Certificate presentation so that only the Certificate of Excellence is present.
- Using Slide Sorter View, use **Edit > Duplicate** to duplicate the Certificate of Excellence slide for each classmate.

Tailor a certificate for each of the three classmates you selected. Certificates should include each student's name and the current date. You can also include your town's name, and the name of any specific projects your classmates have volunteered for. Sign your name as the person presenting the certificate.

Self Assess Use the Have You...? checklist to review the certificates. Proofread each slide and make any necessary edits. With your teacher's permission, print the certificates. Follow your teacher's instructions for naming the presentation and saving it in your Portfolio Folder.

When finished, proceed to Part 3.

Have You...?

- ✓ Selected Certificate in AutoContent Wizard
- ✓ Deleted the first and last slide
- ✓ Duplicated the remaining slide to create three slides
- ✓ Tailored a slide to each classmate
- ✓ Signed your name to each certificate
- ✓ Proofread and made necessary corrections
- ✓ Printed the slides

PART 2 | Software

Operating System Software

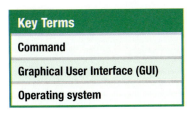

Key Terms
- Command
- Graphical User Interface (GUI)
- Operating system

A computer's **operating system** is a program that runs the computer. It recognizes input from input devices, sends output to output devices, and saves data and information on the hard disk. A computer user controls the operating system with **commands**. A command tells the computer to perform a particular task. Users of operating systems such as Linux and DOS need to type in commands to tell the computer what to do. More popular operating systems such as Windows and Macintosh use a **graphical user interface (GUI)**. A GUI uses images on a monitor to make an operating system easier to use. Instead of learning command words, a GUI user can choose from a list of options.

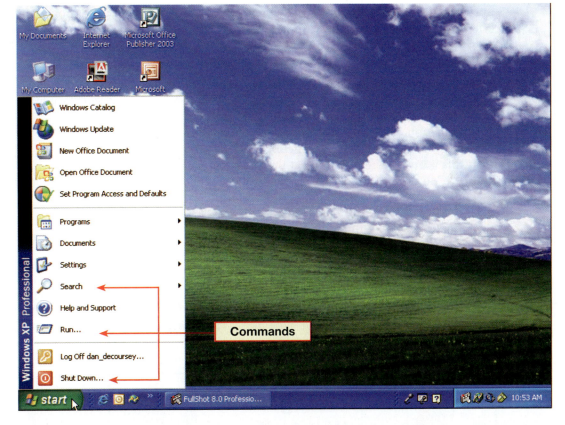

Windows is an operating system that employs a graphical user interface that uses images and a list of options instead of typed commands.

TECH CHECK

1. **Explain** Why are commands important?
2. **Predict** Why do you think operating systems with GUIs are more popular than those that use word commands?

Visit the Student Online Learning Center to learn more about this topic.
iCheckExpress.glencoe.com

UNIT 1 Portfolio Project

Planning a Town Recreation Center

You are a volunteer for your Town Council who recently hired a planner to help stimulate economic growth. Benefits of growth include higher-quality jobs, and the construction of more schools, parks, homes, and roads. The planner has asked you to organize a town meeting to discuss how to increase business from teenagers.

Part 1: Create a Slide

Goal Your first task is to generate interest in the upcoming town meeting. Teens will be invited to offer their ideas about businesses they would like to see in town. You decide to create a flyer to attract their interest.

Create Create a single-slide presentation. You will print this slide and use it as a flyer that informs teenagers of the town meeting. Change the orientation to Portrait. Apply a design and include a title to catch teenagers' interest. Make it clear this is an opportunity to meet the planner and offer ideas directly to her. Also include a description of what the meeting is about as well as the meeting's location, date, and time. Note that attendees will be limited to five minutes to present their ideas.

Self Assess Use the Have You…? checklist to review your slide. Then, print and proofread your flyer. Make necessary corrections. Follow your teacher's instructions for naming the flyer and saving it in your Portfolio Folder.

When finished, proceed to Part 2.

Have You…?
✓ Changed the orientation to Portrait
✓ Selected an appropriate design
✓ Selected a design that is readable when printed
✓ Included a title to capture teenagers' attention
✓ Included a description
✓ Included location, date, and time information
✓ Included a note about a time limit

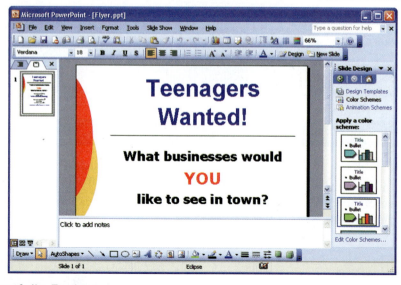

Application Software

Key Terms
- Application
- Database
- Presentation
- Spreadsheet
- Word processor

Today, people use computers for everything from writing a letter to calculating a budget. But it is not a computer's operating system that does these things. The operating system only runs the computer. **Applications** are the programs designed for a particular type of task, like writing a letter or calculating a budget. Applications, however, will not work without an operating system.

Many types of applications serve different purposes. Four of the most common application types are **word processors**, **spreadsheets**, **presentations**, and **databases**. The table below explains each of these types. Other common applications include Internet browsers, used for viewing Internet content; e-mail programs, used for sending and receiving mail electronically; and graphics programs, used to create images on the computer.

Four Common Applications

Application Type	What does it do?	Example
Word Processor	A word processor produces text documents. You key words into the computer using a keyboard just as if you were using a typewriter. However, a word processor is more efficient because you can correct mistakes on the screen before you print a document.	Microsoft Word WordPerfect Wordpro AppleWorks Word Processing Microsoft Works Word Processing
Spreadsheet	A spreadsheet is a table organized into rows and columns. You enter numbers in the table. The spreadsheet can do calculations with the numbers in the table.	Microsoft Excel Lotus 1-2-3 AppleWorks Spreadsheet Microsoft Works Spreadsheet
Presentation	A presentation is composed of slides that contain information and graphics. A presentation program helps you make a presentation look organized and eye-catching.	Microsoft PowerPoint Keynote AppleWorks Presentation
Database	A database is an organized way to store information so that it is easy for the computer to search the information. For instance, you might use a database to store your friends' names, phone numbers, and addresses so that you can easily look up a number or address using a friend's name.	Microsoft Access FileMaker AppleWorks Database Microsoft Works Database

TECH CHECK

1. **Distinguish** How are operating systems and applications different?
2. **Discuss** List three things you could use a word processor for.

Visit the **Student Online Learning Center** to learn more about this topic.
iCheckExpress.glencoe.com

UNIT 1: Ethics in Action

Citizenship

What does it mean to be a citizen? According to early U.S. President Theodore Roosevelt, "The first requisite of a good citizen in this Republic of ours is that he shall be able and willing to pull his own weight." For Roosevelt, a good citizen is an individual who is willing to work hard to support him- or herself and to help the community.

You could also describe a citizen as a person in a nation who is entitled to its protection and its privileges. Citizenship involves putting those privileges into action. For example, if you are 18 years or older, you have the privilege and right to vote.

Getting Involved

Instead of sitting back and letting things happen, involved citizens participate in the decision-making process. They take part in debate, exercise their rights, and try to bring about change. Involved citizens also speak out when they agree—or disagree—with something! Margaret Mead, a famous U.S. anthropologist, author, and environmentalist, once wrote, "Never doubt that a small group of thoughtful, committed citizens can change the world; indeed it's the only thing that ever has."

Consider ways to get involved at your school or in your community. For example, you could support your sports teams, sing in a chorus, or help with a school play. You could volunteer to be an after-school tutor. You could run for class office, or simply make your voice heard by voting for class officers.

In your community, you could participate in town meetings, volunteer at the local library or soup kitchen, or write to your congressman with praise or concerns. You can do so much as a citizen. Take action and get involved!

CASE STUDY

Your class is about to elect a class president. One candidate is very popular, but really seems to be interested only in having the title of class president. Another candidate is very bright and active, but you do not agree with what she wants to accomplish. A third candidate has expressed values that agree with yours, but he does not strike you as a person who can get things done. You want your vote to count but are not sure which candidate you should vote for.

YOU DECIDE

1. **Identify** What is one thing that an involved citizen does?

2. **Evaluate** Make a list of advantages and disadvantages of each candidate in the case study above. Which candidate would you vote for? Explain your reasons.

APPLICATION ACTIVITY

3. **Create a Presentation** You have decided to run for class president. Create a presentation explaining why you think you are the best candidate for the job. Use your proactive attitude toward citizenship to support your candidacy.

Utility Programs

Key Terms
Encryption
File management
Firewall
Utility program
Virus

A **utility program** is a program that performs a specific task within an operating system. Utility programs perform a variety of tasks.

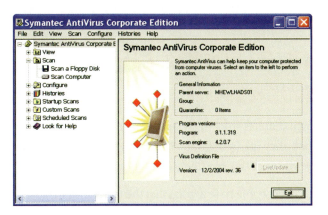

An antivirus program detects and eliminates viruses before they can harm a computer. Good antivirus programs obtain new information about viruses from the Internet.

Computer Security

Computer security is very important because there are more threats to computers than ever before.

One of the most common threats is called a **virus**. A virus is an unwanted program running on a computer. A virus makes copies of itself and, in some cases, sends copies to other computers. Viruses can use up a computer's memory or harm the data stored on the computer. Another threat is unwanted connections to or from the Internet. These connections can be from viruses or from other users who are attempting to gain control of another computer illegally. A **firewall** is a utility that protects computers against unwanted connections.

Some people have information stored on their computer that they do not want everyone to see. For instance, a company that has created a new invention might want to keep the plans secret until they can patent the invention. People can protect their information by using **encryption**, or putting data into a code.

A firewall examines each piece of data that comes into a computer or leaves a computer. If the firewall detects a threat, it will block the data.

```
<a href="&#109;&#97;&#105;&#108;&#116;&#111;&#58;%65%6E%68%61%6E%63
%65%72%40%68%63%70%64%2E%63%6F%6D">&#106;&#97;&#110;&#101;
&#100;&#111;&#101;&#64;&#97;&#111;&#108;&#46;&#99;&#111;&#109;</a>
```

In order to view an encryption, a user must know the key. The key is a string of numbers without which the information will not make sense.

Part 2: Software   Technology Handbook   H15

UNIT 1 Making Connections

SOCIAL STUDIES | MATH | SCIENCE | LANGUAGE ARTS

In this activity, you will create a presentation in which you support a specific point of view.

Create a Town Hall Presentation

You live in a town that has strict leash laws. Pets must be on leashes at all times when they are being walked. The town has a dog run, however, where your pet can run freely in a fenced area.

Recently some townspeople have argued that the town should close the dog run and create a monument park in its place. Residents can voice their opinions about this proposal at a town meeting. This is your only chance to be heard. Create a PowerPoint presentation for or against the closing of the dog run.

1. Create a new presentation. (p. 38)
2. Apply a Design Template to your presentation. (p. 75)
3. Create a Title slide that clearly supports or opposes the closing of the dog run. (p. 39)
4. On Slide 2, introduce yourself and your dog (pretend you own a dog). Include a picture or photograph of a dog on the slide. (p. 50)
5. On Slide 3, list reasons why you are for or against closing the run. (p. 39)
6. On Slide 4, list alternatives to closing the dog run or building a monument park. (p. 39)
7. On Slide 5, include a chart that shows how many people have used the dog run over the last four months. Be creative with your statistics, but make your figures reasonable! (p. 48)
8. Create a final slide with closing comments.
9. Add transitions between slides. (p. 92)

You can use a PowerPoint presentation to let people know your opinion about a topic, such as whether or not your town needs a dog run.

Utility Programs (Continued)

Utility programs accomplish a number of tasks aside from maintaining the security of a computer.

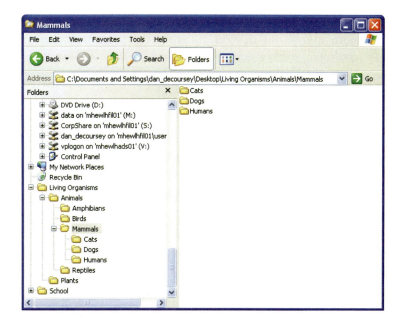

A **file management** utility organizes files and information so that they are easy to locate. The most common file system is called a hierarchical file system. In a hierarchical file system, information is organized by categories, starting with broad categories that get more and more specific as files are opened.

Some utility programs, such as Windows Media Player, allow a user to listen to music or watch movies on his or her computer.

Windows has a group of utilities that make computers easier for people with visual or mobility impairments to use. For instance, a person who cannot type can use the virtual keyboard to click the letters.

TECH CHECK

1. **Discuss** What are the benefits of antivirus programs?
2. **Construct** Create a hierarchical file system for your favorite pastime. The first item should be the broadest category to which your pastime belongs. Each new item should be more specific than the previous item, ending with your pastime.

Visit the **Student Online Learning Center** to learn more about this topic. iCheckExpress.glencoe.com

LESSON 4: Challenge Yourself Projects

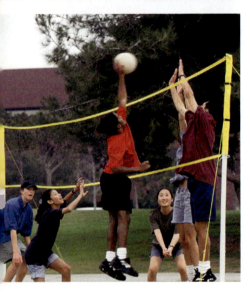

9 A Week in Your Life

Insert Hyperlinks   Using the data file **Activities** as a model, create your own Activity Log presentation. Your activity categories should include homework, television, phone time, sports and after-school activities, volunteer activities, and after-school or weekend jobs. Track the amount of hours you spend on each activity every day of the week. You can either estimate the amount of time you spent on each activity the previous week, or track the hours for the upcoming week. Include a **Summary** slide with a pie chart that illustrates how much time you spend on each activity during one week. Also include a **Goals** slide that lists three ways you intend to modify how you spend your time. In your presentation:

- Include a graphic in every slide. Use the grid feature to position your graphics.
- Add a hyperlink from one slide to another slide in the presentation.
- Add Action Buttons to your presentation.

Save your presentation as: p4rev-[your first initial and last name]9.

10 Lights, PowerPoint, Action!

Deliver a Presentation   Using the presentation you created in Project 9, or the data file **Activities**, show the slide show to a classmate. Use keyboard shortcuts to navigate through the show.

- Make annotations on your **Goals** slide using the Felt Tip Pen.
- On the **Saturday** slide, use the Highlighter.

Save the annotations you made. With your teacher's permission, print the presentation with the annotations showing. Save your presentation as: p4rev-[your first initial and last name]10.

11 Add Finishing Touches

Create a Custom Show   Using the presentation you created in Project 9, or the data file **Activities**, modify the file to create a custom show with less detail. Only include the **Title**, **Summary**, and **Goals** slide. Create a new slide for your presentation that lists all the categories of activities you tracked. Create a hyperlink in your presentation to a new document or to a Web page. When you are finished, package the presentation for a CD. Save your presentation as: p4rev-[your first initial and last name]11.

PART 2 Assessment

Key Term Review

Answer the following questions on a separate piece of paper.

1. A(n) _____ is the program responsible for running a computer. (p. H13)
2. A(n) _____ uses images on a monitor to make an operating system easier to use. (H13)
3. _____ tell the computer what to do and allow the computer user to control the computer. (H13)
4. A program that runs "on top" of an operating system is called a(n) _____. (p. H14)
5. An application that uses values organized into rows and columns is a(n) _____. (p. H14)
6. A(n) _____ is an organized way to store information so that it is easy for the computer to search the information. (H14)
7. A(n) _____ is more efficient than a typewriter because you can correct mistakes on the screen before you print a document. (H14)
8. A _____ is an unwanted program that can copy itself. (p. H15)
9. _____ data is data that has been put into a code. (p. H15)
10. A program that performs a specific task within an operating system is called a _____. (H15)
11. The hierarchical file system is one example of a _____. (H16)
12. A(n) _____ protects computers against unwanted connections. (H15)

Concept Review

Answer the following questions on a separate piece of paper.

13. Explain the relationship between commands and a computer's operating system. (H13)
14. List two differences between word processor applications and spreadsheet applications. (H14)
15. List three things for which you could use a database. (H14)
16. Will an operating system work without an application? (H14)
17. Will an application work without an operating system? (H14)
18. Explain the importance of firewalls. (H15)

Critical Thinking

Complete the following exercises to reinforce your understanding of the lesson.

19. **Predict**   Think of three types of businesses that you think use application software to help make business easier. Write down the type of business and then describe how an application could help that type of business.
20. **Collect**   Think of three school-related activities, such as keeping track of your homework, which you think might be easier with the help of a computer and a software application. Go online and try to locate an application that meets your needs. Try using search terms that combine the words "application" or "software" with the activity (sample search term: homework software).
21. **Compare**   Many people who run their own small office or home office use sophisticated application suites that allow them to create documents, spreadsheets, databases, and presentations. These suites help small business owners solve many of their own problems without the use of accountants, marketers, or designers and without a large financial investment. Research and compare the capabilities of three applications suites. Determine which suite you would prefer to use and explain why.

ISTE Standards

The following ISTE standards are covered in Part 2. Refer to pages xvii to xix for a description of the standards listed here.

NETS•S	Performance Indicator
1, 5	2, 8

Part 2: Software

LESSON 4 Critical Thinking Activities

6 Beyond the Classroom Activity

Create a Custom Show You have started your own lawn mowing business. When you started your business, you created a PowerPoint presentation to recruit employees. You now want to give the presentation to recruit new clients.

Open the data file **Mow**. Create a Custom Show that is directed toward potential clients. Only display the slides that are relevant to customers. Use grids and guides to line up the graphic on the title slide. Add an Action Button to the presentation. Save your presentation as: Mow-[your first initial and last name]6.

7 Standards at Work Activity

Microsoft Office Specialist Correlation PP03S-4-4
Deliver presentations

Use Presentation Tools You work as a spokesperson for the Reading Reach literacy organization. You need to practice delivering the presentation contained on the data file **Publicity**. Open the data file and:

- Practice using the Felt Tip Pen and Highlighter to emphasize important points.
- Rehearse and set timings.
- Copy a slide from the **Literacy** presentation to the **Publicity** presentation.
- Add notes to the Notes pane that you will use when delivering the presentation.
- Print the notes page.
- Print an outline of the presentation.

Save your file as: Publicity-[your first initial and last name]7.

8 21st Century Skills Activity

Show Initiative Create a 5- to 7-slide PowerPoint presentation about a person who took initiative and changed a situation for the better. You can choose a historical person, a public figure, or someone from your family or community. Or, you can describe a time when you yourself took the initiative. Give examples of how initiative was taken, and explain what you think might have happened if nobody had taken the lead. Save your file as: p4rev-[your first initial and last name]8.

Student Online Learning Center

Go to the book Web site to complete the following review activities.

Interactive Review
To review the main points of this lesson, choose **Interactive Review> PowerPoint Lesson 4**.

Online Self Check
Test your knowledge of the material in this lesson by choosing **Self Checks> PowerPoint Lesson 4**.

iCheckExpress.glencoe.com

PART 3 Ready, Set, Process

Getting Ready

Key Terms
Desktop
Icon
Maximize
Menu
Minimize
Recycle bin
Resize
Restore
Scroll box
Shortcut menu
Start menu
Task bar
Window

While computers do not usually require a lot of care and upkeeping, there are many things you can do to help keep your computer functioning properly.

- **Do not eat or drink near the computer.** Food and drinks can ruin the computer. Crumbs from food can get stuck between the keys on the keyboard. Some foods can make the keyboard, mouse, or other computer parts sticky. A spilled drink can cause an electrical shortage.
- **Keep your computer work area free of clutter.** This will help you work more efficiently while at the computer.
- **Insert disks and CDs gently into the disk drive and CD drive.** Never force a disk or CD into the drive.
- **Check that there are no disks or CDs in any of the drives** before turning on the computer.

Now, locate the power button [POWER] on the front of your computer. Press the button to start up the computer. Follow your teacher's instructions to logon once the computer has powered on.

Many hours of typing at a computer can make your wrists, arms, and back tired and sore. Here are a few tips that can help you avoid fatigue and soreness.

1. Sit with your hips as far back in your chair as they will go. Your back should rest against the back of the chair. The chair should support your upper and lower back.
2. Place the keyboard close enough to your body that you don't have to stretch to reach it. Your abdomen should be approximately one hand's span from the keyboard.
3. If you can, adjust the height of your chair so that your knees are even with your hips.
4. Center the keyboard on your body.
5. Place the monitor directly in front of you and slightly below your line of sight. The monitor should be between 20 and 24 inches from your eyes.

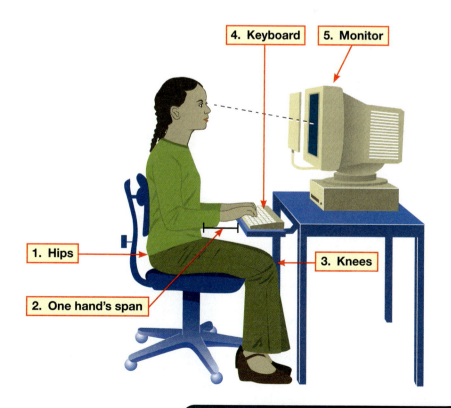

LESSON 4 You Try It Activities

5 Customize a Presentation

Your teacher asked you to give your health presentation to a different audience that is only interested in exercise. You must create a Custom Show for this audience and set the show's timings. You save the presentation as a Web page so that it can be viewed in Web browsers.

Step-By-Step

1. Open your **Habits-4** file. Save as: Habits-[your first initial and last name]5.

2. Choose **Slide Show> Custom Shows**. Create a **New** show named **Exercise**. In your show, include **Slides 1-5**, **8**, **9**, and **11**. Run the Custom Show.

3. Choose **Slide Show> Rehearse Timings**. In the **Slide Show** toolbar, select **Slide>Custom Show> Exercise**.

4. Rehearse and save timings for the **Exercise** slide show.

5. **CHECK** Your screen should look similar to Figure 4.52.

6. Save your presentation as a Web page. Make sure your **File name** has a **.mht** extension.

7. Ask your teacher where to save your Web page. Locate and open your **.mht** file.

8. **CHECK** Your screen should look like Figure 4.53. Save and close your file.

FIGURE 4.52 Timings set for Custom Show

FIGURE 4.53 Presentation saved as a Web page

Lesson 4: You Try It Activities

PowerPoint 141

Getting Ready (Continued)

Once the computer is on, you will see the desktop. In a graphical user interface (GUI), the desktop is the visual representation of the file system on a computer. All of the files and applications on a computer can be accessed through the desktop.

A GUI allows you to issue commands to the computer by using visual objects instead of typing commands. A mouse or other pointing device is used to access the icons and menues in a GUI.

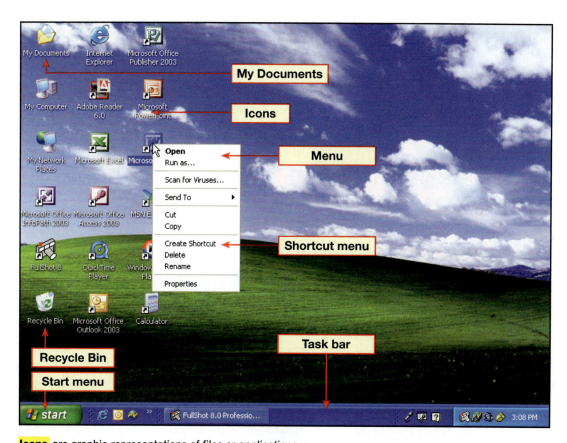

Icons are graphic representations of files or applications.

The Start Menu opens files and applications. It gives you access to all the resources and programs on your computer. A menu is a list of options.

The Task bar shows what files and applications are open. It allows you to launch and manage programs.

The Recycle Bin deletes files or applications from the computer.

Right-click once on the mouse to open a shortcut menu.

Double-click on the My Documents icon to open a list of your documents.

Part 3: Ready, Set, Process

LESSON 4: You Try It Activities

4 Promote Healthy Habits

For your health class, you must create a PowerPoint presentation about healthy exercise and diet habits. Your teacher has asked you to print any notes and package your presentation as a CD.

Step-By-Step

1. Open the data file **Habits.ppt**. Save as: Habits-[your first initial and last name]4.

2. Delete **Slide 3**. Move to **Slide 12**. Click in the slide. Zoom in **150%**.

3. **CHECK** Your screen should look like Figure 4.50. Under **Zoom**, click **Fit**.

4. Move to **Slide 13**. In the **Notes** pane, key: Use a fun activity as a reward.

5. Switch to **Print Preview**. Under **Print What**, select **Notes Pages**. Scroll to **Slide 13**.

6. **CHECK** Your screen should look like Figure 4.51. With your teacher's permission, print **Slide 13**.

7. Choose **File > Package for CD**. Name it **HealthyHabitsCD**. Under **Options**, select **Embedded TrueType fonts**.

8. Copy the presentation to the folder **HealthyHabitsCD**. Save and close your file.

FIGURE 4.50 Slide at 150% zoom

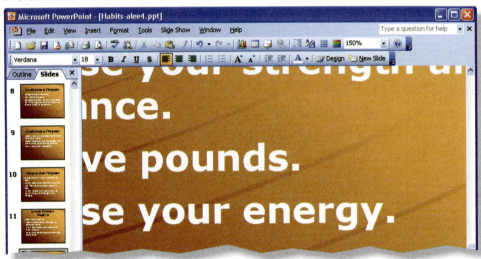

FIGURE 4.51 Preview of notes page

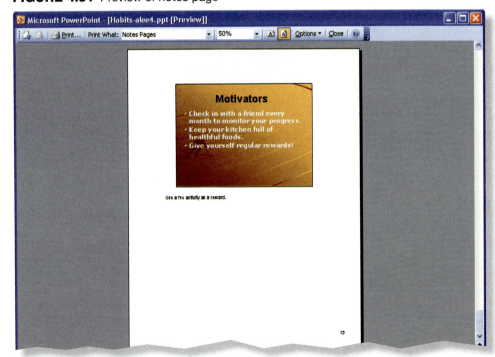

Getting Ready (Continued)

Double-clicking on a folder opens it. The contents of the folder are displayed in a **window**, which is simply a box that shows what is inside a folder or file. A different window can be opened for each file or folder you want to use. You can have many windows open at one time, but you can only work in one window, the active window, at a time.

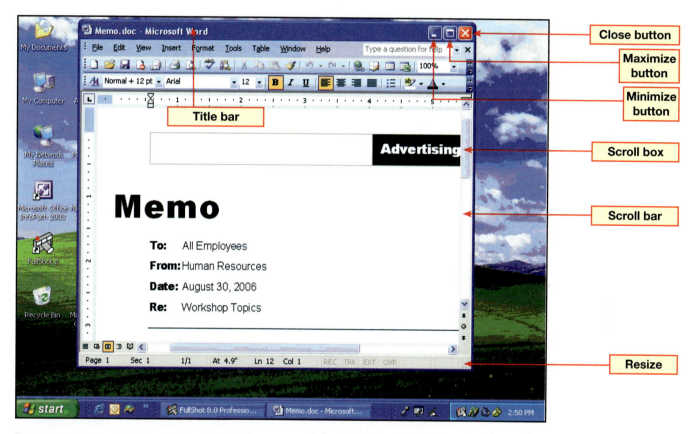

To move a window, place your pointer on the Title bar. Press and hold the left mouse button and then move the pointer to where you want the window to be. Holding down the mouse button and moving the mouse is called dragging.

Often, the entire contents of a window are not visible. To view the rest of the window, grab the scroll bar and drag it downward. The box that moves inside the scroll bar is called the **scroll box**.

To **resize** a window, or to make it larger or smaller, place the pointer over one of the corners of the window. When the small black arrows appear, drag the corner outward to make the window larger. Drag the corner inward to make the window smaller.

To **maximize** a window, or to make it fill up the screen, click the maximize button in the upper right corner of the window. To return the window to its original size, click the button again.

You can **minimize** a window to take the window off the desktop without closing it. To minimize a window, click the minimize button in the upper right corner of the window.

LESSON 4 Practice It Activities

3 Save Files in Different Formats and Print Presentation Items

Step-By-Step

Follow the steps to complete the activity. You must complete Practice It Activity 2 before doing this activity.

1. Open your **Activities-2** file. Save as: Activities-[your first initial and last name]3.

2. Choose **File>Save As**. Click **Create New Folder**. Key: Activities Presentation. Ask your teacher where to save the folder. Click **OK**. Under **Save as type** click **Outline/RTF (*.rtf)**.

3. (CHECK) Your dialog box should look like Figure 4.48. Click **Save**.

4. Choose **File>Save as Web Page**. In the **Save in** box, open your **Activities Presentation** folder. Click **Save**.

5. Choose **File>Print**. Under **Print range**, select **All**. Under **Print what**, select **Handouts**. In **Slides per page**, select **6**.

6. Select **Scale to fit paper**, **Frame slides**, and **Print comments and ink markup**.

7. (CHECK) Your dialog box should look like Figure 4.49. Save and close your file.

FIGURE 4.48 Presentation saved in Rich Text Format

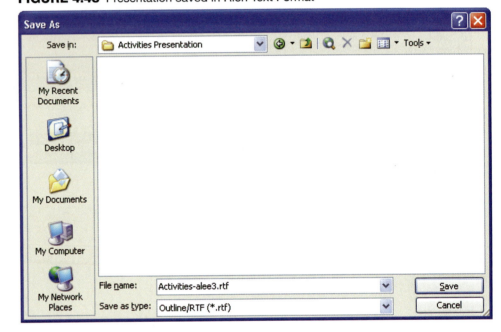

FIGURE 4.49 Print dialog box

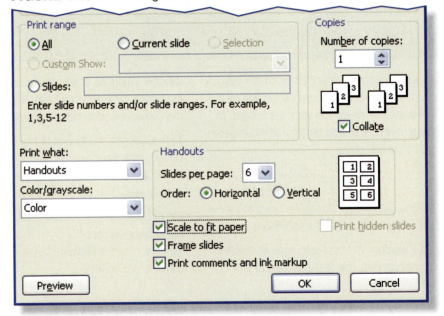

Lesson 4: Practice It Activities

PowerPoint 139

Getting Ready (Continued)

You can **restore** a window that was minimized to make it visible again. To restore a window, click the title of the window in the task bar.

To close a window, click the Close Window button.

To delete a file or folder, drag the item to the Recycle Bin and drop it on top. This places the item in the Recycle Bin, but does not delete the item. To delete the item, right click the Recycle Bin. Locate and click Empty Recycle Bin to permanently delete all of the items in your Recycle Bin.

Icons on the desktop can be arranged and rearranged to fit your needs. You can click and drag icons to various places on the desktop. You can also right click the mouse and choose Arrange Icons By. A submenu will open that allows you to arrange the icons by Name, Size, Type, or Modified. Icons can be arranged using Auto Arrange or they can be placed in a grid by choosing Align to Grid. You can also choose to hide the icons by deselecting Show Desktop Icons.

TECH CHECK

1. **Recall** List three parts of the Windows desktop.
2. **Reproduce** Make a sketch of a window. On the sketch, label the following items: Maximize button, Minimize button, Scroll bar, and Title bar.

Visit the **Student Online Learning Center** to learn more about this topic.
iCheckExpress.glencoe.com

LESSON 4 Practice It Activities

2 Create Action Buttons, Hide Slides, and Use Pens

Follow the steps to complete the activity. You must complete Practice It Activity 1 before doing this activity.

Step-By-Step

1. Open your **Activities-1** file. Save as: Activities-[your first initial and last name]2. On **Slide 9**, choose **Slide Show>Action Buttons**. Click **Action Button: Return**.

2. Click in the slide's lower right corner. In the **Action Settings** dialog box, select **Hyperlink to**. Click **Slide**.

3. In the **Hyperlink to Slide** dialog box, choose **2. Monday**. Click **OK** twice. Choose **Slide Sorter View**. Click **Slide 10**. Click **Hide Slide** .

4. **CHECK** Your screen should look like Figure 4.46. Click **Hide Slide** again.

5. Click **Normal View**. Choose **Slide Show>View Show**. Go to **Slide 8**. Choose **Pen>Felt Tip Pen**. Circle the text **Homework–5 hours**.

6. **CHECK** Your screen should look like Figure 4.47. End the show. Save and close your file.

FIGURE 4.46 Slide hidden in Slide Sorter View

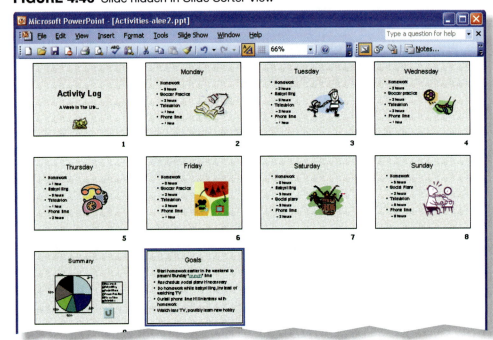

FIGURE 4.47 Slide with pen annotation

Lesson 4: Practice It Activities PowerPoint 138

Getting Set: Working with Files

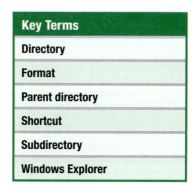

Key Terms
Directory
Format
Parent directory
Shortcut
Subdirectory
Windows Explorer

Windows Explorer is a program that shows the entire file system on a computer. To open Windows Explorer, choose **Start>Programs> Accessories>Windows Explorer**.

At the top left of the Desktop window, click the Desktop icon. All of the files and folders on the desktop will be displayed on the right side of the window.

One of the **directories**, or containers for files and folders, on the desktop is called My Documents. To view the files of this directory, click the My Documents icon on the left. Files can be data, text, programs, and more. To find out more about a file, right-click the file and choose Properties.

A directory can hold other directories. A directory that holds other directories is called a **parent directory**. A directory that is located in another directory is called a **subdirectory**. For instance, My Computer is a parent directory for 3½ Floppy (A:), and 3½ Floppy (A:) is a subdirectory of My Computer.

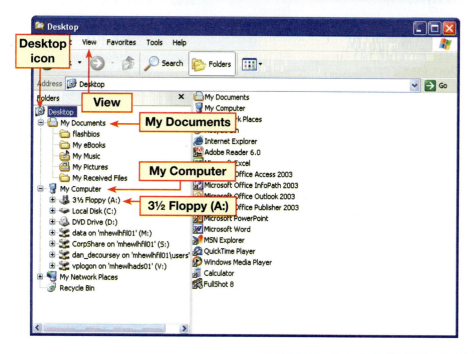

Part 3: Ready, Set, Process

Technology Handbook H22

LESSON 4 Practice It Activities

1 Rearrange Slides, Use Notes Panes, and Create Hyperlinks

Follow the steps to complete the activity.

Step-By-Step

1. Open the data file **Activities**. Save as: Activities-[your first initial and last name]1.

2. Click **Slide Sorter View**. Click **Slide 2** and drag it between **Slides 4** and **5**.

3. Choose **View > Normal**. Move to **Slide 9**. Click in the **Notes** pane and key: Take time to explain pie chart.

4. **CHECK** Your screen should look like Figure 4.44.

5. Move to **Slide 10**. Select the text **crunch**. Choose **Insert > Hyperlink**.

6. In the **Insert Hyperlink** dialog box, click **Place in This Document**.

7. Under **Select a place in this document**, click **8. Sunday**. Click **OK**. Deselect the text.

8. **CHECK** Your screen should look like Figure 4.45.

9. Save and close your file.

FIGURE 4.44 Note added to Notes pane

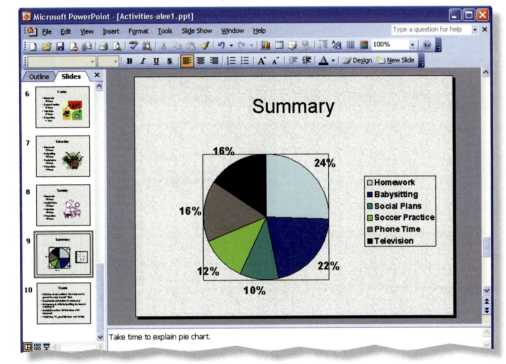

FIGURE 4.45 Hyperlink inserted into slide

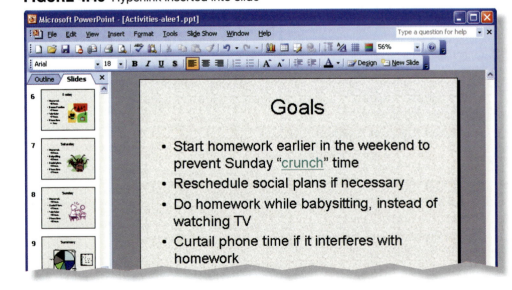

Lesson 4: Practice It Activities

PowerPoint 137

Getting Set: Working with Files (Continued)

With so many places to look, finding folders and files can be difficult. Use the Search window to find files and folders when you do not know where they are.

To search for a folder, you can choose **Start>Search>For Files or Folders**. To search all of the files and folders on the computer, click **All Files and Folders** on the left side of the Search window.

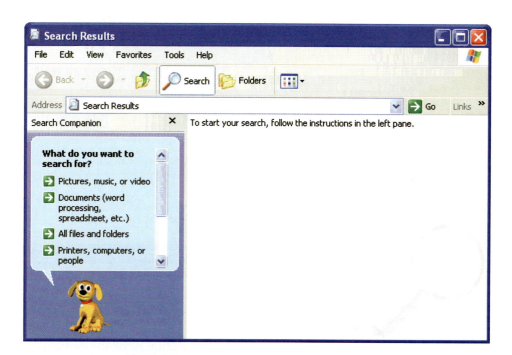

To search for files or folders that contain the word *computer*, key *computer* below **All or part of the file name**. Then click **Search**. If you are not sure if the name of a file is *Computer, Computers,* or *Computing,* use an asterisk for the part you are not sure about. For example, enter *Comput** in **All or part of the file name**. This tells the computer to show all files that start with *Comput.*

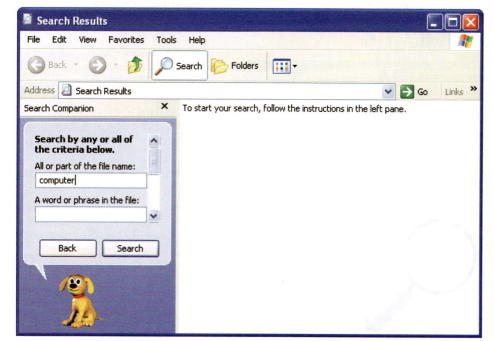

Part 3: Ready, Set, Process

LESSON 4 Concept Review

Key Terms

Action Button
Annotation
Grid
Guide
HTML
Hyperlink
Package for CD
PowerPoint Viewer
Print Preview
Publish
Slide Finder
Snap
Timing
Web Server

Reviewing Key Terms

Complete the following statements on a separate piece of paper. Choose from the Key Terms list on the left to complete the statements.

1. A(n) _____ is a series of horizontal and vertical lines that helps align objects. (p. 117)
2. A(n) _____, when clicked, takes you to another slide, opens another file on your computer, or opens a Web page on the Internet. (p. 114)
3. If you do not have PowerPoint, you can view a presentation using _____. (p. 128)
4. You can use the pen or highlighter to make a(n) _____ on a slide. (p. 126)
5. _____ indicates how long a slide will remain visible during a slide show. (p. 127)

Key Term Activity

6. Select seven Key Terms and create a cryptogram.
   A. For each letter in the alphabet, assign a number. No two letters can have the same number.
   B. For each Key Term, draw a box to represent each letter in the term.
   C. Below each box, write the number that matches that letter.
   D. See if your friends can decode each Key Term. Decode one of the terms to get them started, or give them a hint, such as 3=F.

Reviewing Key Facts

Answer the following questions on a separate piece of paper.

7. Which menu is used to create a Custom Show? (p. 123)
   A. New   C. Slide Show
   B. File   D. View

8. The Zoom button is located on which toolbar? (p. 118)
   A. Standard   C. Drawing
   B. Formatting   D. Outlining

9. Which is the name for a button that connects you to another slide during a Slide Show? (p. 116)
   A. Motion Button   C. Go To Button
   B. Advance Button D. Action Button

10. Which view should you be in to rearrange slides within a presentation? (p. 112)
    A. Normal View   C. Slide Show View
    B. Slide Sorter View D. Slide Finder

Getting Set: Working with Folders

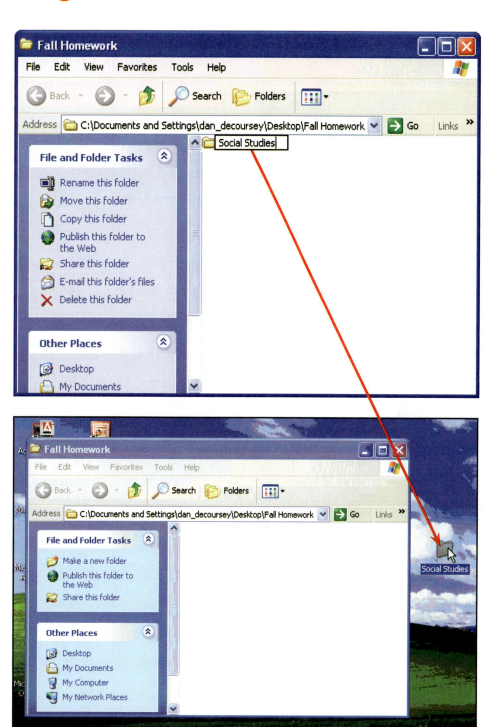

To create a folder, right-click the desktop. Then choose **New> Folder**. When the new folder appears, key Homework and press ENTER on your keyboard. Right-click the **Homework** folder and choose **Rename**. Key Fall Homework. Press ENTER.

To create a subfolder, open the folder in which you want to create the new folder. On the left side of the window, click **Make a new folder**. Finally, key Social Studies and press ENTER.

To move a folder, grab the folder and drop it in its new location. Drag **Social Studies** to the desktop. Then drag it back into the **Fall Homework** folder.

LESSON 4 Quick Reference

The following main commands were covered in the lesson. See Appendix A on page 151 for a listing of all the commands used in this book.

Function	Button	Menu	Keyboard	Speech
Add a slide	New Slide	Insert>New Slide	CTRL + M	☑
Create a Custom Show		Slide Show>Custom Shows	ALT + D / W	☑
Create an Action Button		Slide Show>Action Buttons	ALT + D / I	☑
Delete a slide		Edit>Delete Slide	DELETE	☑
Hide a slide		Slide Show>Hide Slide	ALT + D / H	☑
Insert a hyperlink		Insert>Hyperlink	CTRL + K	☑
Insert slides from other presentations		Insert>Slides from Files	ALT + I / F	☑
Normal View		View>Normal	ALT + V / N	☑
Package a slide show for a CD		File>Package for CD	ALT + F / K	☑
Rehearse timings		Slide Show>Rehearse Timings	ALT + D / R	☑
Set transition times	Slide Transition...	Slide Show>Slide Transition	ALT + D / T	☑
View Grids and Guides		View>Grid and Guides	SHIFT + F9 ALT + F9	☑
View Notes		View>Notes Page	ALT + V / P	☑
Zoom	100%	View>Zoom	ALT + V / Z	☑

Getting Set: Working with Folders (Continued)

To copy the Social Studies folder, right-click the folder and choose **Copy**. Then right-click the empty space in the window and choose **Paste**.

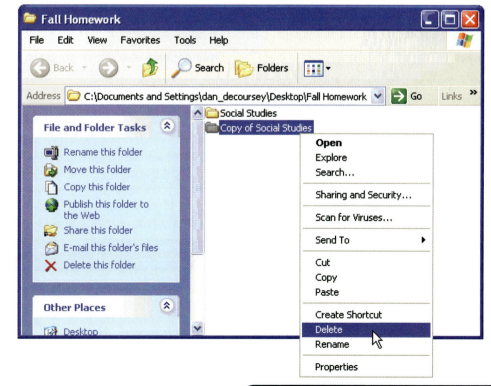

To delete the copy of Social Studies, right-click the copy and choose **Delete**. Then click **Yes** in the Confirm Folder Delete box.

Part 3: Ready, Set, Process

21st Century LEARNER

Communicate Effectively

When you introduce a new idea, you need to determine the best way to communicate with your audience. Thinking about your audience's needs will help you decide how best to deliver your new information. For example, when talking with younger people, it may be better to show them what you mean as opposed to just explaining your ideas in words.

Use Presentation Tools

Using presentation tools can also make you a more effective communicator. For example, if you are presenting complex ideas, you may want to provide handouts that explain your ideas in more detail. Pens, highlighters, and other annotation tools can also help you emphasize important points in a PowerPoint presentation.

MEET THE MANAGER

Maia Rosenfeld is the manager and chief photographer of Maia Rosenfeld Photography in Los Angeles, California. Since she gets many new clients through word-of-mouth recommendations, she knows the importance of effective communication. "If you do a good job and communicate effectively to your client," says Maia, "he will tell one person about your business. If you do a bad job, he'll tell nine." Notes Maia, "In a small business, you can't afford any miscommunication. And it's not just *what* you say; it's *how* you say it."

Interacting with your audience will make you a more effective presenter.

SKILLBUILDER

1. **State** Why is it important to know your audience when you communicate new information?
2. **Create** Develop a set of guidelines for new employees on how to be effective communicators.
3. **Analyze** What does Maia mean when she says, "If you do a good job and communicate effectively to your client, he will tell one person about your business. If you do a bad job, he'll tell nine"?

Getting Set: Using Floppy Disks

Before you can use a blank floppy disk, you must format the disk. When a disk is formatted, the computer first checks to make sure the disk works. Then the computer creates addresses for the information on the disk.

To format a disk, first place the disk in the floppy drive. Then open the **My Computer** directory. Click the **3½ Floppy (A:)** drive. Choose **File>Format**.

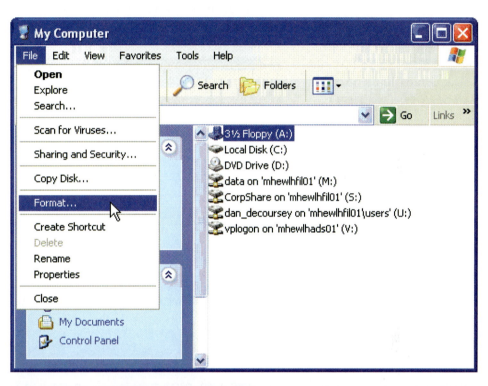

To copy a file to a floppy disk, drag the file to the My Computer window and drop the file on the icon for the 3½ Floppy (A:) drive.

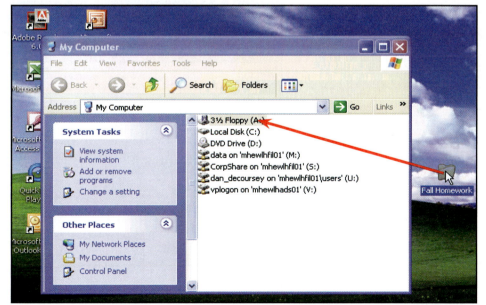

Part 3: Ready, Set, Process

Technology Handbook H26

Step-By-Step

1. Open your **Literacy.ppt** presentation. Choose **File>Send To> Microsoft Office Word**.

2. In the **Send To Microsoft Office Word** dialog box, select **Blank lines next to slides** (see Figure 4.42).

3. Click **OK**.

4. In your Word document, switch to **Print Layout View**.

5. **CHECK** Your screen should look like Figure 4.43.

6. Save the Word document as: Presentation-[your first initial and last name].

7. Close your Word file. Exit Word.

8. Save and close your PowerPoint file. Exit PowerPoint.

EXERCISE 4-19:
Export a Presentation to Microsoft Word

You can export or send a PowerPoint presentation to the Word application. When you export a presentation to Word, the presentation is converted into a Word document. The Word document can be a better format for storing PowerPoint files because they will take up less memory. Converting the presentation into Word can also allow you to send the presentation to someone who does not have PowerPoint.

FIGURE 4.42 Send to Microsoft Office Word dialog box

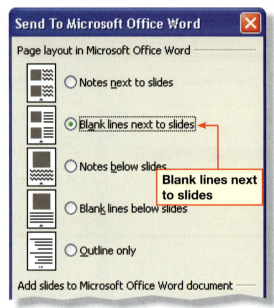

FIGURE 4.43 PowerPoint presentation exported to Word

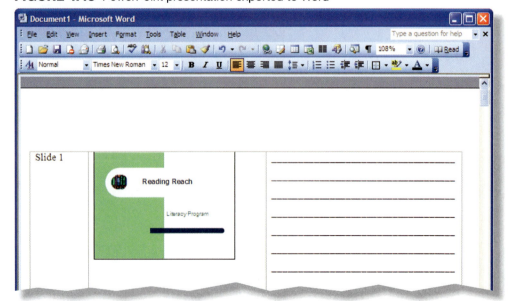

Lesson 4: Exercise 4-19

PowerPoint 133

Getting Set: Using Shortcuts

A <mark>shortcut</mark> is an icon that will automatically open a particular program, folder, or file, no matter where the shortcut is in the file system. For resources that people use often, shortcuts save the time of clicking through multiple folders to get to the program.

Follow these instructions to create a shortcut.

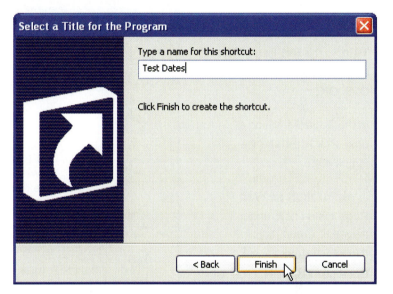

1. Right-click the place where you want to put the shortcut. Choose **New>Shortcut**.

2. In the Create Shortcut box, click **Browse**.

3. Select the location of the program or folder to which you want the shortcut to lead. Click **OK**.

4. In the Create Shortcut box, click **Next**.

5. Key a name for the shortcut in the line at the top of the box. Click **Finish**.

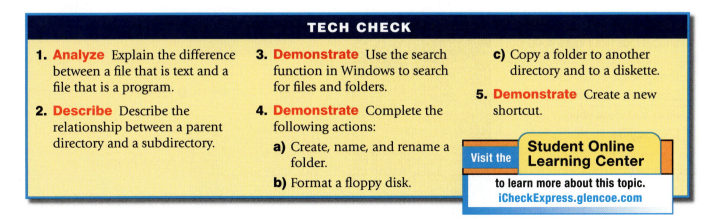

TECH CHECK

1. **Analyze** Explain the difference between a file that is text and a file that is a program.

2. **Describe** Describe the relationship between a parent directory and a subdirectory.

3. **Demonstrate** Use the search function in Windows to search for files and folders.

4. **Demonstrate** Complete the following actions:
   a) Create, name, and rename a folder.
   b) Format a floppy disk.
   c) Copy a folder to another directory and to a diskette.

5. **Demonstrate** Create a new shortcut.

Visit the **Student Online Learning Center** to learn more about this topic.
iCheckExpress.glencoe.com

Part 3: Ready, Set, Process — Technology Handbook H27

Step-By-Step

1. In your **Literacy** file, choose **File>Save as Web Page**.

2. In the **Save As** dialog box, click **Create New Folder**.

3. Key: Published Web Pages. Click **OK**. Click **Change Title**. In the **Set Page Title** dialog box, key: Library Staff. Click **OK**.

4. In the **Save As** dialog box, click **Publish** (see Figure 4.40).

5. In the **Publish as Web Page** dialog box, under **Publish what?**, click **Custom show**. Under **Browser support**, click **All browsers listed above (creates larger files)**.

6. Select **Open published Web page in browser**. With your teacher's permission, click **Publish**.

7. **CHECK** Your screen should look like Figure 4.41.

8. Navigate the presentation. Close your Web browser. Save and close your **Literacy** file.

EXERCISE 4-18:
Publish Presentations as Web Pages

Once you save a presentation in HTML format, you can **publish** the Web page by putting it on a Web server. A **Web server** is a computer on the Internet that stores Web pages. Publishing a presentation is different from saving it as a Web page, which allows only those on your network to view it. When you publish a presentation, anyone with a Web browser can view it.

FIGURE 4.40 Publish as Web Page dialog box

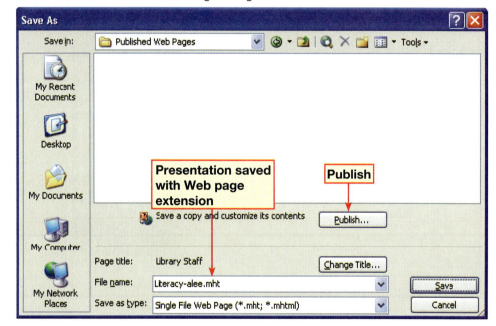

FIGURE 4.41 Published Web page

Lesson 4: Exercise 4-18

PowerPoint 132

Processing: Using Windows Applications

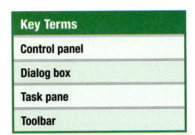

Key Terms
- Control panel
- Dialog box
- Task pane
- Toolbar

In Windows, the Start menu launches applications. To launch an application, click the Start button and then choose Programs. Click the application you want to launch.

After launching a Microsoft application, notice the following parts of the screen.

The **Control Panel** contains tools that allow a user to change the way Windows appears and functions. Visit the Student Online Learning Center to learn about using the control panel to change monitor, mouse, and printer settings.

The **task pane** helps complete basic tasks.

The **toolbars** provide a quick way to give the application commands. The menus also contain commands. A **dialog box** is a window that appears inside an application and has buttons and menus to carry out various commands.

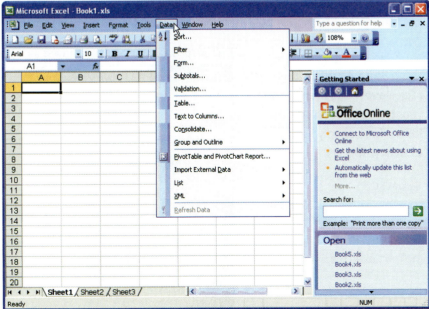

Visit the **Student Online Learning Center** to learn more about this topic. iCheckExpress.glencoe.com

EXERCISE 4-17: Save Presentations as Web Pages

You can save a presentation as a Web page. The presentation is saved as **HTML**, a programming language that Web browsers use to read and display Web pages. Use Web Page Preview to preview how your Web pages will look in a Web browser.

FIGURE 4.38 Presentation in Web Page Preview

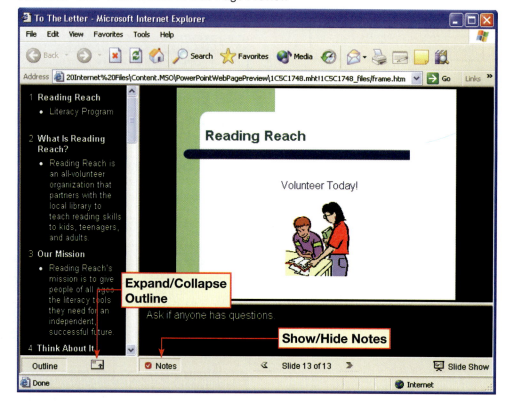

FIGURE 4.39 Presentation saved as a Web page

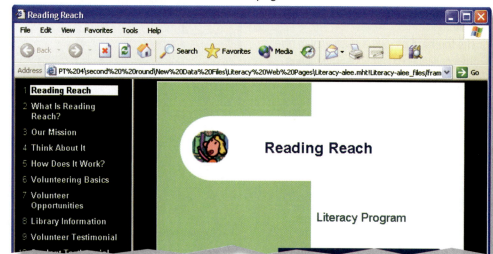

Step-By-Step

1. In your **Literacy** file, choose **File>Web Page Preview**.

2. In the **Outline** pane, click the **13 Reading Reach** hyperlink.

3. Click **Expand/Collapse Outline**. Click **Show/Hide Notes**.

4. **CHECK** Your screen should look like Figure 4.38. Close the browser.

5. Choose **File>Save as Web Page**. In the **Save As** dialog box, click **Create New Folder**.

6. Key: Literacy Web Pages. Click **OK**.

7. Click **Change Title**. In the **Set Page Title** dialog box, key: Reading Reach. Click **OK**.

8. In the **Save As** dialog box, click **Save**. Locate and open your **Literacy Web Pages** folder. Then open your **Literacy.mht** file.

9. **CHECK** Your screen should look like Figure 4.39.

10. Save your file. Continue to the next exercise.

Processing: Shutting Down Windows

Follow these steps to shut down, or turn off, Windows once you have finished using the computer.

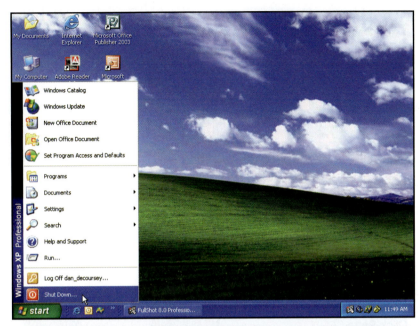

① Close all files and programs.

② Click **Start**.

③ Choose **Shut Down**...

④ When the Shut Down Windows dialog box appears, click the drop-down arrow and choose **Shut down** if necessary.

⑤ Click **OK**.

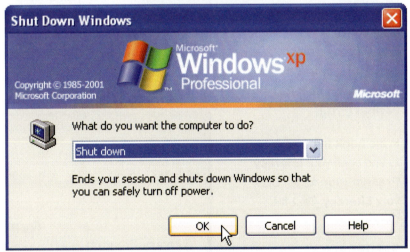

TECH CHECK

1. **Demonstrate** Use the Control Panel to do the following:
   a) Change screen displays.
   b) Change mouse settings.
   c) Change the date and time.

2. **Demonstrate** Use the Printers and Faxes option in the Control Panel to perform the following tasks:
   a) Change the default printer.
   b) Change printer properties.

3. **Recall** What are two places in a Microsoft application that commands can be found?

Visit the **Student Online Learning Center** to learn more about this topic.
iCheckExpress.glencoe.com

Part 3: Ready, Set, Process

Technology Handbook   H29

Step-By-Step

EXERCISE 4-16:
Save Slides with Different Names and Formats and in Different Folders

You can save presentations with different names and in different formats. For example, you can save presentations in Rich Text Format, which allows you to open and edit the presentation in Word. Use different folders to organize different versions of a presentation.

1. In your **Literacy** file, choose **File>Save As**. In the dialog box, click **Create New Folder**.

2. Key: **Literacy Presentation**. Click **OK**.

3. In the **File name** box, key: **Literacy_Text-[your first initial and last name]**. Click the **Save as type** drop-down arrow. Click **Outline/RTF (*.rtf)**.

4. **CHECK** Your dialog box should look like Figure 4.36. Click **Save**.

5. Start **Word**. In Word, choose **File>Open**. In the **Open** dialog box, under **Files of Type**, select **Rich Text Format (*rtf.)**.

6. In the **Look in** box, browse to and open your **Literacy Presentation** folder. Click your **Literacy_Text** file. Click **Open**.

7. **CHECK** Your screen should look like Figure 4.37. Save and close the .rtf file. Exit Word.

8. Save your **Literacy** file. Continue to the next exercise.

FIGURE 4.36 Presentation saved in Rich Text Format

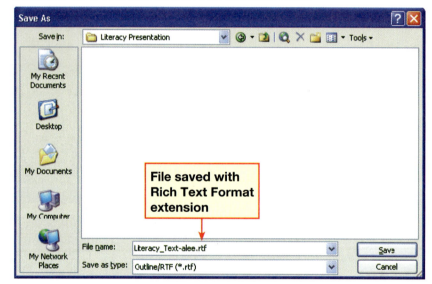

FIGURE 4.37 Rich Text Format file viewed in Word

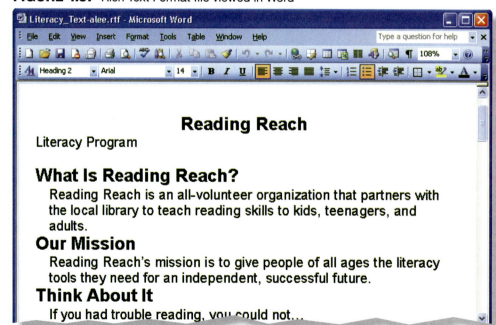

Lesson 4: Exercise 4-16

PART 3 Assessment

Key Term Review

Answer the following questions on a separate piece of paper.

1. A(n) _____ is a container for files and folders. (p. H22)
2. The _____ is the visual representation of a file system on a computer. (p. H19)
3. A directory that contains other directories is called a _____. (p. H22)
4. The _____ is used to delete items permanently. (p. H19)
5. A(n) _____ is a list of options. The _____ opens files and applications. A(n) _____ can be opened by right-clicking the mouse. (p. H19)
6. Graphic representations of files or applications are called _____. (p. H19)
7. A(n) _____ is the box that moves inside the scroll bar. (p. H20)
8. _____ is a program that shows the entire file system on a computer. (p. H22)
9. A(n) _____ is an icon that will automatically open a particular program, folder, or file, no matter where the shortcut is in the file system. (p. H27)
10. A window that appears inside an application and has buttons and menus to carry out various commands is called a _____. (p. H28)
11. The _____ contains tools that allow a user to change the way Windows appears and functions. (p. H28)
12. To _____ a window means to make it larger or smaller. (p. H20)
13. The _____ shows what file and applications are open. (p. H19)
14. The _____ deletes files or applications from the computer. (p. H19)
15. A(n) _____ is a box that shows what is inside a file or folder. (p. H20)

Concept Review

Answer the following questions on a separate piece of paper.

16. Explain the difference between maximizing a window and minimizing a window. (p. H20)
17. How would you move a window? (p. H20)
18. Describe how to delete a file or folder. (p. H21)
19. Explain what the desktop is in a graphical user interface. (p. H19)
20. Explain where the monitor should be located to help avoid soreness while working at the computer. (p. H18)
21. Write detailed directions explaining to a friend how to use Search to find a particular file or folder. (p. H23)
22. Explain the similarities and differences between folders and subfolders. (p. H24)
23. What steps would you take to copy a folder? (p. H25)

Critical Thinking

Complete the following exercises to reinforce your understanding of the lesson.

24. **Design** Design a file system to store information, such as homework, related to school. Sketch the file system with the highest directory at the top of the page. Use lines to show which folders are in each directory. Be sure to label each folder.
25. **Explain** Write a paragraph in which you explain the different parts of a Windows desktop to someone who has never seen it before. Mention at least three parts of the desktop and explain the function of each part.

ISTE Standards

The following ISTE standards are covered in Part 3. Refer to pages xvii to xix for a description of the standards listed here.

NETS•S	Performance Indicator
3	5

Part 3: Ready, Set, Process

Step-By-Step

EXERCISE 4-15: (Continued)
Package Presentations for Storage on a CD

7. Click **Options**. Be sure both the **PowerPoint Viewer** and **Linked files** check boxes are checked.

8. Check the **Embedded TrueType fonts** check box.

9. **CHECK** Your **Options** dialog box should look like Figure 4.34. Click **OK**.

10. Click **Copy to Folder**. In the **Folder name** box, key: LiteracyCD.

11. **CHECK** Your dialog box should look like Figure 4.35. Click **Browse**. Ask your teacher which location to select in the **Location** box. Click **OK**.

12. If a warning box opens, click **Continue**.

13. In the **Package for CD** dialog box, click **Close**.

14. Locate and open your **LiteracyCD** folder. Note the different files in the folder. Close the folder.

15. Save your file.

16. Continue to the next exercise.

FIGURE 4.34 Package for CD Options dialog box

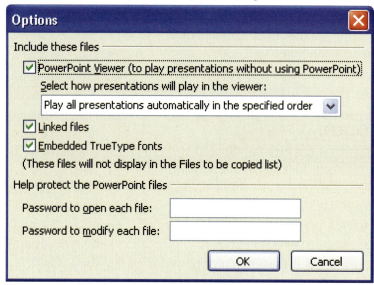

FIGURE 4.35 Copy to Folder dialog box

You Should Know

In the **Package for CD Options** dialog box, you can set a password to either open a file or modify a file. These passwords apply only to the packaged versions of the presentation. They do not affect passwords you set in the original files.

PART 4 Living Online

Impact of Computers on Society

Key Terms

Moore's law

Some of the first computers were built during WWII. They were built to perform the many calculations necessary to break codes.

The first American computer, which was built during WWII, was called the ENIAC. The ENIAC filled a 30 by 50 foot room and had 18,000 vacuum tubes and 6,000 switches. At 5,000 calculations per second, the ENIAC was much faster than any computer before it. However, it had to be rewired for each new calculation.

In **1944**, Howard Aiken introduced the first fully functional computer: the Harvard Mark I.

The Harvard Mark I was 55 feet long and 8 feet high. It was slower than the ENIAC, but it did not have to be rewired for new calculations.

2005 saw more advances in wireless networking. The ability to access the Internet by wireless connections with handheld computers was a main focus in business and school environments.

The first "personal computer" was the Altair 880. It became available for commercial purchase in **1975** and cost about $400. The Altair 880 came in a kit that the user had to assemble.

A personal digital assistant called the Pilot was released in **1996**. It was extremely popular because of its capabilities and ease of use.

The Apple II came out in **1977**. It came fully assembled with a built-in keyboard. However, users had to plug the computer into their own television sets to use the monitor.

In **1989** the World Wide Web was created at a physics laboratory in Geneva, Switzerland. It was originally intended for use by scientific researchers.

Step-By-Step

1. In your **Literacy** file, choose **File>Package for CD**.

2. In the **Package for CD** dialog box, in the **Name the CD** box, key: LiteracyCD-[your first initial and last name] (see Figure 4.32).

3. Click **Add Files**. In the **Files of type** box, click **All Files (*.*)**.

4. Locate and select the data file **Worksheet.doc**.

5. Click **Add**.

6. **CHECK** Your dialog box should look like Figure 4.33. Click **OK**.

Continued on the next page.

Tips and Tricks

If you have a CD writer connected to your computer, choose **Copy to CD** to burn your presentation onto a CD.

EXERCISE 4-15:
Package Presentations for Storage on a CD

Burning a presentation to a CD makes it easy to store and transport your work. Many different text and graphics files are used to create one presentation. When you use the **Package For CD** feature, PowerPoint automatically creates a folder that stores all these files. If you have hyperlinked to a file, you must add this file to the folder so PowerPoint can locate the file to which the presentation is linked. **PowerPoint Viewer** allows someone to view a slide show without PowerPoint.

FIGURE 4.32 Package for CD dialog box

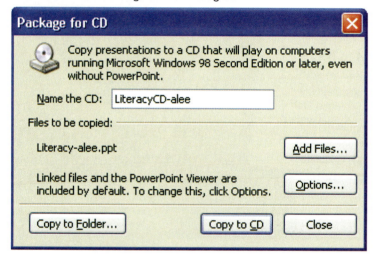

FIGURE 4.33 Package for CD with file added

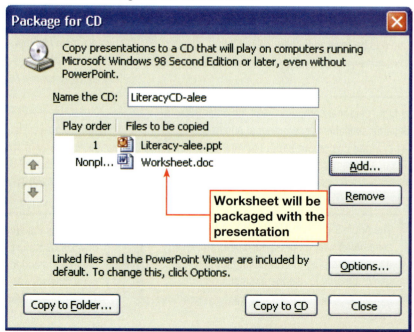

Lesson 4: Exercise 4-15

PowerPoint 128

Impact of Computers on Society (Continued)

Moore's Law

Computers were mostly used by large businesses and by the government until the mid-1970s when personal computers were first built. However, in 1965 Gordon Moore made a prediction that became known as **Moore's Law**. Moore predicted that the number of transistors in computer circuits would double every couple of years. As it turns out, his prediction has been fairly accurate.

The increase in the number of transistors made it possible for computers to become much smaller than the ENIAC and the Harvard mark I. Compared to the room-filling ENIAC, today's laptops are about the size of a coffee table book. And they are far more powerful. An average laptop today is about 300,000 times faster than the ENIAC.

Circuit board used in the 1960s.

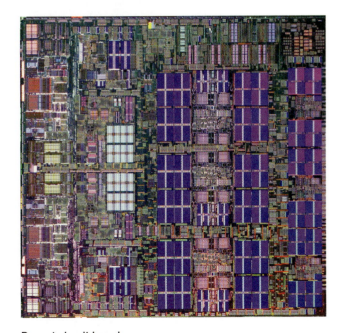

Recent circuit board.

Step-By-Step

1. In your **Literacy** file, choose **Slide Show>Slide Transition**.

2. Under **Advance slide**, select **Automatically after**. Key: **00:15**.

3. **CHECK** Your screen should look like Figure 4.30. Click **Apply to All Slides**.

4. Choose **Slide Show>Rehearse Timings**.

5. Slowly read each slide aloud. Practice any comments you plan to say. Click **Next** on the **Rehearsal** toolbar (upper-left corner of the screen) to move to the next slide.

6. After you have read the last slide, in the **Rehearsal** toolbar, click **Close**. Click **Yes** to save the timing for each slide.

7. **CHECK** Your screen should look similar to Figure 4.31.

8. Close the task pane. Switch to **Normal View**.

9. Save your file. Continue to the next exercise.

EXERCISE 4-14: Rehearse and Save Timings

To set a show's timing, or how long each slide appears, rehearse the presentation. Make sure you and your audience have enough time to read each slide. Use the Rehearsal toolbar to move from slide to slide, to track the presentation's total time, and to pause if necessary while setting timings. When finished, test your timings by viewing the slide show again.

FIGURE 4.30 Automatic timing set at 15 seconds

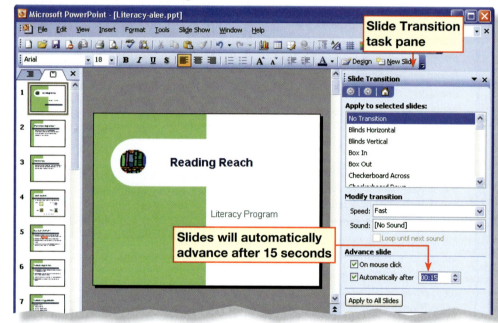

FIGURE 4.31 Saved timings

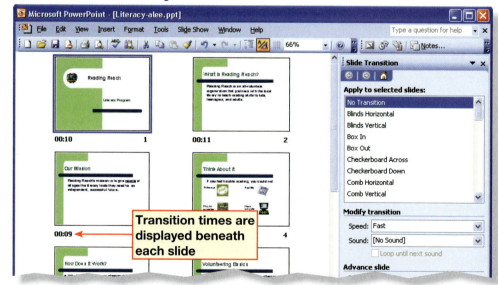

Lesson 4: Exercise 4-14

PowerPoint 127

Impact of Computers on Society (Continued)

Computers have changed the world. They have changed everything from shopping, to movies, to the kinds of jobs that are available.

Overall, computers have made it easier for businesses to exchange information. E-mail and access to information, such as stock market data, has increased the speed of business. Computers have made surveillance (monitoring and watching people) easier than ever. Privacy and security issues are being debated in courtrooms every day. Data is being collected on millions of people and sold to virtually all types of businesses. People who work together today do not have to do so at the same time. Many services and information are available 24 hours per day. Technologists believe that we have only begun to imagine the impact of computers on our society.

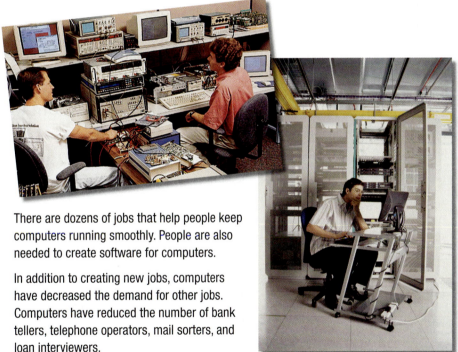

There are dozens of jobs that help people keep computers running smoothly. People are also needed to create software for computers.

In addition to creating new jobs, computers have decreased the demand for other jobs. Computers have reduced the number of bank tellers, telephone operators, mail sorters, and loan interviewers.

TECH CHECK

1. **Reproduce** What is Moore's Law?
2. **Summarize** Write a paragraph that summarizes the invention and development of computers.
3. **Discuss** Write a paragraph that discusses the positive and negative impacts that computers have had on society.

Visit the **Student Online Learning Center** to learn more about the impact of computers on consumers.
iCheckExpress.glencoe.com

Part 4: Living Online

Technology Handbook H33

EXERCISE 4-13:
Use Pens, Highlighters, and Arrows

Use a pen to highlight or circle items, or use an arrow to point to parts of a slide. You can change the color of the pen or erase the **annotations**, or marks. You can save or not save your annotations. Select **Print Comments and Ink Markup** from print options to print annotations.

FIGURE 4.28 Text circled with Felt Tip Pen

1. In your **Literacy** file, choose **Slide Show>View Show**. Move the mouse to display the **Slide Show** toolbar.

2. Forward to slide **5. How does it work?**

3. In the **Slide Show** toolbar, click **Pen**. Choose **Ink Color>Red**. Click **Pen**. Choose **Felt Tip Pen**.

4. Hold down the mouse button to circle **weekday** (see Figure 4.28).

5. Click **Pen**. Choose **Highlighter**. Hold down the mouse button to highlight **library** in the last bullet point.

6. **CHECK** Your screen should look like Figure 4.29.

7. Click **Pen**. Choose **Eraser**. Hold down the mouse button to erase the highlighted word.

8. Click **Pen**. Choose **Arrow**. Right-click the slide. Click **End Show**. In the dialog box, click **Keep**.

9. Switch to **Normal View**. Save your file. Continue to the next exercise.

FIGURE 4.29 Highlighted text

Lesson 4: Exercise 4-13

PowerPoint 126

Staying Safe Online

The Internet can be a wonderful place. There is much to learn, explore, and discover. But it can also be a dangerous place. Many Web sites seek information from their users. Although some of these Web sites are legitimate, there are many questionable sites that are looking for data as well. Before you type any information into an online form or chat room, you need to evaluate that Web site. Take the following precautions to stay safe online.

Know to whom you are giving the information. Check the URL in your browser. Does it match the domain you visited? Or were you redirected to another site without your knowledge?

Why are you giving the information? For example, if you are ordering something online, you will need to give your address in order for the product to be shipped. There should always be a good reason for all the information you provide.

Never give out your social security number, your birth date, or your mother's maiden name without adult consent. This information is often used to secure credit reports, and giving this information to a dishonest source can ruin your credit.

Never give personal information of any sort to someone you meet in a chat room. Always remain anonymous.

If you are still unsure whether it is safe to give the information, check with a parent or another trusted adult.

EXERCISE 4-12:
Navigate in Slide Show View

If you move the mouse during a slide show, the Slide Show toolbar appears. Use the Slide Show toolbar arrows and the Slide shortcut menu to navigate forward, backward, or to a specific slide. You can also use the Slide shortcut menu to access a custom show, help information, or screen options. Some shortcut functions are shown in Table 4.1.

TABLE 4.1 Slide shortcut menu navigation options

Shortcut Commands	Function
Next	Moves to next slide
Previous	Moves to previous slide
Last Viewed	Moves to last slide viewed
Go to Slide	Moves to a specified slide
Pause	Pauses show
End Show	Ends show

FIGURE 4.27 Slide Show toolbar with shortcut menu open

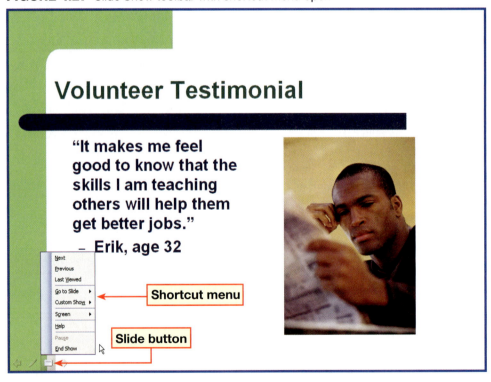

Step-By-Step

1. In your **Literacy** file, Choose **Slide Show>View Show**. The slide show begins.

2. Move your mouse to display the **Slide Show** toolbar.

3. Click the **Next** arrow to move to **Slide 2**.

4. Click **Slide** to open the shortcut menu. Review the commands described in Table 4.1.

5. Click **Slide**. Choose **Next** to go to **Slide 3**.

6. Click **Slide**. Choose **Go to Slide**. Click **9. Volunteer Testimonial**. Click **Slide** to open the shortcut menu.

7. **CHECK** Your screen should look like Figure 4.27.

8. Click **Slide**. Choose **End Show**.

9. Save your file.

10. Continue to the next exercise.

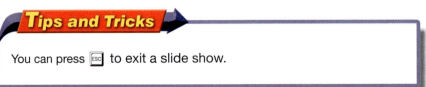

You can press [ESC] to exit a slide show.

Netiquette

New rules of etiquette have evolved for the communication media provided by the Internet: e-mail, chat rooms, and newsgroups. Nicknamed "netiquette," these basic guidelines are important to keep in mind whenever you are communicating with someone online.

NETIQUETTE GUIDELINES

E-MAIL

- ✓ Do not send large attachments, unless the recipient is expecting them.
- ✓ When forwarding e-mails, trim off unnecessary information like old headers and quotes—these can build up quickly!
- ✓ Do not say anything about someone that you would not want them to hear. Even after you click Delete, the e-mail is not really gone. E-mail records stay in the system for a long time.
- ✓ Never send or forward chain letters. Even if they seem like a good idea, they are often fraudulent.
- ✓ Do not "spam." Spam, or junk e-mail, is a billion-dollar problem, clogging e-mail systems and wasting time. Do not add to the problem.
- ✓ Do not SHOUT. Make sure your Caps Lock key is off.

CHAT ROOMS

- ✓ Choose chat rooms wisely. Some chat rooms have questionable people, so do some research first.
- ✓ Behave in a chat room as though you were communicating face-to-face. Remember that words can be misinterpreted, and things like sarcasm and body language may not come across online.
- ✓ Do not threaten, harass, or abuse any participants in a chat room.
- ✓ Take turns with the conversation. Just like in a real conversation, allow people to finish their thoughts, and do not interrupt.
- ✓ Be aware of "lurkers," people who are reading the conversation but not taking part.

NEWSGROUPS

- ✓ Stay on topic. Most newsgroups are very specific, and readers do not appreciate posts (contributed information) that do not fit the topic.
- ✓ Do not "flame." A flame is an aggressive or insulting letter. People in newsgroups often get passionate or excited in these conversations, which makes it easy to flame. Never key something that you would not want to say out loud.
- ✓ Know your facts. There is no fact-checking process in newsgroups. Just because someone makes a statement does not mean it is true. Remember this when quoting or replying to someone.
- ✓ Behave online as you normally would—honestly, ethically, and wisely.

TECH CHECK

1. **Predict** What information will you need to give if you order something online?
2. **Summarize** What are some general "netiquette" rules?
3. **Discuss** Write a paragraph that discusses the benefits and dangers of the Internet.

Visit the **Student Online Learning Center** to learn more about this topic.
iCheckExpress.glencoe.com

Step-By-Step

EXERCISE 4-11: (Continued)
Create and Edit a Custom Show

9. Click **Edit**.

10. In the **Define Custom Show** dialog box, under **Slides in presentation**, click **13. Reading Reach**.

11. Click **Add**.

12. Under **Slides in custom show**, click **3. Our Mission**.

13. Click the **up arrow** button once.

14. **CHECK** Your dialog box should look like Figure 4.25. Notice **Slide 3** has become the second slide in the list.

15. Under **Slides in custom show**, click **8. Library Information**.

16. Click **Remove**.

17. **CHECK** Your dialog box should look like Figure 4.26. Click **OK**.

18. In the **Custom Shows** dialog box, click **Show**.

19. View your custom show.

20. Save your **Literacy** file. Continue to the next exercise.

FIGURE 4.25 Rearranging slides in the custom presentation

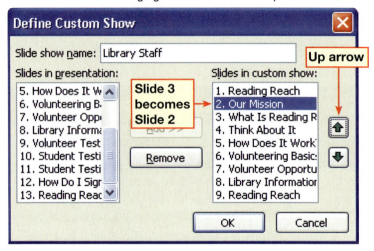

FIGURE 4.26 Edited Custom Show

Tips and Tricks

To select multiple slides in the **Define Custom Show** dialog box, hold down CTRL as you click the slides.

You Should Know

You can use the **Custom Shows** dialog box to add, modify, remove, or copy a custom show.

Lesson 4: Exercise 4-11   PowerPoint   124

Ethics and Technology

Computers can be used to do wonderful things, but they can also be misused. Knowing some simple ethical guidelines will ensure that you are always doing the right thing.

USING THE INTERNET RESPONSIBLY

- ✓ Because your school may have a fast Internet connection, you may be tempted to use these connections to download large files. Check with your teacher first, as there may be policies forbidding this.
- ✓ Remember that the school computer is there to help you get your work done. If you instead use the computer to play games, check your personal e-mail, or look at offensive material on the Internet, you are inappropriately using the resource that is being provided for you.
- ✓ If you engage in inappropriate activity on a school computer, you could be suspended from school, or perhaps even prosecuted.
- ✓ Do not do anything on a computer that you would not do if your teacher or parents were standing behind you, watching.
- ✓ E-mail systems leave a "digital paper trail." This means that what you type into an e-mail can be found by a system administrator. Be sure not to abuse company or school e-mail systems—it may come back to haunt you!

- ✓ You would not steal office supplies from your office or school, so make sure you do not take home computer-related resources like CD-ROMs or floppy disks.
- ✓ If you download any files or applications, be sure to check with your system administrator before using them. Downloaded files are a chief source of viruses, which cause millions of dollars in damages to computer networks every year.
- ✓ Avoid plagiarism, or copying someone else's work. It is acceptable to quote online sources in your work, but you must make sure you identify those sources and give them proper credit.
- ✓ Follow copyright laws. If you want to use part of an online work that has been copyrighted, contact the Webmaster of the site or the author of the article to request permission.
- ✓ It is not legal to download copyrighted music and videos and share them for free. Only use legal file sharing sites, which usually charge a small fee.

- ✓ If you need graphic images for a document you are creating, look for sources of license-free images that you do not have to pay to use. The owner of the image should be able to provide proof of ownership of the image and grant or deny permission to use it. If you cannot get this type of documentation in writing, do not use the image.
- ✓ Evaluate the information listed in a Web site. Sites that include bibliographical information tend to be more reliable.
- ✓ Do not engage in cyberbullying. Cyberbullying involves using the Internet or other digital communication devices to send or post information that is harmful or cruel. It might include harassment, put-downs, or making private information about an individual public. Be sure to report any instances of cyberbullying.
- ✓ Do not interfere with or tamper with anyone else's computer files.
- ✓ Always show consideration and respect for others in the way you use your computer.

TECH CHECK

1. **Explain** What is a "digital paper trail"?
2. **Predict** When is it acceptable to quote from someone else's work?
3. **Analyze** Why do you think music companies are trying to stop illegal downloading of music files?

Visit the **Student Online Learning Center** to learn more about the legal and ethical problems associated with computer technology.
iCheckExpress.glencoe.com

EXERCISE 4-11:
Create and Edit a Custom Show

Another way to tailor an existing presentation for different audiences is to create a custom show. A custom show includes slides from an existing slide show. You can edit a custom show by adding, removing, and rearranging slides.

FIGURE 4.23 Custom Shows dialog box

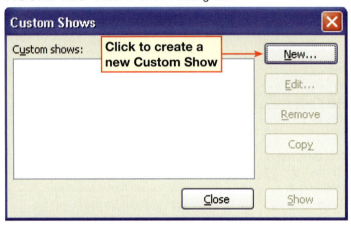

FIGURE 4.24 Define Custom Show dialog box

Step-By-Step

1. In your **Literacy** file, choose **Slide Show>Custom Shows**.

2. In the **Custom Shows** dialog box, click **New** (see Figure 4.23).

3. In the **Define Custom Show** dialog box, click in the **Slide show name** box. Key: Library Staff.

4. Hold down CTRL. Select Slides **1–8**. Click **Add**.

5. ⓘCHECK Your dialog box should look like Figure 4.24. Click **OK**.

6. In the **Custom Shows** dialog box, click **Show**. View your custom show.

7. Choose **Slide Show> Custom Shows**.

8. Under **Custom shows**, select **Library Staff** (if necessary).

Continued on the next page.

Tips and Tricks

To open the **Custom Shows** dialog box quickly, press ALT + D. Then press W.

Lesson 4: Exercise 4-11

Navigating the Internet

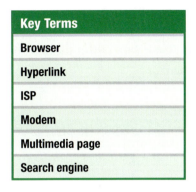

Key Terms
- Browser
- Hyperlink
- ISP
- Modem
- Multimedia page
- Search engine

Computers are connected to the Internet in different ways. Homes and businesses pay an **ISP**, or Internet Service Provider, to connect to the Internet. A **modem** allows a computer to be connected to the Internet. Dialup modems and DSL modems use phone lines to connect to the Internet. A cable modem uses cable TV wires to connect. A **browser** is the software that sends and retrieves information on the Internet. Study the figure below to learn about some important browser functions.

Click back to return to the previous Web page

Key the URL or Web address here

Click a hyperlink to view a page it is linked to

A **hyperlink** is an item on a Web page that links to another Web page. When you click a hyperlink, the browser will display the page the hyperlink connects to.

The Favorites menu allows you to bookmark Web pages. A bookmark sends the browser automatically to a page that you specify. Web pages that contain information in many forms, like sound and movies, are called **multimedia pages**.

Favorites

Linked page

Visit the Student Online Learning Center to learn about using Internet resources.
iCheckExpress.glencoe.com

Part 4: Living Online

Technology Handbook H37

Step-By-Step

1. In your **Literacy** file, click **Slide Sorter View**.

2. Click **Slide 4**.

3. Choose **Slide Show > Hide Slide**.

4. **CHECK** Your screen should look like Figure 4.21.

5. Click **Slide 6**. Press CTRL. Hold the button and click **Slides 7**, **9**, **12**, and **13**.

6. On the **Slide Sorter** toolbar, click **Hide Slide** to hide the five slides.

7. **CHECK** Your screen should look similar to Figure 4.22. View the show.

8. In **Slide Sorter View**, click **Slide 4**. Press CTRL and click **Slides 6**, **7**, **9**, **12**, and **13**.

9. Click **Hide Slide** again to unhide the slides.

10. Switch to **Normal View**. Save your file.

11. Continue to the next exercise.

EXERCISE 4-10:
Hide Slides

If you show the same presentation to different audiences, there may be some slides that are appropriate for one audience and not for the other. You can use the Hide Slide button to hide slides that you do not want to appear when you run a slide show. The Hide Slide button is only available in Slide Sorter view. Select **Print hidden slides** in the Print dialog box to print slides you have hidden.

FIGURE 4.21 Hidden slide in Slide Sorter View

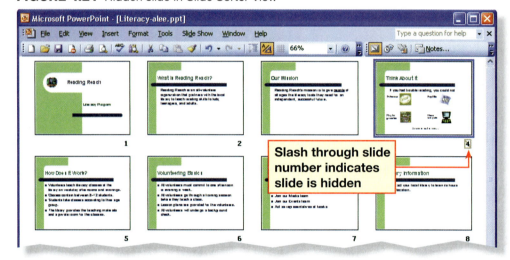

Slash through slide number indicates slide is hidden

FIGURE 4.22 Multiple slides hidden

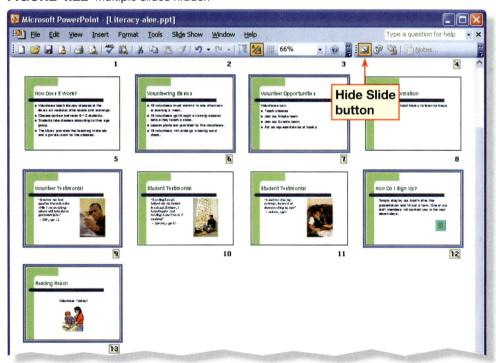

Hide Slide button

Unit 1, Lesson 4: Exercise 4-10

Navigating the Internet (Continued)

The Internet contains so much information that it is often hard to find what you are looking for. **Search engines** search the Internet for keywords that you provide.

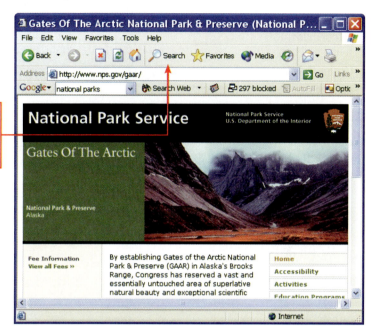

Click here to use the search engine Internet Explorer

In addition to the search engine in Internet Explorer, there are several very good search engines such as Google, on the Internet. Regardless of which search engine you use, it is important for you to be able to search effectively.

The first step towards searching effectively is choosing appropriate keywords. When you are searching for something that is not easily summed up in one word, you can enter two or more words.

Many search engines also have an advanced search that allows you to indicate exactly what you want the engine to search for and what you want it to ignore.

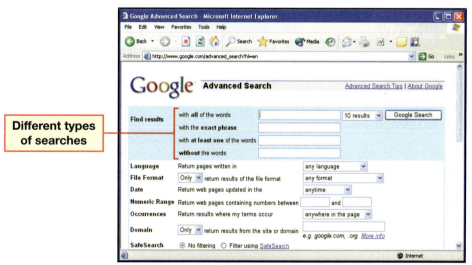

Different types of searches

TECH CHECK

1. **Define** What is a browser?
2. **Explain** Why are bookmarks useful?
3. **Predict** Describe a situation in which it would be best to use an advanced search.

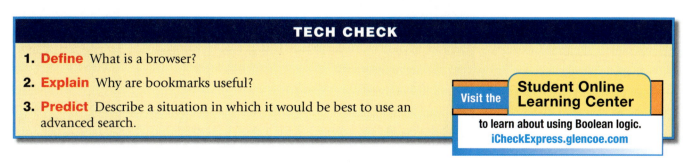

Visit the **Student Online Learning Center** to learn about using Boolean logic.
iCheckExpress.glencoe.com

Part 4: Living Online

Technology Handbook H38

EXERCISE 4-9: Modify Printing Options

By modifying printing options, you can choose to print slides, handouts, notes pages, or outline view. You can print every slide in a show, or only selected slides.

Step-By-Step

1. In your **Literacy** file, choose **File > Print**.
2. Under **Print range**, select **All**.
3. Click in the **Number of copies** box. Key: 2.
4. Click the **Print what** drop-down arrow. Click **Handout**.
5. Click the **Slides per page** drop-down arrow. Select **9**.
6. Make sure the **Scale to fit paper** and **Frame slides** check boxes are selected.
7. **CHECK** Your dialog box should look like Figure 4.19.
8. Click **Preview**.
9. **CHECK** Your screen should look like Figure 4.20.
10. With your teacher's permission, click **Print** to print your handouts.
11. Save your file. Continue to the next exercise.

FIGURE 4.19 Print dialog box with options selected

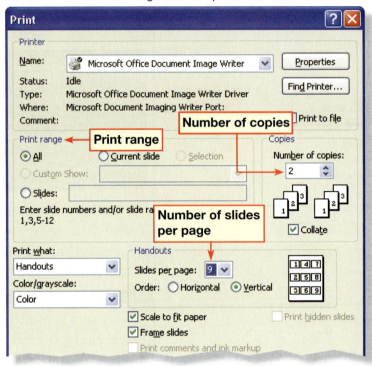

FIGURE 4.20 Print Preview

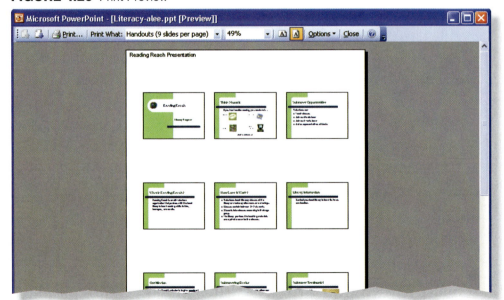

Emerging Technology

Key Terms
- Smart appliance
- Smart house

Computer technology is constantly changing. Today, many workers carry a laptop PC, a cell phone, and a PDA. Single, small devices able to do the work of all three are gaining in popularity. With improvements in wireless technology, workers are able to work in many different places—the kitchen table, a park bench, or a lounge chair by the pool.

Smart appliances with computers that are connected to the Internet are also becoming a reality. Refrigerators could warn you when the milk is about to spoil, order more eggs for you, or schedule a repair visit. Microwaves could have an Internet browser to search the Web for recipes. Such inventions could lead to smart houses with networks that control Internet-enabled appliances. Technology already exists to automatically monitor and adjust lights, temperature, and TV or stereo volume. Smart houses might be able to open doors automatically for an elderly or disabled resident. A smart house might include motion sensors to track movement—if they detect no motion for a certain amount of time, the house could call for help in case the person has fallen or lost consciousness.

TECH CHECK

1. **Define** What is a smart appliance?
2. **Predict** Name three features that a smart house might have.
3. **Create** Draw a diagram of your own smart appliance. Label all of its features.

Visit the Student Online Learning Center to learn more about emerging trends in computing.
iCheckExpress.glencoe.com

Part 4: Living Online

EXERCISE 4-8:
Change Preview Options

Use **Print Preview** to see how slides, notes pages, outlines, and handouts will look when you print them. Use the Print What drop-down arrow to preview different views. Preview in grayscale or in black and white to see how printouts will look on a black and white printer. You can also decide to add frames and other features.

FIGURE 4.17 Preview of slide with options applied

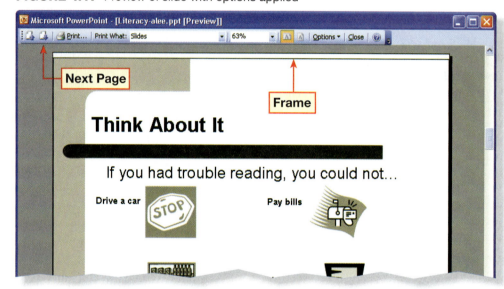

FIGURE 4.18 Preview of handout with options applied

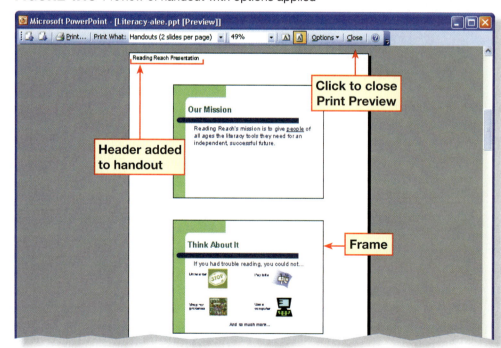

Step-By-Step

1. In your **Literacy** file, click **Print Preview**. Click the **Print What** drop-down arrow. Select **Slides**.

2. Click the **Options** drop-down arrow. Select **Scale to Fit Paper** and **Frame Slides**.

3. Under **Options**, choose **Color/Grayscale > Grayscale**. Click **Next Page** three times (see Figure 4.17).

4. **CHECK** Your screen should look like Figure 4.17.

5. Click the **Print What** drop-down arrow. Select **Handouts (2 slides per page)**.

6. Under **Options**, select **Scale to Fit Paper** and **Frame Slides**. Choose **Color/Grayscale > Color**.

7. Click **Header and Footer**. On the **Notes and Handouts** tab, select only **Header**. In the **Header** box, key: Reading Reach Presentation. Click **Apply to All**.

8. **CHECK** Your screen should look like Figure 4.18. Close Print Preview.

9. Save and continue to the next exercise.

PART 4 Assessment

Key Term Review

Answer the following questions on a separate piece of paper.

1. A(n) _____ is the software that sends and retrieves information on the Internet. (p. H37)
2. Web pages that contain information in many forms, like sound and movies, are called _____ pages. (p. H37)
3. A(n) _____ searches the Internet for keywords or phrases that a user enters. (p. H38)
4. _____ states that the number of transistors in a computer circuit will double every couple of years. (p. H32)
5. A(n) _____ connects homes and businesses to the Internet. (p. H37)
6. Dialup, DSL, and cable are three types of _____ that connect a computer to the Internet. (p. H37)
7. A(n) _____ is an item on a Web page that links to another Web page. (p. H37)
8. A refrigerator that could order more eggs for you is an example of a _____. (p. H39)
9. A(n) _____ might have technology that automatically adjusts lights and temperature, opens doors for residents, and include motion sensors to track movement. (p. H39)

Concept Review

Answer the following questions on a separate piece of paper.

10. What was the first fully functional computer? (p. H31)
11. Describe the ENIAC, first American computer. (p. H31)
12. What was one major outcome of the increase in the number of transistors in a computer? (p. H32)
13. Explain how computers have both increased and decreased the demand for jobs. (p. H33)
14. Give one example of when it would be appropriate to key your address in a Web site. (p. H34)
15. Why should you never give out your social security number, your birth date, or your mother's maiden name without the consent of an adult? (p. H34)
16. When using e-mail, why should you not say something about someone that you would not want them to hear? (p. H35)
17. Why should you never send "spam" or junk e-mail? (p. H35)
18. What is a "flame"? (p. H35)
19. How does a search engine find information on the Internet? (p. H38)
20. How might a smart house help an elderly or disabled person? (p. H39)

Critical Thinking

Complete the following exercises to reinforce your understanding of the lesson.

21. **Defend** Is the Internet a positive or negative influence on society? Write a short three-paragraph essay in which you argue that the Internet is either a positive or negative influence on society.
22. **Compile** With a classmate, create a list of ten Web sites that would be useful for school research. All the Web sites should contain information on a variety of topics, and all of the sites should contain reliable and accurate information.
23. **Develop** Create a diagram similar to the one below. Fill in the diagram with five events in the history of computers. (p. H31)

ISTE Standards

The following ISTE standards are covered in Part 4. Refer to pages xvii to xix for a description of the standards listed here.

NETS•S	Performance Indicator
2	3, 4

Part 4: Living Online

EXERCISE 4-7:
Print Outlines and Speaker Notes

Step-By-Step

1. In your **Literacy** file, switch to the **Outline** pane.

2. Choose **View>Toolbars>Outlining**. On the toolbar, click **Collapse All**.

3. Choose **File>Print**. In the **Print** dialog box, click the **Print what** drop-down arrow. Click **Outline View**.

4. Click **Preview**. Zoom to **100%** and scroll up.

5. **CHECK** Your screen should look similar to Figure 4.15. With your teacher's permission, click **Print**.

6. On the **Outlining** toolbar, click **Expand All**. Switch to the **Slides** pane.

7. Choose **File>Print**. Click the **Print what** drop down arrow. Click **Notes Pages**.

8. Click **Preview**. Scroll to **Page 13**.

9. **CHECK** Your screen should look like Figure 4.16.

10. With your teacher's permission, click **Print**. Close the **Outlining** toolbar. Save your file. Continue to the next exercise.

You can use Outline View to print only the text of a presentation. Before you print, use the Outlining toolbar in the Outline pane to choose the number of levels of text that you want to print. You can also print notes pages, which display each slide and its notes. Use these pages to remind yourself what you want to say for each slide.

FIGURE 4.15 Preview of Outline View at 100% zoom

FIGURE 4.16 Preview of notes page

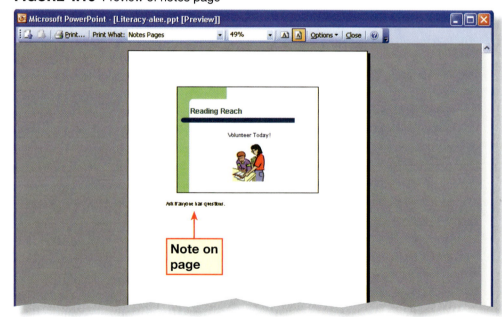

PART 5 | Outlook and Productivity Tools

Outlook

Key Terms
E-mail
Outlook

E-mail is a system for sending electronic messages from one computer to another. The messages can be text entered on the keyboard or they can be from files stored on a computer. Outlook is a program that sends and receives e-mail.

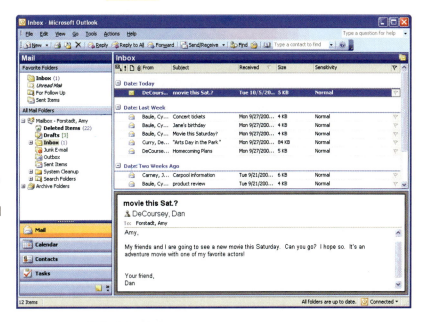

In addition to sending and receiving e-mail, Outlook saves contact information, such as phone numbers and e-mail addresses. Outlook also has a calendar for scheduling.

The Outlook calendar is a useful time-management tool. You can view your schedule by the month, by the week, or by the day. The Day view, shown here, allows you to schedule your time by the hour.

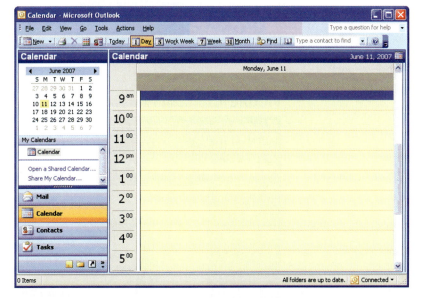

TECH CHECK

1. **Define** Define e-mail.
2. **Reproduce** Name three functions for which Outlook is useful.

Step-By-Step

1. In your **Literacy** file, move to **Slide 13**. Make sure you are in **Normal View**.

2. Click in the **Notes** pane. Key: **Ask if anyone has questions.**

3. **(i)CHECK** Your screen should look like Figure 4.13.

4. Choose **View>Notes Page**.

5. Click the **Zoom** drop-down arrow. Click **75%**.

6. **(i)CHECK** Your screen should look like Figure 4.14.

7. Click the **Zoom** drop-down arrow. Click **Fit**.

8. Click **Normal View**.

9. **(i)CHECK** Your screen should again look like Figure 4.13.

10. Save your file.

11. Continue to the next exercise.

EXERCISE 4-6:
Use Notes Pages and Zoom Views

In Normal View, use the Notes pane to add notes to the presentation. Use Notes Page view to see your notes. Use Zoom to increase and decrease the display size.

FIGURE 4.13 Normal View with note added to Notes pane

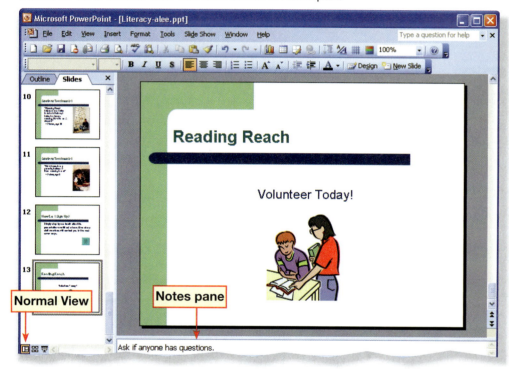

FIGURE 4.14 Notes Page view at 75% zoom

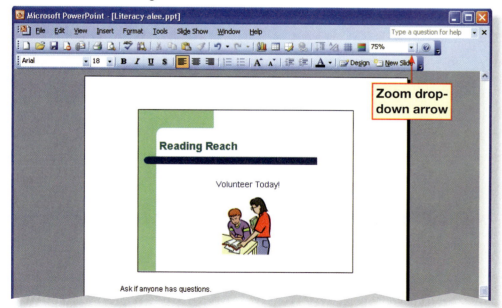

Lesson 4: Exercise 4-6

PowerPoint 118

Online Communication

Key Terms
- Distribution list
- Instant messaging
- Newsgroup

You can share information with whole groups at one time using online communication. A **newsgroup** is an online discussion group where people can discuss specific topics.

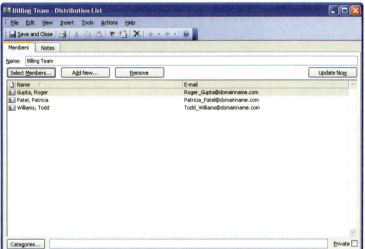

A **distribution list** identifies people who share a common interest. When an e-mail is sent to a distribution list, every e-mail address on the list receives the e-mail.

Instant messaging is like having a telephone conversation with text. As soon as you key a message, everyone in the conversation will receive it. They can then respond with their own messages.

TECH CHECK

1. **Use** Send your teacher an e-mail explaining instant messaging.
2. **Explain** How are distribution lists and newsgroups different?

Visit the Student Online Learning Center to learn more about e-mail, distribution lists, instant messaging, and newsgroups.
iCheckExpress.glencoe.com

Part 5: Outlook and Productivity Tools

Technology Handbook **H42**

Step-By-Step

1. In your **Literacy** file, move to **Slide 12**.

2. Choose **View > Grid and Guides**. In the **Grid and Guides** dialog box, under **Snap to**, select **Snap objects to grid**.

3. Under **Grid settings**, select **Display grid on screen**.

4. Under **Guide settings**, select **Display drawing guides on screen**.

5. **CHECK** Your dialog box should look like Figure 4.11. Click **OK**.

6. Select the Action Button. Drag it up and position it within the grid lines. Press CTRL and use ↑ and ↓ to position the button more accurately.

7. **CHECK** Your screen should look similar to Figure 4.12.

8. Choose **View > Grid and Guides**. Uncheck **Display grid on screen** and **Display drawing guides on screen**. Click **OK**.

9. Save your file. Continue to the next exercise.

EXERCISE 4-5:
Display Grids and Guides

Grids and guides make it easier to create, modify, and align text and graphics. A **grid** is a series of horizontal and vertical lines that look similar to graph paper. A **guide** is a horizontal or vertical line you place on a slide to help you align objects. When you drag an object close to a grid or guide, it **snaps** into place.

FIGURE 4.11 Grid and Guides dialog box

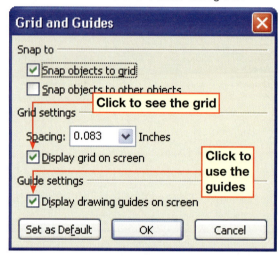

FIGURE 4.12 Action Button positioned using grids and guides

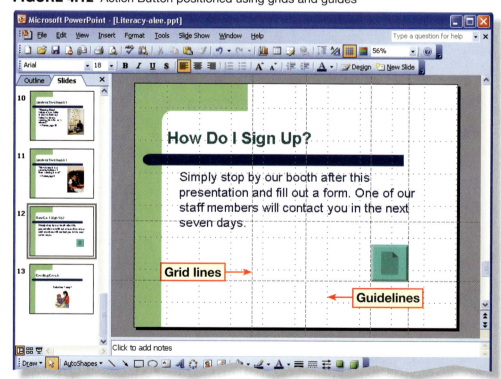

Using Help and Other Productivity Tools

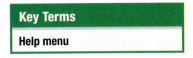

Key Terms

Help menu

Outlook, like the other applications in Microsoft Office, has many features, so it can sometimes be difficult to remember how to do something. The **Help menu** feature offers instructions and tips about many topics.

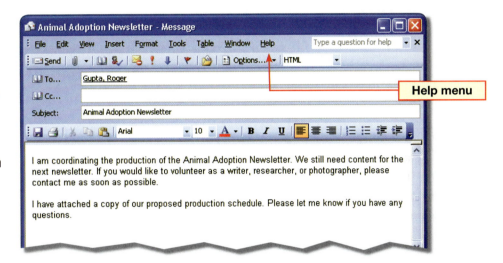

To use Help, open the Help menu and choose Outlook Help. Enter a keyword or keywords to search for the topic you want.

The Microsoft Office Web site provides help and other useful information.

TECH CHECK

1. **Demonstrate** Use Online Help to retrieve information about sending e-mail.
2. **Demonstrate** Use the Microsoft Office Online Web site to retrieve online tools.

Visit the **Student Online Learning Center** to learn more about Help and the Microsoft Office Online Web site.
iCheckExpress.glencoe.com

Part 5: Outlook and Productivity Tools

Technology Handbook **H43**

Step-By-Step

1. In your **Literacy** file, move to **Slide 12**.

2. Choose **Slide Show>Action Buttons**. Click **Action Button: Document**.

3. Click once in the slide's lower right corner to create the button.

4. In the **Action Settings** dialog box, select **Hyperlink to**. Click the **Hyperlink to** drop-down arrow. Select **Slide**.

5. In the **Hyperlink to Slide** dialog box, click **1. Reading Reach**. Click **OK**.

6. **CHECK** Your dialog box should look like Figure 4.9. Click **OK**.

7. **CHECK** Your screen should look like Figure 4.10.

8. Right-click the button. Select **Edit Hyperlink**. Click the **Hyperlink to** drop-down arrow. Select **Other File**.

9. Select the data file **Worksheet.doc**. Click **OK** twice.

10. **CHECK** Your screen should again look like Figure 4.10. Save and continue to the next exercise.

EXERCISE 4-4:
Create and Modify an Action Button

An **Action Button** is a visual button displayed on a slide. An Action Button is like a hyperlink in that it links a slide to other slides, presentations, documents, or Web pages. Graphic icons indicate where you are sent when you click the button. Some buttons help you navigate among slides. Others will take you to the first slide in your presentation (Home), to Information, to Help, or to a selected Document.

FIGURE 4.9 Action Button settings

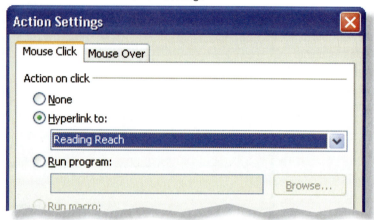

FIGURE 4.10 Action Button added to slide

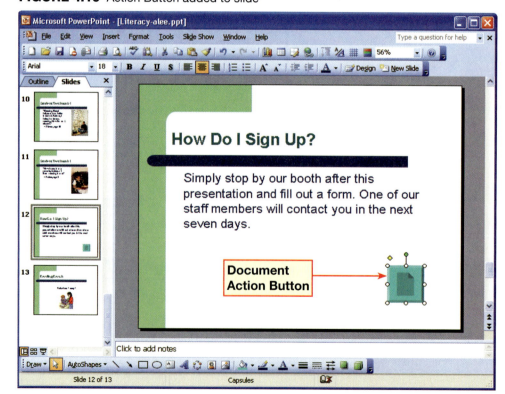

Lesson 4: Exercise 4-4

PowerPoint 116

PART 5 Assessment

Key Term Review

Answer the following questions on a separate piece of paper.

1. The Microsoft Office software that sends and receives e-mail is _____. (p. H41)
2. _____ is a system for sending messages and files electronically from one computer to another. (p. H41)
3. A(n) _____ is a list of e-mail addresses. (p. H42)
4. A(n) _____ is an online discussion of a particular issue. (p. H42)
5. _____ is like having a telephone conversation using text. (p. H42)
6. The _____ feature in Microsoft Office can answer questions you might have about how to do something in Outlook. (p. H43)

Concept Review

Answer the following questions on a separate piece of paper.

7. What are two ways messages can be entered into an e-mail? (p. H41)
8. Name two things Outlook can do in addition to sending and receiving e-mail. (p. H41)
9. What are four types of online communication? (p. H42)
10. Explain how instant messaging is similar to having a telephone conversation. (p. H42)
11. What is a newsgroup? (p. H42)
12. Where can you access Help in Outlook? (p. H43)
13. What is the function of the Help feature? (p. H43)
14. Which of the following is *not* true about Outlook? (p. H41)
    a. You can view your schedule by the year.
    b. You can view your schedule by the month.
    c. You can view your schedule by the week.
    d. You can view your schedule by the day.
15. To use Help in Outlook (p. H43)
    a. Open the Help menu and choose Outlook Tools.
    b. Open the Help menu and choose Outlook Help.
    c. Open the Outlook menu and choose Help.
    d. Open the Outlook menu and choose Go Online.

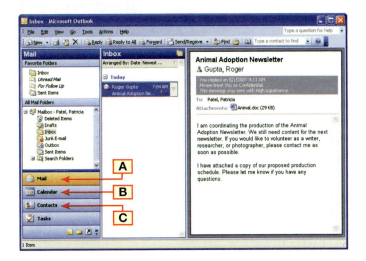

16. Match the labeled buttons on the Outlook screen with the following tasks:
    a. Check incoming messages (p. H41)
    b. View a list of stored e-mail addresses (p. H41)
    c. Switch to Day view (p. H41)
17. In the Outlook screen above, how many messages are in the Inbox? (p. H41)
18. In the Outlook screen above, whose Outlook mailbox is shown? (p. H41)

Critical Thinking

Complete the following exercises to reinforce your understanding of the lesson.

19. **Explain** Write a paragraph in which you explain how you think e-mail has changed the way people do business and communicate.
20. **Use** Use the Outlook calendar to create a weekly schedule for yourself. Include the times that your classes meet as well as time for extracurricular activities and time for homework.

ISTE Standards

The following ISTE standards are covered in Part 5. Refer to pages xvii to xix for a description of the standards listed here.

NETS•S	Performance Indicator
4, 5, 6	5, 7

Step-By-Step

EXERCISE 4-3: (Continued)
Add Hyperlinks to Slides

11. Click **Slide Show from current slide**. Click the hyperlink. Press ESC. Click **Slide 3**.

12. **CHECK** Your screen should look like Figure 4.7.

13. Click **Slide 12**. In the slide, select the text **form**. Click **Insert Hyperlink**.

14. In the dialog box, under **Link to**, click **Existing File or Web Page**. In the **Look in** box, browse to and select the data file **Worksheet.doc**.

15. Click **ScreenTip**. In the dialog box, key: Click to go to worksheet. Click **OK** twice.

16. Repeat Step 11 to follow the hyperlink. Close the Word document. Press ESC to exit the show.

17. Switch to the **Outline** pane. In the **Outline** pane, right-click the text **form**. Select **Remove Hyperlink**.

18. **CHECK** Your screen should look like Figure 4.8.

19. Switch to the **Slides** pane. Save your file. Continue to the next exercise.

FIGURE 4.7 Hyperlink after it is clicked

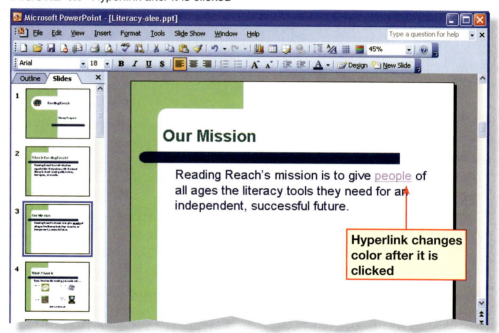

FIGURE 4.8 Hyperlink removed from slide

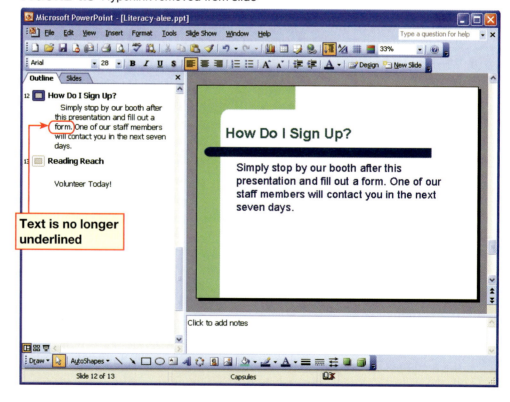

Lesson 4: Exercise 4-3

PowerPoint 115

UNIT 1: PowerPoint®: The Power of Presentations

Unit Contents:

LESSON 1:
PowerPoint® Basics

LESSON 2:
Create Content and Collaborate

LESSON 3:
Formatting Content

LESSON 4:
Managing Presentations

Why It Matters

Share Information Effectively In today's world, it is important to know how to share information. At school, teachers and students share the information needed to master essential concepts and skills. At work, employees use documents and presentations to share data, statistics, and other types of information that help a business run smoothly. For many schools and businesses, Microsoft PowerPoint has become an essential means of sharing information. *How might a club or activity that you are involved with use PowerPoint?*

PowerUp Activity **Online Learning Center** Go to **iCheckExpress.glencoe.com**. Select your book and click PowerPoint **Unit 1** to learn more about how different organizations use PowerPoint presentations.

iCheckExpress.glencoe.com

EXERCISE 4-3:
Add Hyperlinks to Slides

Adding a **hyperlink** to a slide makes it easy to quickly display different types of information during a presentation. A hyperlink moves to another slide within the same presentation, to another file on your computer, or to a Web page.

FIGURE 4.5 Insert Hyperlink dialog box

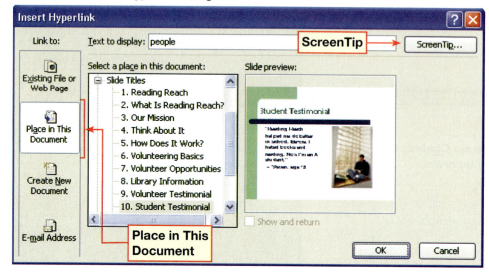

FIGURE 4.6 Hyperlink inserted into slide

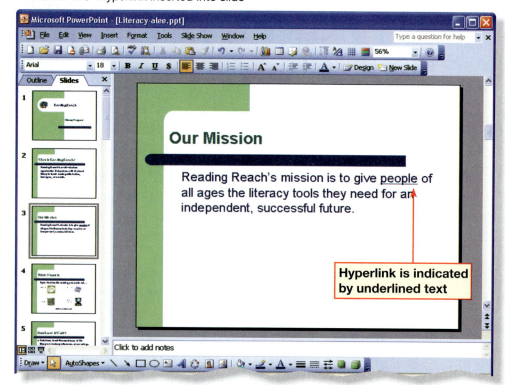

Step-By-Step

1. In your **Literacy** file, move to **Slide 3**.

2. In the slide, select the text **people**.

3. Choose **Insert > Hyperlink**.

4. In the **Insert Hyperlink** dialog box, under **Link to**, click **Place in This Document**.

5. Under **Select a place in this document**, click **10. Student Testimonial**.

6. Click **ScreenTip**.

7. In the **Set Hyperlink ScreenTip** dialog box, key: Click to go to Slide 10. Click **OK**.

8. **CHECK** Your dialog box should look like Figure 4.5.

9. Click **OK**. Click outside the text box to deselect the text.

10. **CHECK** Your screen should look like Figure 4.6.

Continued on the next page.

Lesson 4: Exercise 4-3

PowerPoint 114

UNIT 1: Career Facts

- In 1997, only about 13% of farms had Internet access. More recently, that figure has grown to 48%, although some states have much higher figures. Oregon and Montana have rates of 72% and 68%.

- Many athletes now use computers to help them train to become more physically fit and to improve their performances.

The U.S. Department of Labor has organized the country's different occupations into 23 major occupational groups. The chart below shows the number of people expected to work in selected groups. Having computer skills is an essential part of succeeding in each occupational group.

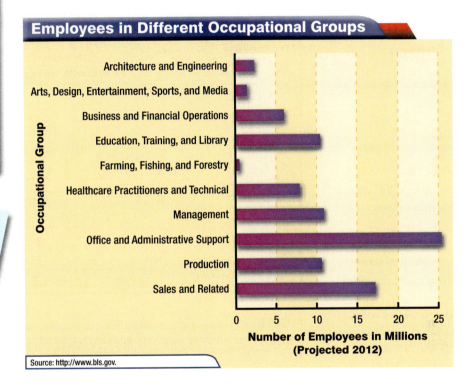

 FACT CHECK

1. **Identify** What do the labels on the y-axis (vertical axis) indicate?
2. **Compute** Which occupational group is the largest? Which has the fewest number of employees?
3. **Evaluate** Choose one of the occupations in the graph that interests you. Write down three ways that you think computers might be useful in that occupation.

Step-By-Step

1. In your **Literacy** file, move to **Slide 6**.
2. Choose **Insert > Slides from Files**.
3. In the **Slide Finder** dialog box, click **Browse**.
4. Locate and click the data file **Publicity.ppt**.
5. Click **Open**.
6. In the **Slide Finder** dialog box, click slide **3. Volunteer Opportunities** (see Figure 4.3).
7. Make sure **Keep source formatting** is not checked.
8. Click **Insert**. Click **Close**.
9. **CHECK** Your screen should look like Figure 4.4.
10. Save your file.
11. Continue to the next exercise.

EXERCISE 4-2:
Copy Slides Between Presentations

Use the **Slide Finder** to copy slides between presentations. Select the slide you want in the Slide Finder dialog box. If you select Keep source formatting, the slide keeps its original formatting. If you do not, the slide takes on the design of the new presentation.

FIGURE 4.3 Slide Finder dialog box

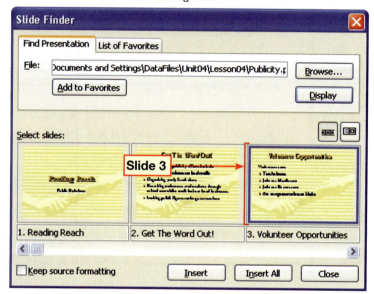

FIGURE 4.4 New slide inserted from different presentation

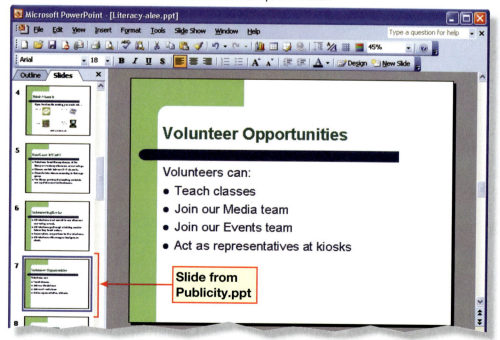

UNIT 1 Before You Begin

Before you begin the unit on creating presentations, you should understand these basic terms and concepts.

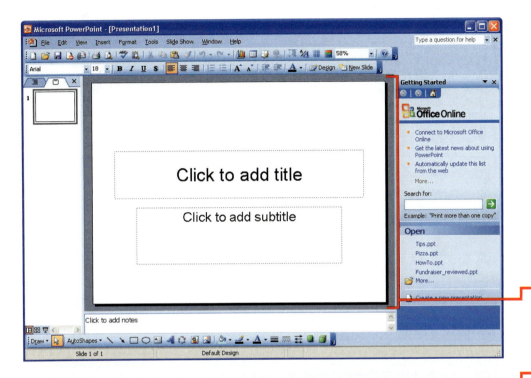

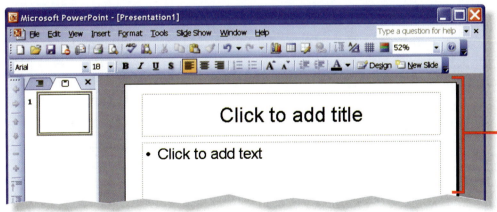

Terms:

Presentation — a PowerPoint file. A presentation can contain text, pictures, charts, links to other pages, and other objects.

Slide Show — a presentation that is shown one slide at a time using a computer monitor or projector.

Slide — one page in a presentation.

Title slide — slide that contains a presentation's title. Usually the first slide in a presentation.

Title and text slide — slide that contains a title with text underneath. Text is often formatted as a bulleted list.

Placeholder text — text that tells you what type of content should be placed in different areas of a slide.

Format — to change the look of a presentation.

Edit — to make changes to the content of a presentation.

1. **Define** What is a Title slide?
2. **Predict** Why does placeholder text make it easier to create a PowerPoint presentation?

Unit 1: Before You Begin

PowerPoint 3

Step-By-Step

1. Open the data file **Literacy.ppt**. Save as: Literacy-[your first initial and last name]. (For example, *Literacy-alee*.)

2. In the **Slide** pane, click **Slide 7**. On the **Formatting** toolbar, click **New Slide**. Close the **Slide Layout** task pane.

3. In the title box of the new slide, key: Library Information.

4. Click in the text box. Press BACKSPACE. Press TAB. Key: Contact your local library to learn its hours and location. (see Figure 4.1).

5. Click **Slide Sorter View**. Click **Slide 2** and drag it between **Slides 6** and **7**.

6. Click **Slide 4**. Choose **Edit > Delete Slide**.

7. **CHECK** Your screen should look like Figure 4.2.

8. Switch to **Normal View**.

9. Save your file.

10. Continue to the next exercise.

EXERCISE 4-1:
Add, Delete, and Rearrange Slides

As you create a presentation, you can add, delete, and rearrange slides at any time so the presentation flows in a logical order and all desired information is displayed.

FIGURE 4.1 New slide inserted into presentation

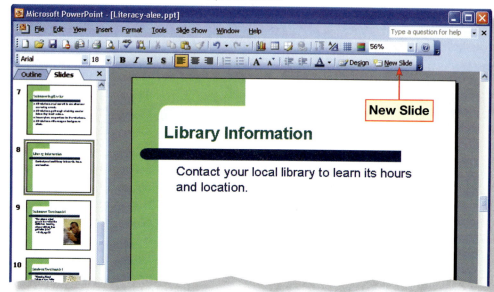

FIGURE 4.2 View with slides deleted and rearranged

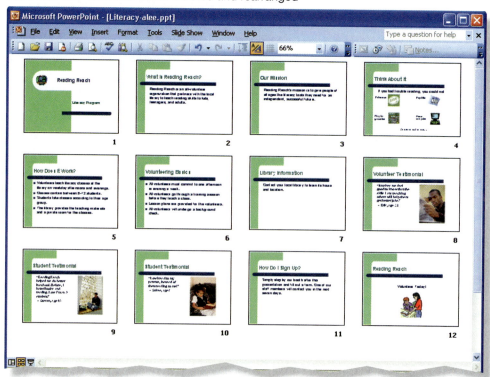

Lesson 4: Exercise 4-1

PowerPoint 112

LESSON 1: PowerPoint Basics

From the classroom to the board room, people love to use PowerPoint when giving presentations. PowerPoint gives you an easy way to display information in an interesting and visual way. In this lesson, you will become familiar with PowerPoint by learning how to open, run, modify, and print an existing presentation.

You Will Learn To:

- Identify parts of the PowerPoint screen
- Work with menus, toolbars, and task panes
- Open an existing presentation
- Insert and edit text on slides
- Start and run slide shows
- Preview and print a presentation

21st CENTURY SKILLS

Understand Your Audience As you plan a presentation, ask yourself some questions. How can I make my presentation interesting to my audience? Who are they? What will keep their attention? What do they already know, and what do they need to know? These questions will help you understand your audience. Understanding your audience will help you make a presentation that gives your audience the information they need in a way that is interesting to them. *Why is it important to catch your audience's interest when you are giving a presentation?*

Standards

The following standards are covered in this lesson. Refer to pages xvii and 156 for a description of the standards listed here.

ISTE Standards Correlation

NETS•S	Performance Indicator
1, 3, 4	5, 9, 10

Microsoft Office Specialist Correlation

PP03S

1-2, 4-1, 4-6, 4-7

Study Skill

Organize Your Thoughts
If you have trouble organizing your ideas, try creating a list, outline, or diagram. These tools will help you organize your thoughts so you can create presentations that are easy to follow.

Lesson 1: PowerPoint Basics

LESSON 4: Key Concepts

You can have the best slide show imaginable, but if it is not professionally presented, much of its impact is lost. In this lesson, you will learn how to add finishing touches to your presentation and prepare for the big show.

Linking Up

Linking to other locations makes presentations flexible and is an easy way to bring in additional information. In this lesson, you will learn to create hyperlinks to link a slide to another slide, another file, and even a Web page. You also can create Action Buttons that work as hyperlinks. Action Buttons contain icons that tell you where they will take you.

Making Notes and Handouts

When giving a presentation, it is often helpful to have notes to remind you of major points. You can enter these notes into PowerPoint's Notes pane. When you print notes pages, both the notes and a small image of the accompanying slide are printed. Some presenters like to provide handouts for audience members. In a handout, multiple slides are printed on each page.

Creating Custom Shows

If you give a presentation about Saturn to your astronomy club and later want to give the same presentation to your sister's fifth grade class, you may wish to modify the presentation. For example, you may want to skip some of the more complicated material. Hiding slides is an easy way to customize a presentation for different audiences. You can also use the Custom Show feature to create custom shows from existing presentations.

Presenting a Slide Show

Good speakers interact with their audiences. Using on-screen devices such as pens and highlighters helps direct your audience's attention.

Sometimes you will want to tell PowerPoint when to advance to the next slide. In other shows, you may want to move through the show automatically. This is referred to as setting the show's timing. You determine how long each slide should remain on the screen, and these timings are then saved as part of the presentation.

Slide shows can be presented in a variety of ways. For example, you may want to send a presentation to clients or post it on your company's Web site. Presentations can easily be packaged for CD or converted to Web pages.

Reading Skill

Take Guilt-Free Days of Rest The reason for resting is to refresh oneself. However, if you feel guilty ("I really should be reading") then your precious rest period has been used to create more stress. The brain will not absorb new data if it is stressed. Your reading skills will be much more effective if you are relaxed and ready to learn.

LESSON 1: Key Terms

Knowing these terms will help you complete the exercises in this lesson. Use this chart as a study guide when you review the lesson.

Key Term	Definition	Page Number
Button	A graphic item that can be clicked to perform a specific task.	8
Cursor	A blinking mark that indicates where the text you key will appear on the screen. Also known as an insertion point.	17
Dialog box	A box that is used to enter specific information to perform a particular task such as naming and saving a document.	11
Folder	An item that helps the user organize files.	11
Insertion point	A blinking mark that indicates where the text you key will appear on the screen. Also known as a cursor.	17
Key	To type text.	17
Menu	A list of related commands.	8
Menu bar	A bar that displays the names of available menus.	7
Menu command	An individual option on a menu.	8
Outline pane	The pane that displays the outline view, or text, of the presentation.	13
Pointer	The arrow used to select on-screen items, such as menus and buttons.	7
ScreenTip	The description of an object such as a button that appears when you point to the object.	8
Scroll bar	A bar at the right side or bottom of the screen that allows you to move up and down or left and right in a document.	15
Slide icon	In the Outline pane, the small slide image that is located next to the slide content. Click the image to move among slides.	13
Slide pane	The part of the PowerPoint screen where you key in text.	17
Slide Sorter View	View you can use to add more slides, to delete slides, or to rearrange the order of slides.	14
Slides pane	The pane that displays miniatures of the slides in a presentation.	13
Status bar	The bar at the bottom of the screen that displays information such as the current slide number and the total number of slides in the presentation.	7
Task pane	An optional part of the PowerPoint screen that provides easy access to common tasks.	9
Title bar	The bar at the top of the screen that displays the name of the current presentation.	7
Toolbar	The bar that contains buttons that can be clicked to perform different tasks.	8

LESSON 4 Key Terms

Knowing these terms will help you complete the exercises in this lesson.
Use this chart as a study guide when you review the lesson.

Key Term	Definition	Page Number
Action Button	A button that, when clicked, performs an action during a slide show, such as advancing to another slide.	116
Annotation	A mark or note made with a pen tool when viewing a slide show.	126
Grid	A series of horizontal and vertical lines laid over a slide to help align items on a slide.	117
Guide	A horizontal or vertical line you place on a slide to help align objects.	117
HTML	A programming language used by Internet browsers to read and display Web pages.	131
Hyperlink	Text or button that, when clicked, takes you to another slide within your presentation, opens another file, or opens a Web page.	114
Package for CD	A fast way to group a PowerPoint presentation and all related files (such as linked files and PowerPoint Viewer) into one folder.	128
PowerPoint Viewer	A computer application that allows people to view a slide show without using PowerPoint.	128
Print Preview	A preview of slides to be printed.	120
Publish	To copy necessary HTML files to a Web server so that they can be seen over the Internet.	132
Slide Finder	Displays a miniature of each slide in a presentation that you can select and insert into the current presentation.	113
Snap	To line up with a grid or guide when something is dragged close to it.	117
Timing	A PowerPoint feature that determines how long a slide should remain visible during a slide show before automatically moving to the next slide.	127
Web server	A computer on the Internet that stores Web pages.	132

You Should Know

You can create a hyperlink to send e-mail messages. Choose the **Insert** menu and click **Hyperlink**. In the **Insert Hyperlink** dialog box, click **E-mail Address**. Key the recipient's e-mail address and subject.

LESSON 1 Key Concepts

You have probably heard the expression "A picture is worth a thousand words." Nothing proves this better than Microsoft PowerPoint. PowerPoint helps you display information visually. Making presentations is similar to making other documents in Microsoft Office. If you are familiar with Office components such as toolbars, menus, and task panes, you will feel right at home.

Target Your Audience

Anybody who knows how to use PowerPoint can create a presentation, but not everybody can create an effective presentation. It is important to know your audience. A presentation for third graders on good citizenship should be a lot different than one for adults on the importance of voting. Aim your presentation to the viewers' ages and interests.

Working with Your Slides

While creating your slide show, you can view it in several ways. Normal View lets you see one slide at a time. In this view, you can make changes to the slide's content. Slide Sorter View lets you see "thumbnails" of all the slides in a presentation. When you are in this view, you can easily change the order of slides, or add and delete them. Slide Sorter View gives you the "big picture."

Using Placeholders

It is important to properly position each item on a slide. You want the slide to be attractive. You also want the main points to stand out. Placeholders help you properly position different components. For example, if a slide has both a bulleted list and a chart, you would place the bulleted list in one placeholder and the chart in another.

Viewing a Presentation

Finally, you will want to view your presentation. When viewing a slide show, each slide appears on the screen, one after the other. Like most things in PowerPoint, you can control the way a slide show is displayed in many ways. For example, you can have PowerPoint automatically move from one slide to the next, or tell it when to move on. By the time you are done with Lesson 1, you will begin to appreciate the power and flexibility of PowerPoint.

Reading Skill

How Can You Improve?
What do you do after you take a test on the material you have studied? If you do well, your reading strategies were successful. If you do poorly, think about how to improve your reading for the next test. It can be very helpful to think about the process you use to learn material. How can you improve your understanding? Discuss reading techniques with classmates. But remember, what works for one person might not work for you. Pay attention to your reading methods and find out how you learn best.

LESSON 4: Managing Presentations

An essential part of using PowerPoint is actually giving the presentation. Presentations can include the actual slide show, and any handouts or notes you want to give to your audience. In this lesson, you will learn how to use features that make it easier to navigate and give a presentation. You will also learn how to package presentations in different formats so they can be accessed and viewed by people using a variety of technological tools such as CD players and Web browsers.

21st CENTURY SKILLS

Take Initiative Imagine a time when you were faced with a very challenging problem, either at school, at work, or with friends. Did you avoid the problem, or did you take the initiative and tackle the problem head-on? Taking initiative means making informed decisions and acting on them. You can take initiative by focusing on a challenge, writing down your goals, and taking steps to achieve them. *When was the last time you took initiative?*

You Will Learn To:

- Add, delete, and rearrange slides
- Add hyperlinks and Action Buttons
- Use grids and guides
- Create Custom Shows
- Rehearse timings and create annotations
- Package presentations and save them in different formats
- Preview slides and modify printing options

Standards

The following standards are covered in this lesson. Refer to pages xvii and 156 for a description of the standards listed here.

ISTE Standards Correlation

NETS•S	Performance Indicator
1, 3, 4	5, 9

Microsoft Office Specialist Correlation

PP03S
4-1, 4-2, 4-3, 4-4, 4-5, 4-6, 4-7

Study Skill

Use Mnemonics A mnemonic is a sentence or phrase that jogs your memory. For instance, ROY G BIV is an easy way to remember the colors of the rainbow.

Lesson 4: Managing Presentations

PowerPoint 109

Step-By-Step

1. To start PowerPoint, choose **Start>Programs> Microsoft Office®> Microsoft Office PowerPoint 2003**.

2. **CHECK** Your screen should look like Figure 1.1.

3. Find the **title bar**. The name of your presentation is **Presentation1**.

4. Locate the **Standard** toolbar. The first button on the toolbar is **New**.

5. Locate the **Formatting** toolbar. The first item on the toolbar is the **Font** box.

6. Find the **status bar**. You are on **Slide 1 of 1**.

7. Click **File** on the **menu bar**. Read the list of menu options. Click in a blank area to close the menu.

8. Continue to the next exercise.

EXERCISE 1-1:
Identify Parts of the PowerPoint Screen

You need to know your way around the PowerPoint screen before you can create a presentation. The **title bar** displays the name of the current presentation. The **menu bar** shows you the available menus. The **status bar** displays information such as the number of the slide you are viewing. You use the **pointer** to select tools on the screen.

FIGURE 1.1 PowerPoint screen

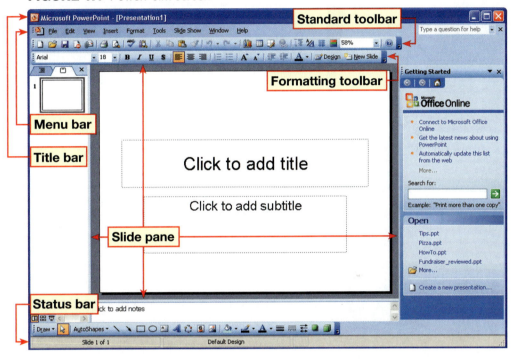

You Should Know

The PowerPoint screen is divided into three sections. The **Slides** and **Outline** pane is on the left. The slide pane is in the middle. The task pane is on the right.

Tips and Tricks

The **Standard**, **Formatting**, and **Drawing** toolbars open automatically when you create a new PowerPoint presentation.

LESSON 3 Challenge Yourself Projects

9 Promote a Restaurant

Format Slides You work for a public relations firm that has been hired to promote a new Italian restaurant. Your job is to create a presentation that tells the owners how you plan to promote their restaurant.

- Identify the restaurant's main customers—will the restaurant target an older or a younger crowd? Is it a casual pizza parlor, or a fancy gourmet restaurant?
- Create a 5- to 7-slide presentation that describes how you will promote the restaurant (by using flyers, advertisements, free offers, etc.). Make sure your promotion ideas match the restaurant's main customer base.
- Format your presentation to match the restaurant's image. Use fonts, colors, backgrounds, and graphics that reflect whether the restaurant is casual or more formal.

Save your presentation as: p3rev-[your first initial and last name]9.

10 Present a Business Proposal

Apply Effects First, think of a business or service to promote. Perhaps you want to start a new Web site. Or, you want to start a recycling service that will help people transport their recyclables to a recycling center. Then, create a 5- to 7-slide presentation promoting your idea. In your presentation, include:

- At least three images that have effects applied to them (fill color, transparency, custom animation, etc.)
- Slide transitions and an animation scheme on at least one slide

Save your presentation as: p3rev-[your first initial and last name]10.

11 Create an Employee Orientation

Use Slide Masters You work for a company that is opening a branch in a new country. You have been asked to create a presentation that will help your coworkers learn more about this country. Create a 5- to 10-slide presentation about a country of your choice. Include information that will help your coworkers better understand the country's customs, lifestyle, and history. Use slide masters to keep formatting consistent. Create a company logo and place it on the masters so it appears on every slide. Apply a design template and customize its color scheme to better suit your presentation. Save your presentation as: p3rev-[your first initial and last name]11.

Step-By-Step

1. In **Presentation1**, on the **Standard** toolbar, move the pointer over the **Paste** button.

2. **CHECK** Your screen should look like Figure 1.2.

3. Read the ScreenTip for each button on the **Standard** toolbar.

4. Read the ScreenTip for each button on the **Formatting** toolbar.

5. Click **Edit** on the menu bar. A list of menu commands opens.

6. Move the pointer over the name of each menu on the menu bar. Each menu opens.

7. Click in a blank area to close the menu.

8. Continue to the next exercise.

EXERCISE 1-2:
Use Toolbars and Menus

A **toolbar** contains **buttons** that you can click to perform specific tasks. When you point to a button, a **ScreenTip** appears that tells you what the button does. A **menu** contains a list of commands. Each **menu command** allows you to do something to your presentation, such as print or close.

FIGURE 1.2 Using ScreenTips

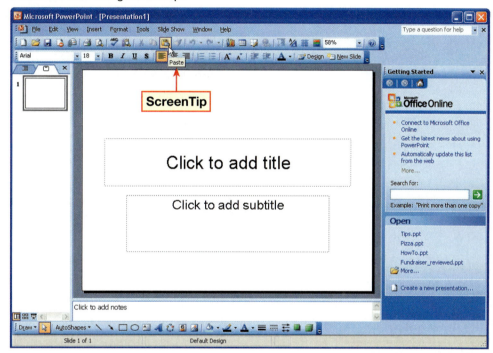

You Should Know

ScreenTips do more than just show you the names of toolbar buttons. A ScreenTip will appear if you point to the **Close** button, the buttons in the lower left corner of the window, or other items on the PowerPoint screen.

Tips and Tricks

If you do not see a ScreenTip on screen, select **Tools>Options**. On the **View** tab, click **ScreenTips**.

LESSON 3 Critical Thinking Activities

6 Beyond the Classroom Activity

Format Slides You volunteer at a home for senior citizens. The facility just upgraded its computers. The supervisor has asked you to make a presentation to the senior citizens about how they can use and enjoy the Internet.

- Create a presentation with five slides. Add content that highlights how your audience can use the Internet. You may want to discuss using e-mail to communicate with loved ones, finding message boards to meet others with common interests, or keeping up with current events around the world.
- Format your presentation so it is appropriate for an older audience. Make sure your fonts, colors, graphics, and other objects are large and readable.

Save as: p3rev-[your first initial and last name]6.

7 Standards at Work Activity

 Microsoft Office Specialist Correlation PP03S-2-5
Apply slide transitions

Apply Slide Transitions You are scheduled to give a presentation tomorrow to your marketing team. The presentation's content and formatting are both complete. Before you give the presentation, however, you need to add transition effects to the slides.

- Open the data file **p3rev7**.
- Apply a transition effect to the entire presentation.
- Modify the speed of the effect and add a sound effect. Make sure that the effects you select are appropriate for your presentation's tone and audience.

Save as: p3rev-[your first initial and last name]7.

8 21st Century Skills Activity

Identify Role Models Individuals often look to their role models for ethical guidance. Think about someone who you think is a good role model. This person may be a family member, a teacher, or even an historical figure. Create a brief presentation about this person. Identify why you think he or she is a good role model, and explain how your actions have been influenced by this person. Use at least three PowerPoint features learned in this lesson in your presentation. Save as: p3rev-[your first initial and last name]8.

Student Online Learning Center

Go to the book Web site to complete the following review activities.

Interactive Review
To review the main points of this lesson, choose **Interactive Review> PowerPoint Lesson 3**.

Online Self Check
Test your knowledge of the material in this lesson by choosing **Self Checks> PowerPoint Lesson 3**.

iCheckExpress.glencoe.com

Step-By-Step

1. Locate the task pane (see Figure 1.3). Notice that the **Getting Started** task pane is open.

2. Click the **Other Task Panes** drop-down arrow.

3. Click **Slide Layout**. The **Slide Layout** task pane opens.

4. **✓CHECK** Your screen should look like Figure 1.4.

5. At the top of the task pane, click **Back** to return to the previous task pane.

6. Click **Close** to close the task pane.

7. Choose **View > Task Pane**.

8. **✓CHECK** Your screen should again look like Figure 1.3.

9. Click **Close Window** to close the presentation (see Figure 1.3).

10. Continue to the next exercise.

EXERCISE 1-3:
Use the Task Pane

A **task pane** gives you quick access to tools that you use frequently. You can choose from several task panes, depending on the type of work you are doing.

FIGURE 1.3 The Getting Started task pane

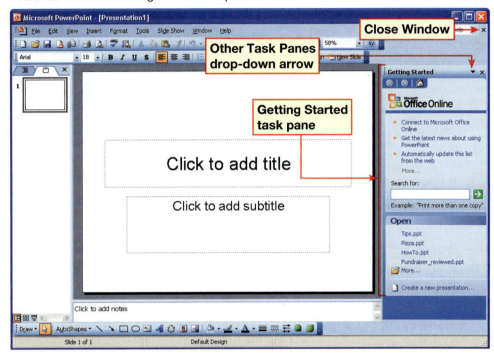

FIGURE 1.4 The Slide Layout task pane

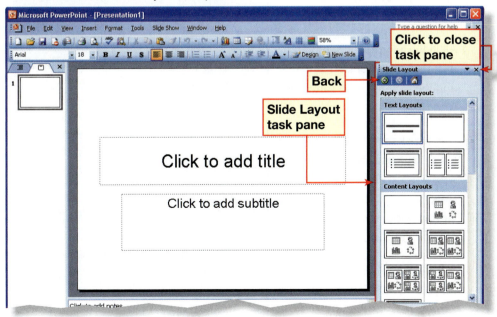

Lesson 1: Exercise 1-3

PowerPoint 9

LESSON 3 You Try It Activities

5 Rotate, Align, and Add Effects to Graphics

Your presentation is almost ready to show. All you have to do is finish the final slide. To do this, you must modify Clip Art, WordArt, and shapes to make your content presentable. You must complete You Try It Activity 4 before doing this activity.

FIGURE 3.57 Rotated and recolored images

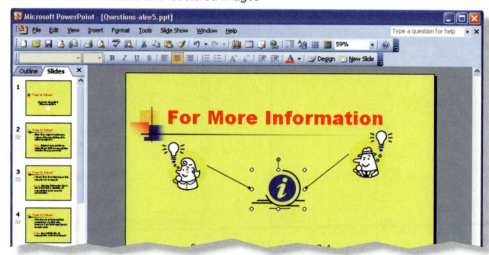

FIGURE 3.58 Modified graphics

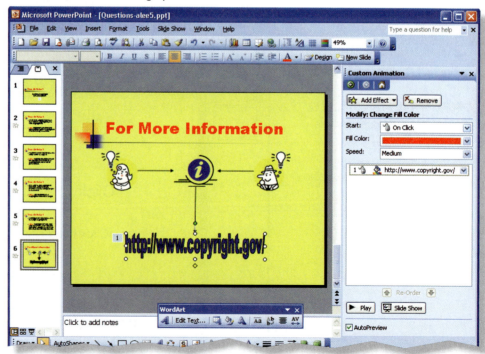

Step-By-Step

1. Open your **Questions** file. Save as Questions-[your first initial and last name]5.

2. Select **Slide 6**. Rotate the image of the man to the right **90°**.

3. Use **Format Picture** to recolor the central image from green to blue.

4. **CHECK** Your screen should look like Figure 3.57.

5. Select the URL address. Change its **Fill Color** to blue. Use a **Straight arrow connector** to connect the information symbol to the URL.

6. Align the information symbol with the images of the man and the woman using **Align Middle**.

7. Right-click the URL. Select **Custom Animation**. Click **Add Effect**. Choose **Emphasis>Change Fill Color**. Under **Modify**, change **Fill Color** to **Red**.

8. **CHECK** Your screen should look like Figure 3.58. Save and close your file.

Lesson 3: You Try It Activities

Step-By-Step

1. In **PowerPoint**, close the task pane.
2. Choose **File > Open**.
3. In the **Open** dialog box, click the **Look in** box drop-down arrow.
4. Select the location of your data files. Ask your teacher for the correct location.
5. Click **Tips.ppt** (see Figure 1.5).
6. Click **Open**. The **Tips** presentation opens in **Normal View**.
7. **CHECK** Your screen should look like Figure 1.6.
8. Continue to the next exercise.

EXERCISE 1-4:
View a Presentation in Normal View

A presentation is a group of slides that can be printed or presented as a slide show. PowerPoint automatically opens presentations in Normal View. In this view, the screen is divided into two sections.

FIGURE 1.5 Open dialog box

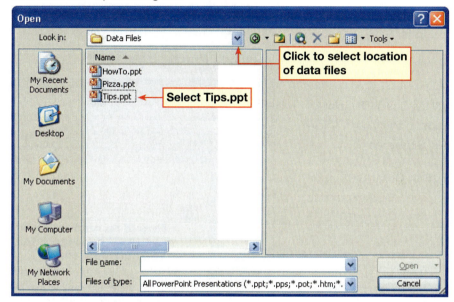

FIGURE 1.6 Tips presentation open in Normal View

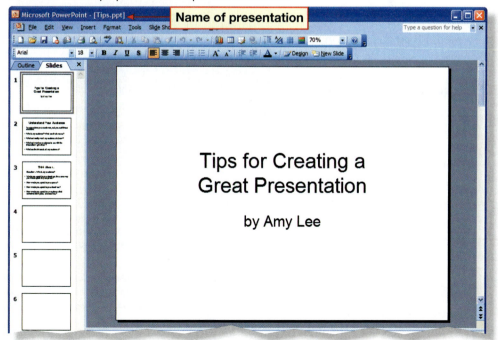

Lesson 1: Exercise 1-4

PowerPoint 10

LESSON 3 — You Try It Activities

4 Format Slides and Add Animation Effects

You work on your school's Web site. Your supervisor has asked you to put together a brief presentation to help new students understand what materials they can and cannot include on the Web site. You have created the content for your presentation and are ready to format the slides and apply animation effects.

Step-By-Step

1. Open the data file **Questions**. Save as Questions-[your first initial and last name]4.

2. Apply the Design Template **Blends** to every slide. Click **Color Schemes**.

3. Click **Edit Color Schemes**. Change the **Background** to light yellow. Change **Title text** to red.

4. Use the slide masters to change all the text to **Arial Black**. Close the slide masters.

5. On Slides 2 to 5, make the words **True** and **False** in the slide body red. Click **Slide 2**.

6. **CHECK** Your screen should look like Figure 3.55.

7. In the task pane, click **Animation Schemes**. In the **Slides** pane, click **Slide 2**. Press SHIFT. Hold and click **Slides 3, 4,** and **5**. In the task pane, click **Fade in one by one**.

8. **CHECK** Your screen should look like Figure 3.56. Close the task pane. Save your file.

FIGURE 3.55 Slide 2 with new formatting

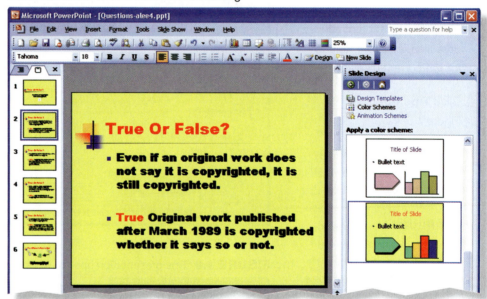

FIGURE 3.56 Animation effect applied to selected slide

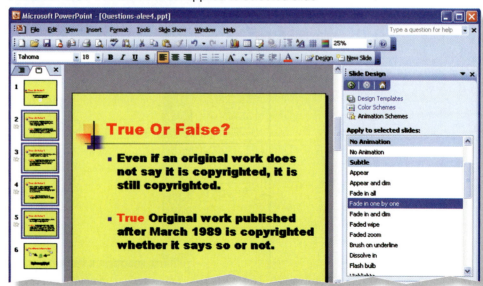

EXERCISE 1-5:
Create a New Folder

Instead of storing all of your presentations in one place, you can store them in folders. A **folder** helps you organize your presentations by grouping related presentations together. One way to create a new folder is to use the Save As dialog box. A **dialog box** is used to enter specific information to perform a task, such as naming and saving a document.

Step-By-Step

1. In your **Tips** file, choose **File>Save As**. The **Save As** dialog box opens.

2. In the **Save As** dialog box, click the **Save in** drop-down arrow (see Figure 1.7).

3. Select the location provided by your teacher.

4. With your teacher's permission, right-click in the blank area of the **Save As** dialog box. Click **New**.

5. Click **Folder**.

6. **CHECK** Your screen should look similar to Figure 1.7.

7. Key: [your first initial and last name] as the new folder name. (For example, *alee*.) Press ENTER.

8. **CHECK** Your screen should look like Figure 1.8.

9. Click **Close** X to close the dialog box.

10. Continue to the next exercise.

FIGURE 1.7 Creating a new folder

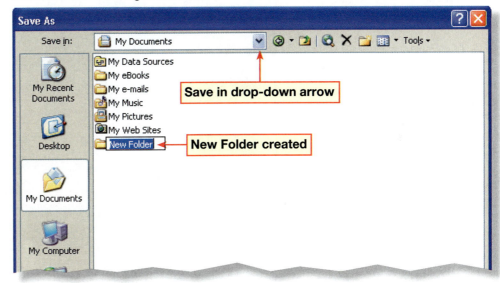

FIGURE 1.8 Naming a new folder

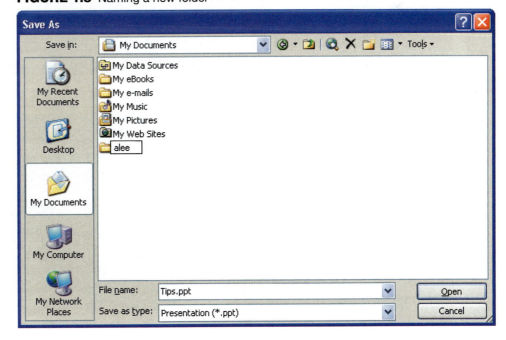

LESSON 3 Practice It Activities

3 Insert Footers and Headers

Follow the steps to complete the activity. You must complete Practice It Activity 2 before doing this activity.

Step-By-Step

1. Open your **Copyrights-2** file. Save as Copyrights-[your first initial and last name]3.

2. Click **Slide 2**. Choose **View>Header and Footer**.

3. On the **Slide** tab, select **Date and Time**. Select **Fixed**. In the **Fixed** box, key today's date.

4. Select **Slide number**. Select **Footer**. In the **Footer** box, key: Copyrights. Select **Don't show on title slide**. Click **Apply to All**.

5. **CHECK** Your slide's footer should look like Figure 3.53.

6. Choose **View>Header and Footer**. On the **Notes and Handouts** tab, select **Header**.

7. In the **Header** box, key: Copyright Presentation. Click **Apply to All**. Choose **View>Notes Page**.

8. **CHECK** Your screen should look like Figure 3.54.

9. Click **Normal View**. Save and close your file.

FIGURE 3.53 Footer added to slide

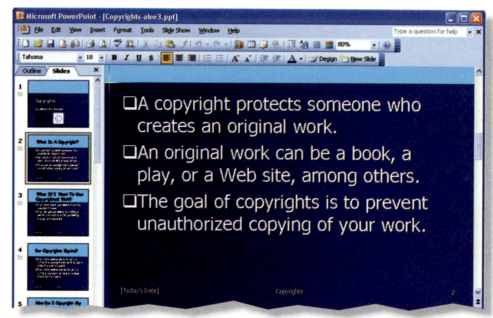

FIGURE 3.54 Header added to notes page

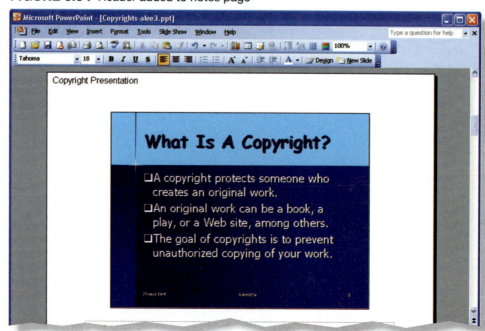

Lesson 3: Practice It Activities

PowerPoint 104

Step-By-Step

1. In your **Tips** file, choose **File > Save As**.

2. In the **Save As** dialog box, in the **File name** box, key: Tips-[your first initial and last name]. (For example, *Tips-alee*).

3. Click the **Save in** drop-down arrow.

4. Navigate to the folder you created in Exercise 1-5, or to the location provided by your teacher. Select the location and click **Open**.

5. **CHECK** Your screen should look similar to Figure 1.9.

6. Click **Save** in the **Save As** dialog box.

7. **CHECK** Your screen should look like Figure 1.10.

8. Continue to the next exercise.

EXERCISE 1-6:
Name and Save a Presentation

When you save a presentation for the first time, give your presentation a meaningful name. Give it a name that makes sense to you and that will be easy to remember.

FIGURE 1.9 Save As dialog box

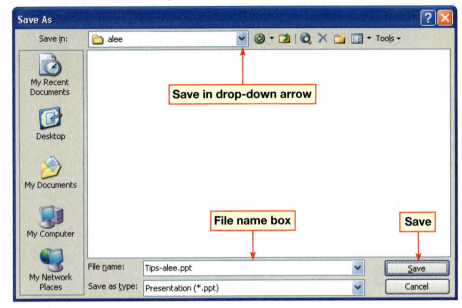

FIGURE 1.10 Saved presentation

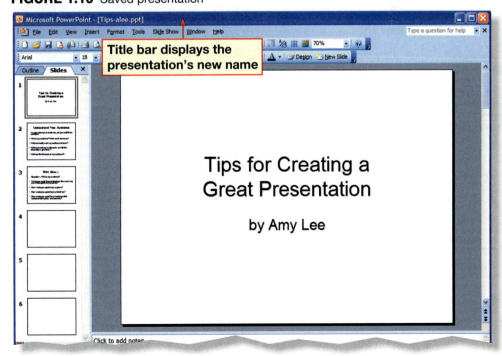

Lesson 1: Exercise 1-6

PowerPoint **12**

LESSON 3 Practice It Activities

2 Format Text, Modify Graphics, and Manage Masters

Follow the steps to complete the activity. You must complete Practice It Activity 1 before doing this activity.

Step-By-Step

1. Open your **Copyrights-1** file. Save as Copyrights-[your first initial and last name]2.

2. On **Slide 1**, select **Copyrights**. Change the **Font Color** to **White**. Click **Bold**.

3. Right-click the graphic. Select **Format Picture**. On the **Size** tab, change **Height** to **2"**. Press TAB. Click **OK**.

4. **CHECK** Your screen should look like Figure 3.51.

5. Click **Slide 2**. Choose **View>Master>Slide Master**. Click the **Master title style** text. Format: **Comic Sans MS**, **48** pt. Click the **Font Color** drop-down arrow. Click the first blue box under **Automatic**.

6. Select all five lines in the second box. Choose **Format>Bullets and Numbering**. Choose the square bullets. Click **OK**. Click **Close Master View**.

7. **CHECK** Your screen should look like Figure 3.52. Save and close your file.

FIGURE 3.51 Formatted Title slide

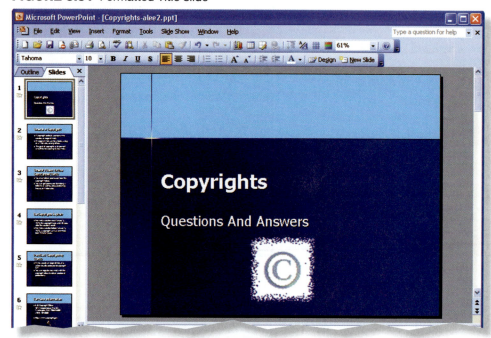

FIGURE 3.52 Formatted text on Text slide

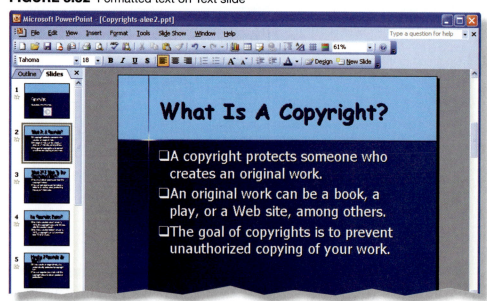

EXERCISE 1-7:
Switch Between Slides Pane and Outline Pane

The **Slides pane** shows you a miniature of each slide in your presentation. The **Outline pane** displays the content of your presentation in outline form. You can use both panes to move around in your presentation. In the Outline pane, you can click the **slide icon** next to each slide to move among slides.

FIGURE 1.11 Slides pane

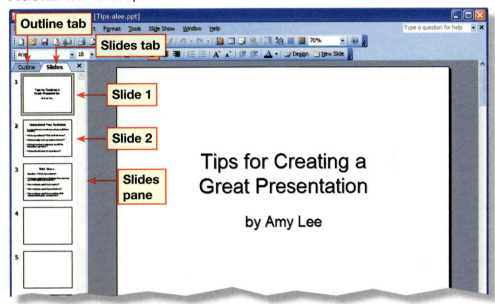

FIGURE 1.12 Outline pane

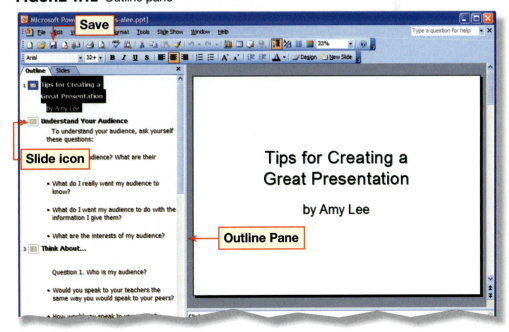

Step-By-Step

1. In your **Tips** file, locate the **Outline** tab and the **Slides** tab (see Figure 1.11).

2. In the **Slides** pane, click **Slide 2** (see Figure 1.11). This moves the presentation to Slide 2.

3. Click **Slide 1**. Your screen should again look like Figure 1.11.

4. Click the **Outline** tab.

5. ✓CHECK Your screen should look like Figure 1.12.

6. In the **Outline** pane, click the slide icon next to **2**.

7. Click the slide icon next to **1**.

8. Click the **Slides** tab.

9. ✓CHECK Your screen should again look like Figure 1.11

10. Click **Save** to save your work. Continue to the next exercise.

Lesson 1: Exercise 1-7

LESSON 3 Practice It Activities

1 Format Slides and Add Transition Effects

Follow the steps to complete the activity.

Step-By-Step

1. Open the **Copyrights** data file. Save as: Copyrights [your first initial and last name]1.

2. Select **Slide 1**. Choose **Format>Slide Layout**. In the **Slide Layout** task pane, click **Title Slide**.

3. Click **Slide Design** . Click the **Shimmer** drop-down arrow. Click **Apply to All Slides**.

4. **CHECK** Your screen should look like Figure 3.49.

5. Choose **Format> Background**. Click the **Background** fill drop-down arrow. Under **Automatic**, click the fifth box from the left. Click **Apply to All**.

6. Choose **Slide Show>Slide Transition**. In the task pane, click **Fade Smoothly**. Click **Apply to All Slides**.

7. **CHECK** Your screen should look like Figure 3.50.

8. Close the task pane. Save and close your file.

FIGURE 3.49 Slide with modified layout and design

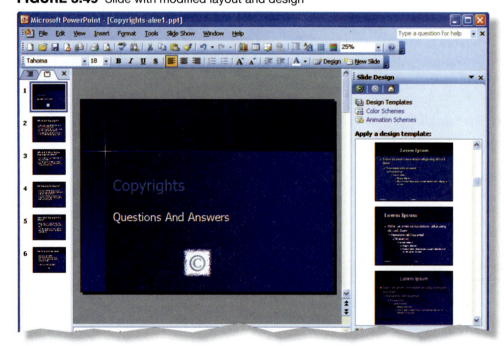

FIGURE 3.50 Slide with modified background and transition effect applied

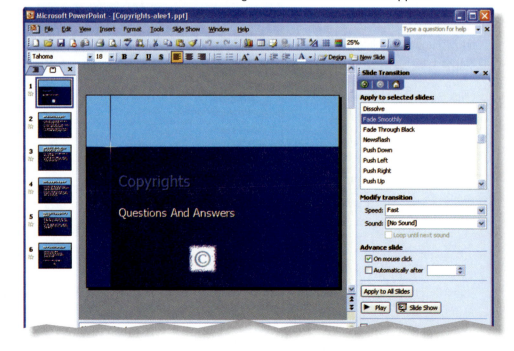

Step-By-Step

1. In your **Tips** file, click **Slide Sorter View** (see Figure 1.13).

2. **✓CHECK** Your screen should look like Figure 1.14.

3. Point to **Slide 1**. Click the slide and drag it to the right of Slide 2. The slide order changes.

4. Point to the new **Slide 1**. Click the slide and drag it to the right of Slide 2. Click **Slide 1**.

5. **✓CHECK** Your screen should again look like Figure 1.14.

6. Double click **Slide 1**.

7. **✓CHECK** Your screen should again look like Figure 1.13.

8. Save your file.

9. Continue to the next exercise.

EXERCISE 1-8:
Use Slide Sorter View

You can use **Slide Sorter View** to add more slides, to delete slides, and to change the order of slides in a presentation.

FIGURE 1.13 Presentation in Normal View

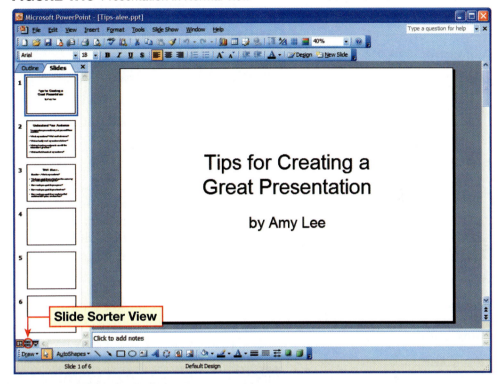

FIGURE 1.14 Presentation in Slide Sorter View

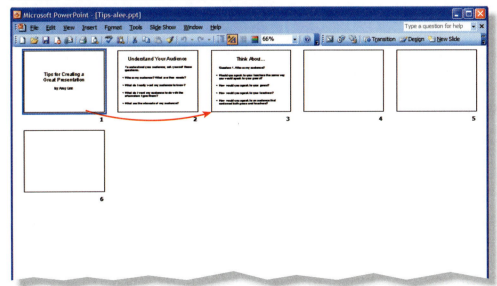

Lesson 1: Exercise 1-8

PowerPoint 14

LESSON 3 Concept Review

Key Terms

Alignment
Animation scheme
Background
Color scheme
Fill color
Font
Font style
Footer
Formatting
Gradient
Header
Landscape
Line color
Portrait
Rotate
Slide layout
Slide master
Title master
Transition
Typeface

Reviewing Key Terms

Complete the following statements on a separate piece of paper. Choose from the Key Terms list on the left to complete the statements.

1. A text's _____ refers to whether it is lined up along the left margin, along the right margin, along both margins, or in the center of the text box. (p. 80)
2. A(n) _____ is the eight colors used in a slide's design. (p. 76)
3. The color inside a shape is called _____. (p. 82)
4. Bold, italic, underline, and shadow are all types of _____. (p. 78)
5. You can use a(n) _____ to make objects on a screen appear one by one. (p. 91)

Key Term Activity

6. Create a PowerPoint Key Term quiz.
   A. Organize into groups of four or five students.
   B. Have each group member select a different Key Term.
   C. Have each member create one slide. Place the Key Term definition at the top of the slide. Use the **Fade in one by one** animation scheme to have the Key Term drop into the slide.
   D. Run the slide show. Have each group member guess which Key Term is being defined before revealing the Key Term on the slide.

Reviewing Key Facts

Answer the following questions on a separate piece of paper.

7. Which of the following can you use to join two graphics? (p. 87)
   A. Rotate or Flip
   B. Align or Distribute
   C. Connectors
   D. Join

8. If you want to change all of the bullets in a presentation, where should you change them? (p. 96)
   A. Presentation master
   B. Slide master
   C. Title master
   D. Show master

9. The footer of a presentation can contain which of the following information? (p. 98)
   A. Date
   B. Presentation
   C. Slide title
   D. All of the above

10. Which task pane do you use to change the arrangement of text and graphics on a slide? (p. 77)
    A. Slide Design
    B. Slide Layout
    C. Slide Sorter
    D. Slide Transition

Lesson 3: Concept Review

Step-By-Step

1. In your **Tips** file, click the **down arrow** on the scroll bar once (see Figure 1.15).

2. **CHECK** Your screen should look like Figure 1.16.

3. On the scroll bar, click the **up arrow**.

4. **CHECK** Your screen should again look like Figure 1.15.

5. Click **Next Slide**. Your screen should again look like Figure 1.16.

6. Click **Previous Slide**. Your screen should again look like Figure 1.15.

7. On the keyboard, press [PAGE DOWN]. You move to Slide 2.

8. On the keyboard, press [PAGE UP]. You move back to Slide 1.

9. **CHECK** Your screen should again look like Figure 1.15. Save your file.

10. Continue to the next exercise.

EXERCISE 1-9:
Move Among Slides

You can move from slide to slide using the **scroll bar** on the right edge of the screen. The Next Slide and Previous Slide buttons will also help you move among slides. Use the navigation keys on the keyboard to move through a presentation quickly.

FIGURE 1.15 The scroll bar

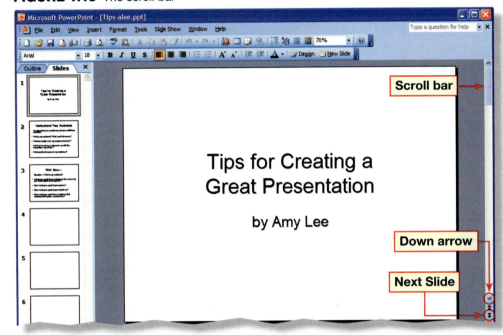

FIGURE 1.16 Slide 2

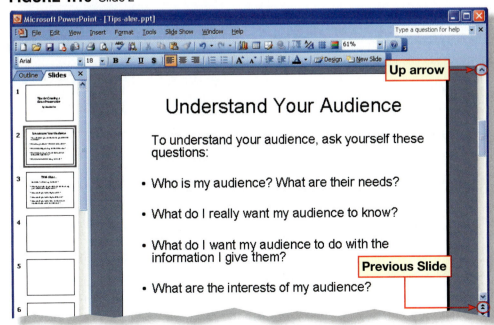

Lesson 1: Exercise 1-9

PowerPoint 15

LESSON 3 Quick Reference

The following main commands were covered in the lesson. See Appendix A on page 151 for a listing of all the commands used in this book.

Function	Button	Menu	Keyboard	Speech
Change alignment		Format>Alignment	ALT + O / A	☑
Choose Animation Schemes		Slide Show>Animation Schemes	ALT + D / C	☑
Choose Slide Design	Design	Format>Slide Design	ALT + O / D	☑
Choose Slide Layout	[icon]	Format>Slide Layout	ALT + O / L	☑
Choose Slide Transition		Slide Show>Slide Transition	ALT + D / T	☑
Format AutoShape, Picture, or WordArt		Format>Object	ALT + O	☑
Group objects		Draw>Group	CTRL + SHIFT / G	☑
Header and Footer		View>Header and Footer	ALT + V / H	☑
Modify background		Format>Background	ALT + O / K	☑
Modify bullets		Format>Bullets and Numbering	ALT + O / B	☑
Modify font		Format>Font	ALT + O / F	☑
Page Setup		File>Page Setup	ALT + F / U	☑
Ungroup objects		Draw>Ungroup	CTRL + SHIFT / H	☑
View Slide Master	SHIFT + [icon]	View>Master>Slide Master	ALT + V / M / S	☑

Step-By-Step

1. In your **Tips** file, in the **Slides** pane, click **Slide 4**.
2. Click in the text box that reads **Click to add title**.
3. Key: How Would You Speak to Your Peers?
4. **CHECK** Your screen should look like Figure 1.17.
5. Click in the text box that reads **Click to add text**.
6. Key the text that appears after the first bullet in Figure 1.18. Press ENTER.
7. Key the text that appears after the second bullet in Figure 1.18. Press ENTER.
8. Key the text that appears after the third bullet in Figure 1.18. Click in a blank space in the slide.
9. **CHECK** Your screen should look like Figure 1.18. Save your file.
10. Continue to the next exercise.

EXERCISE 1-10:
Add Text to a Slide

When you create a new title slide, it contains preset text boxes called placeholders for the title and subtitle. When you create a new bulleted list slide, it contains text boxes for the title and bulleted list. Each text box contains instructions such as "Click to add title." To add text, click in one of these boxes and begin keying text.

FIGURE 1.17 Slide 4 with title keyed in

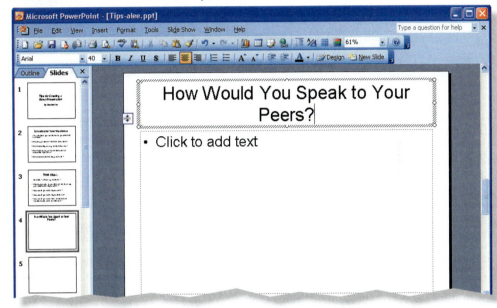

FIGURE 1.18 Text added to a slide

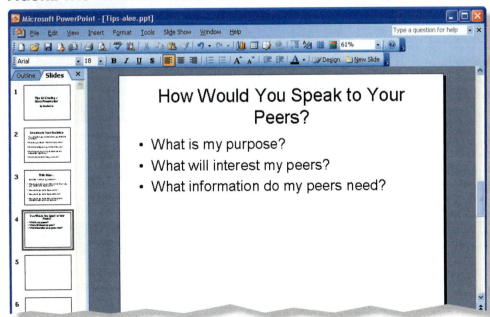

Lesson 1: Exercise 1-10   PowerPoint **16**

Writing MATTERS

Copyrights

You have written a great short story for your creative writing class. When a friend asks to read it, you are flattered at his interest. Later, you learn that your friend has taken your ideas, changed the words slightly, and turned the story in to his teacher without giving you any credit. What would you say to this friend?

Copyrights

When a work is copyrighted, it is illegal for someone else to use it and pass it off as his or her own. When you create an original work, it is automatically copyrighted. That means even if you do not see the copyright symbol (©) on an item, the artist or writer is protected by copyright law. Published authors usually apply for a copyright notice through the U.S. Copyright Office. Books, artistic works, and ideas are all copyrighted. Material found on the Internet is also protected by the same copyright laws.

How to Use Copyrighted Material

Sometimes when you are preparing a report or presentation, you find a piece of writing, music, or video clip that perfectly illustrates your point. While all of these items are copyrighted, this does not necessarily mean that you cannot use them. Rules for using copyrighted material are different depending upon whether the purpose is educational or commercial. To get permission to use copyrighted material:

- Find out who owns the material you want to use. Many Web sites have a Terms of Use page that lets you know who owns the material and what you can and cannot use from the site.

- Write a letter to the copyright owner and ask for written permission to use the material.

- Cite your source in a footnote, endnote, or credit line.

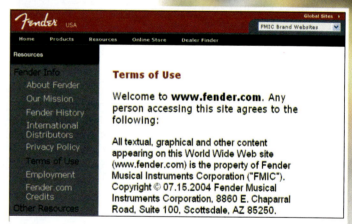

Read a Web site's Terms of Use page to find out who owns the material on a site.

SKILLBUILDER

1. **Identify** What is the purpose of a copyright?

2. **Apply** What are some examples of copyrighted materials that might work in a presentation about famous movie soundtracks?

3. **Evaluate** Why do you think copyright laws are important? In your own words, describe what you think would happen if these laws did not exist. Give examples.

Lesson 3: Writing Matters

EXERCISE 1-11:
Edit Text on a Slide

You might want to add a word, delete text, or make other edits to a presentation. To edit or add text to a slide, use the I-pointer to place the **insertion point** (also called a **cursor**) where you want new text to go. Then click and **key**, or type, the new text into the **slide pane**.

Step-By-Step

1. In your **Tips** file, move to **Slide 1**. Click to the left of the word **by**.

2. Key: Written. Press the **spacebar** once. Click in a blank part of the slide.

3. **CHECK** Your screen should look like Figure 1.19.

4. On the keyboard, press `PAGE DOWN`.

5. Double-click the word **really**. The word is selected (see Figure 1.20).

6. On the keyboard, press `DELETE`. The word is deleted.

7. Press `PAGE UP`.

8. **CHECK** Your screen should again look like Figure 1.19.

9. Save your file.

10. Continue to the next exercise.

FIGURE 1.19 Edited text

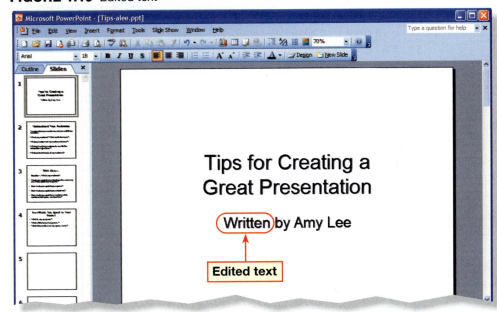

FIGURE 1.20 Selected word

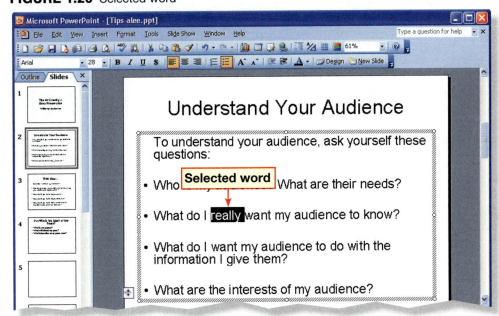

Lesson 1: Exercise 1-11   PowerPoint 17

Step-By-Step

1. In your **Staff** file, click **Slide 3**. Choose **View> Header and Footer**.

2. In the **Header and Footer** dialog box, on the **Slide** tab, select **Date and time**.

3. Select **Fixed**. In the **Fixed** box, key: October 2007.

4. Select **Slide number**.

5. Select **Footer**. In the **Footer** box, key: Music On The Run Staff.

6. Select **Don't show on title slide**.

7. **CHECK** Your dialog box should look like Figure 3.47.

8. On the **Notes and Handouts** tab, select **Header**. In the **Header** box, key: Staff Orientation. Click **Apply to All**.

9. Select **View>Notes Page**. Increase the **Zoom** to **115%**.

10. **CHECK** Your screen should look similar to Figure 3.48.

11. Click **Normal View**. Save and close your file.

EXERCISE 3-22:
Use Footers and Headers

A **footer** is text that appears at the bottom of every slide in a presentation. Footers often contain the date, presentation title, and slide number. You can choose not to include footers on specific slides, such as Title slides. A **header** is information that appears at the top of every notes page or presentation handout.

FIGURE 3.47 Header and Footer dialog box

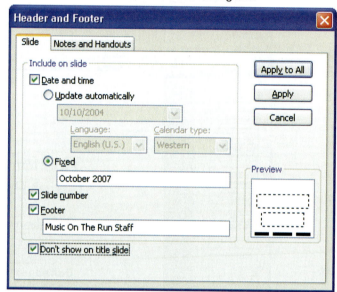

FIGURE 3.48 Header and footer on notes page

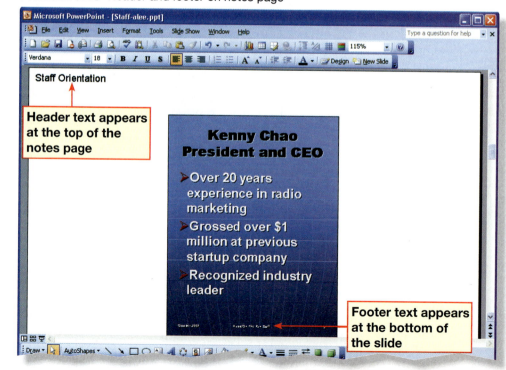

Lesson 3: Exercise 3-22

PowerPoint 98

Step-By-Step

1. In your **Tips** file, choose **Slide Show>Set Up Show**.

2. In the **Set Up Show** dialog box, under **Show type**, make sure **Presented by a speaker (full screen)** is selected.

3. Under **Show slides**, make sure **All** is selected.

4. Under **Advance slides**, click **Manually**.

5. **CHECK** Your dialog box should look like Figure 1.21. Click **OK**.

6. Choose **Slide Show>View Show**.

7. **CHECK** Your screen should look like Figure 1.22.

8. Click the mouse OR press the **spacebar** to advance to the next slide.

9. Repeat Step 8 twice to view the remaining two completed slides in the presentation.

10. To exit the slide show, click the mouse twice OR press the **spacebar** twice. Save your file.

11. Continue to the next exercise.

EXERCISE 1-12:
Set Up and Run a Slide Show

You can set up a slide show to run automatically, or you can manually move from slide to slide. In this exercise, you will use the Set Up Show dialog box to run a show manually. When setting up the show, you will use some of PowerPoint's preset, or default, settings.

FIGURE 1.21 Set Up Show dialog box

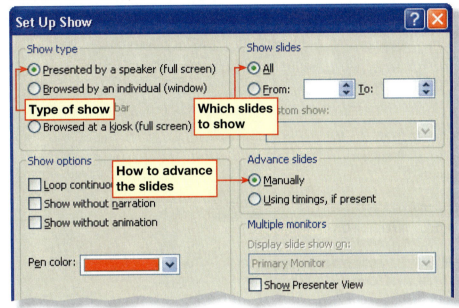

FIGURE 1.22 Slide show

Tips for Creating a Great Presentation

Written by Amy Lee

Lesson 1: Exercise 1-12

PowerPoint 18

Step-By-Step

1. In your **Staff** file, select **Slide 2**. Press SHIFT and click **Slide Master View**.

2. Click the **Click to edit Master subtitle style** placeholder box. Press DELETE.

3. **CHECK** Your screen should look like Figure 3.45.

4. On the **Slide Master View** toolbar, click **Master Layout**.

5. In the **Master Layout** dialog box, click **Text**. Click **OK**.

6. Select **Click to edit Master subtitle style**. Click the **Font Color** drop-down arrow. Under **Automatic**, select the dark yellow color.

7. Click the top placeholder box. Select the middle sizing point. Increase the size of the box to include all of the text.

8. Click **Close Master View**.

9. **CHECK** Your screen should look like Figure 3.46.

10. Save your file and continue to the next exercise.

EXERCISE 3-21:
Add, Delete, and Modify Placeholders

A placeholder indicates where content should be inserted on a slide. A presentation's master slides determine the size and position of placeholders. As with text boxes, you use sizing handles to change a placeholder's size. You can also select a placeholder, reposition it on a slide, or delete it.

FIGURE 3.45 Text placeholder deleted

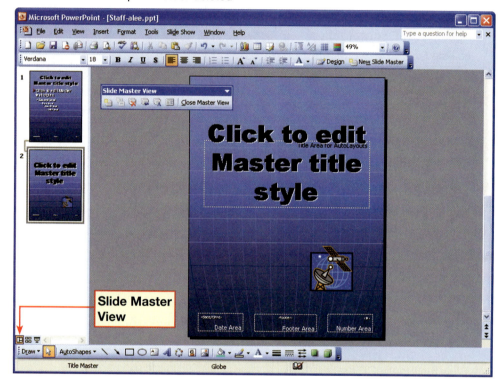

FIGURE 3.46 Text placeholder added and formatted

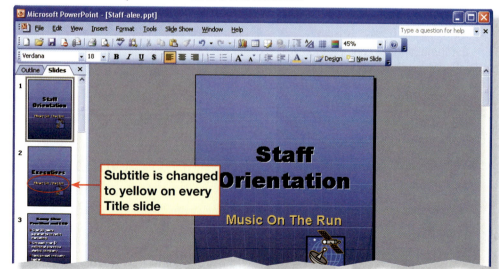

Lesson 3: Exercise 3-21

PowerPoint 97

Step-By-Step

1. In your **Tips** file, choose **Slide Show>Set Up Show**.

2. Under **Show slides**, click **From**. The numbers **1** and **6** appear in the **From** and **To** boxes.

3. In the **From** box, key: **2**. Press TAB.

4. Key: **4**.

5. *CHECK* Your screen should look like Figure 1.23.

6. Click **OK**.

7. Choose **Slide Show> View Show**.

8. *CHECK* Your screen should look like Figure 1.24. Notice that the slide show now begins on Slide 2.

9. Press ESC to exit the slide show. Save your file.

10. Continue to the next exercise.

EXERCISE 1-13:
Select Slides for a Show

If necessary, you can choose to show only selected slides instead of an entire presentation. You use the Set Up Show dialog box to identify the slide numbers you want to include in your customized presentation.

FIGURE 1.23 Set Up Show dialog box

FIGURE 1.24 Slide show beginning with Slide 2

Understand Your Audience

To understand your audience, ask yourself these questions:

- Who is my audience? What are their needs?

- What do I want my audience to know?

- What do I want my audience to do with the information I give them?

- What are the interests of my audience?

Lesson 1: Exercise 1-13   PowerPoint **19**

Step-By-Step

1. In your **Staff** file, select **Slide 3**. Choose **View>Master>Slide Master**.

2. On the **Slide Master** slide, select **Click to edit Master title style**.

3. Format the text: **Arial**, **48** pt., **Bold**. Keep the **Shadow** formatting.

4. In the **Click to edit Master text styles** box, select **Click to edit Master text styles**.

5. Format the text: **Arial**, **40** pt., **Bold**. Keep the **Shadow** formatting.

6. Select **Format>Bullets and Numbering**. Select the arrow bullet style. Change **Size** to **110%** of text, **Color** to **Dark Red**. Click **OK** twice. Deselect the text.

7. **CHECK** Your screen should look like Figure 3.43.

8. On the **Master View** toolbar, click **Close Master View**.

9. **CHECK** Your screen should look like Figure 3.44. Save your file.

10. Continue to the next exercise.

EXERCISE 3-20:
Use a Slide Master

Title slides are based on the title master. Slides that are not Title slides are based on the slide master. As with the title master, modifications made to the slide master are reflected on every non-Title slide in the presentation.

FIGURE 3.43 Text slide in Slide Master View

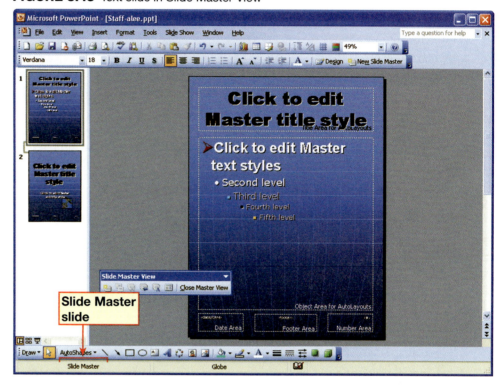

FIGURE 3.44 Modified Text slide

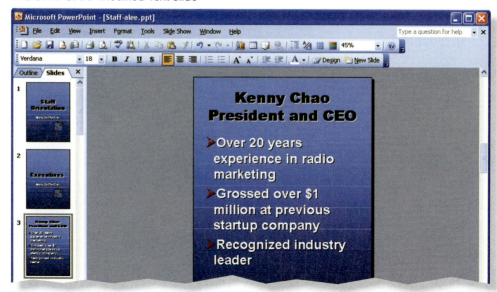

Lesson 3: Exercise 3-20

Step-By-Step

1. In your **Tips** file, choose **Help>Microsoft Office PowerPoint Help**. The **PowerPoint Help** task pane opens.

2. In the **Search for** box, key: move slides around. Press ENTER.

3. **CHECK** Your screen should look similar to Figure 1.25.

4. In the results list, click **Change slide order**.

5. A **Help** window opens with information about changing slide order (see Figure 1.26).

6. Click **Close** ✖ in the **Help** window.

7. Click **Close** ✖ in the **Search Results** task pane (see Figure 1.25).

8. Save your file.

9. Continue to the next exercise.

EXERCISE 1-14:
Use the Help Feature

Use the **Help** feature to answer questions as you work. Enter the topic you want to find in the Help task pane, and PowerPoint will produce a list of search results.

FIGURE 1.25 Search Results task pane

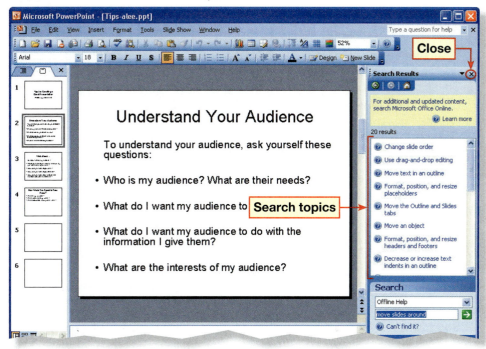

FIGURE 1.26 Help window

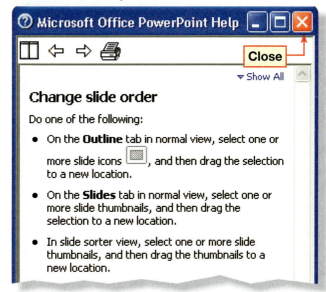

Lesson 1: Exercise 1-14

PowerPoint **20**

Step-By-Step

1. In your **Staff** file, click the graphic on **Slide 1**. Click **Cut**.

2. Choose **View>Master>Slide Master**.

3. On the slide, click in the **Click to edit Master subtitle style** box.

4. Click **Paste**. Position the graphic in the lower-right corner of the placeholder box.

5. Click the text **Click to edit Master subtitle style**. Format the text: **Arial**, **40** pt., **Bold**. Keep the **Shadow** formatting.

6. Click the text **Click to edit Master title style**.

7. Format the text: **Arial**, **66** pt., **Bold**. Keep the **Shadow** formatting. Deselect the text.

8. **CHECK** Your screen should look like Figure 3.41.

9. On the **Slide Master View** toolbar, click **Close Master View**.

10. **CHECK** Your screen should look like Figure 3.42. Save your file.

11. Continue to the next exercise.

EXERCISE 3-19:
Use a Title Master

Each slide in a presentation is based on a master slide. The master slide stores information such as which fonts, font sizes and styles, bullet styles, background colors, and color schemes are used in the presentation. Changes made to a master slide are repeated on every slide in the presentation. When you modify a ==title master== slide, every Title slide in the presentation reflects your modifications.

FIGURE 3.41 Title Slide in Slide Master View

FIGURE 3.42 Modified Title slide

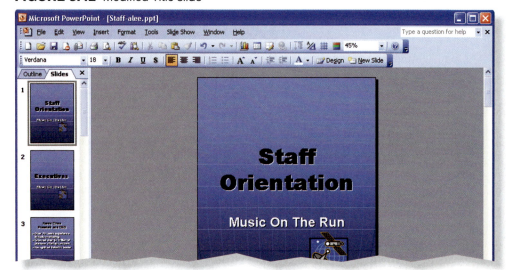

Step-By-Step

1. In your **Tips** file, go to **Slide 1**.

2. Choose **File>Print Preview**.

3. **(CHECK)** Your screen should look like Figure 1.27.

4. Click the slide to zoom in. Notice the text in the slide gets larger.

5. Click again on the slide to zoom out.

6. Press [PAGE DOWN]. You are now previewing Slide 2.

7. Press [PAGE UP]. You are again previewing Slide 1.

8. Click **Close** to close Print Preview (see Figure 1.27).

9. **(CHECK)** Your screen should look like Figure 1.28. Save your file.

10. Continue to the next exercise.

EXERCISE 1-15:
Preview a Presentation

Print Preview shows you what a slide will look like when you print it. Using Print Preview before you print can help you to catch and fix mistakes in your presentation.

FIGURE 1.27 Print Preview

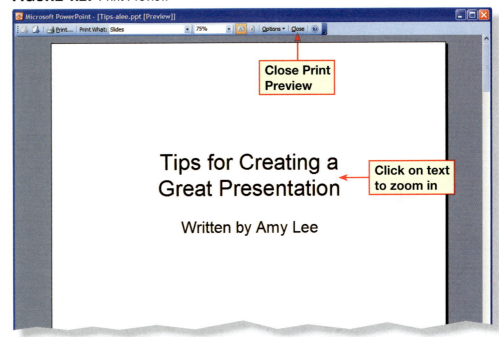

FIGURE 1.28 PowerPoint screen after closing Print Preview

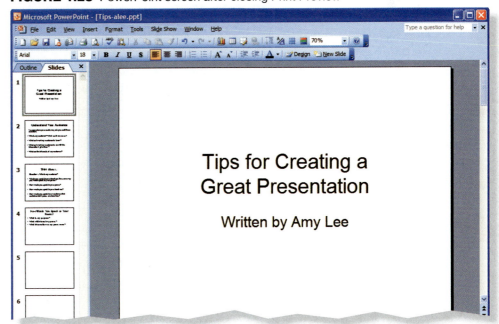

Lesson 1: Exercise 1-15

PowerPoint 21

EXERCISE 3-18:
Customize a Template

One way to customize a template to fit your presentation is to change its color scheme. Each design template has a specific eight-color scheme that is used for the presentation's background, text and lines, shadows, Title text, fills, accents, and hyperlinks. You can use the Edit Color Scheme option to change one or all of these eight-colors to create your own custom template.

FIGURE 3.39 Edit Color Schemes dialog box

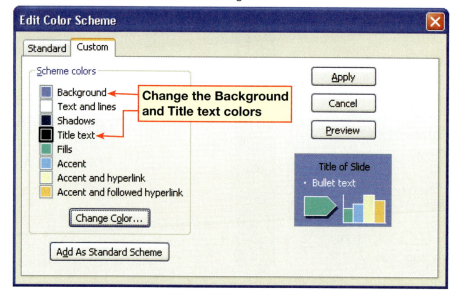

FIGURE 3.40 Template with customized color scheme

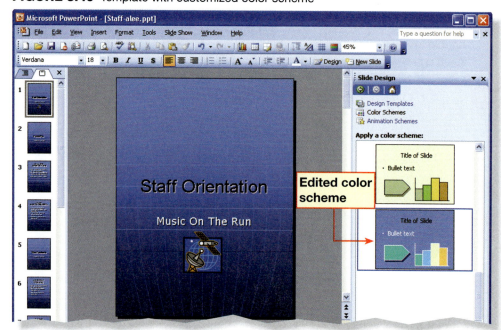

Step-By-Step

1. In your **Staff** file, click **Slide Design**. Click **Design Templates**.

2. Click the **Globe** drop-down arrow. Select **Apply to All Slides**.

3. At the top of the task pane, click **Color Schemes**. At the task pane's bottom, click **Edit Color Schemes**.

4. In the **Edit Color Scheme** dialog box, choose **Background**. Click **Change Color**.

5. In the **Background Color** dialog box, on the **Standard** tab, choose the color in the fourth row, fourth from the right. Click **OK**.

6. Click **Title text**. Click **Change Color**. Choose **Black**. Click **OK**.

7. **CHECK** Your dialog box should look like Figure 3.39. Click **Apply**.

8. **CHECK** Your screen should look like Figure 3.40.

9. Close the task pane. Save your file and continue to the next exercise.

Step-By-Step

1. In your **Tips** file, choose **File>Print**.

2. In the **Print** dialog box, in the **Name** box, click the drop-down arrow to select a printer. Ask your teacher which printer you should use.

3. Check that there is a **1** in the **Number of copies** box.

4. Under **Print range**, click **Slides**. In the **Slides** box, key: **1**.

5. **CHECK** Your dialog box should look similar to Figure 1.29. With your teacher's permission, click **OK**.

6. **CHECK** Your screen should look like Figure 1.30.

7. Choose **File>Print**. Under **Print range**, click **Slides**. In the **Slides** box, key: **2-4**.

8. With your teacher's permission, click **OK**.

9. **CHECK** Your screen should again look like Figure 1.30. Save your file.

10. Continue to the next exercise.

EXERCISE 1-16:
Print Slides

You can choose to print any number of slides—from a single slide to the entire presentation. Indicate which slides you want to print in the Print dialog box.

FIGURE 1.29 Print dialog box

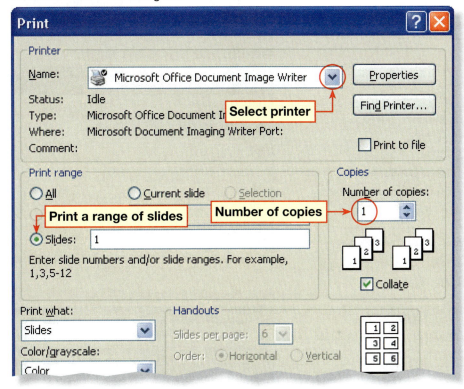

FIGURE 1.30 PowerPoint screen after printing

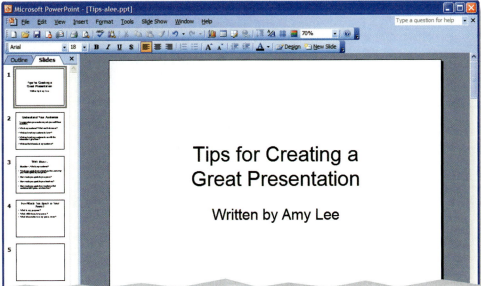

Lesson 1: Exercise 1-16

PowerPoint **22**

Step-By-Step

1. Open the data file **Staff.ppt**. Save as: Staff-[your first initial and last name].

2. Choose **File > Page Setup**.

3. Under **Slides**, click **Portrait**.

4. **CHECK** Your dialog box should look like Figure 3.37. Click **OK**.

5. Click in the Slide pane. Click the **Zoom** drop-down arrow. Click **Fit**.

6. If necessary, resize the **Slide 1** Clip Art to: Height **1.75"**, Width **1.65"**.

7. **CHECK** Your screen should look like Figure 3.38.

8. Save your file.

9. Continue to the next exercise.

EXERCISE 3-17:
Modify Page Setup

Use Page Setup to change a presentation's size and orientation. If you want your slides to be wider than they are tall, set the orientation to landscape. Set the orientation to portrait for slides to be taller than they are wide. If you plan to print your presentation, you can also use Page Setup to change the orientation of your printed slides and of handouts.

FIGURE 3.37 Page Setup dialog box

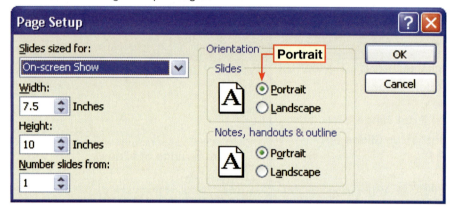

FIGURE 3.38 Portrait view

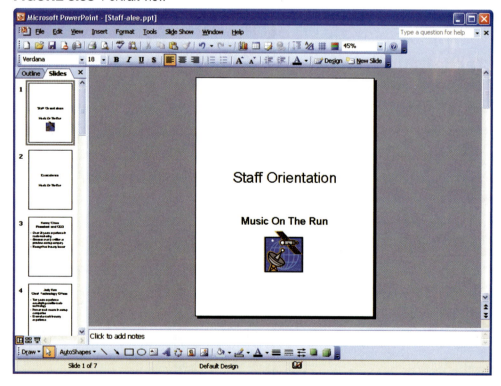

Step-By-Step

1. In your **Tips** file, choose **File > Print**.

2. In the **Print** dialog box, under **Print what**, click the drop-down arrow to see the list of options.

3. Click **Handouts** (see Figure 1.31).

4. Under **Handouts**, click the drop-down arrow in the **Slides per page** box.

5. Click **6**.

6. **CHECK** Your dialog box should look like Figure 1.32.

7. With your teacher's permission, click **OK** to print.

8. Save your file.

9. Continue to the next exercise.

Tips and Tricks

Click **Save** frequently as you work. Then you will never lose your hard work if your computer freezes or you lose power.

EXERCISE 1-17:
Print a Presentation Handout

Instead of printing slides, you can print handouts. Handouts have one or more slides on each page and space to take notes.

FIGURE 1.31 Printing handouts

FIGURE 1.32 Choosing the number of slides per page

Lesson 1: Exercise 1-17   PowerPoint   23

Step-By-Step

1. In your **Music** file, select **Slide 1**.

2. Choose **Slide Show > Slide Transition**.

3. In the **Slide Transition** task pane, select **Box Out** (see Figure 3.35).

4. Under **Modify transition**, click the **Speed** drop-down arrow. Select **Medium**.

5. Click the **Sound** drop-down arrow. Select **Laser**. Click **Apply to All Slides**.

6. ✓CHECK Your screen should look like Figure 3.36.

7. At the bottom of the task pane, click **Slide Show**. Press → to move from slide to slide.

8. On **Slide 5**, press → to display each bulleted point.

9. On **Slide 7**, press → to display each image and its connector line.

10. Close the task pane. Save and close your **Music** file.

EXERCISE 3-16:
Apply Transition Effects and Run the Slide Show

To choose the way one slide changes to the next during a slide show, apply a transition effect. You can apply a transition effect to one slide or to an entire presentation. You can also modify the speed of transition effects, and add sound effects that play when you move from slide to slide. To remove transitions, select No Transition in the task pane.

FIGURE 3.35 Slide Transition task pane

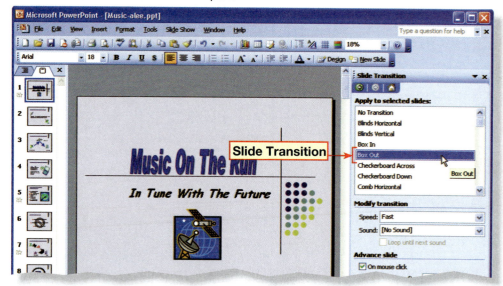

FIGURE 3.36 Slide Transition selections

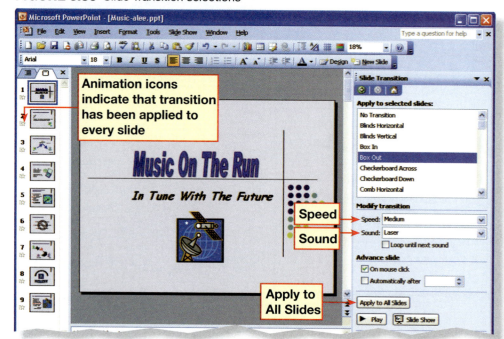

Step-By-Step

1. In your **Tips** file, click **File**.

2. Locate but do NOT click the **Close** command in the **File** menu. This is one way to close a presentation.

3. Click in the middle of the screen to close the **File** menu.

4. Click **Close Window** ⊠ (see Figure 1.33). Your presentation closes.

5. **✓CHECK** Your screen should look like Figure 1.34.

6. To close the PowerPoint program, click **Close** ⊠ on the title bar.

You Should Know

If you have saved your changes prior to closing PowerPoint, you will not be asked to save when you close your presentation.

EXERCISE 1-18:
Close a Presentation

Close your presentation once you have finished working with it. In this exercise, you will learn two different ways to close a presentation.

FIGURE 1.33 Close Window button

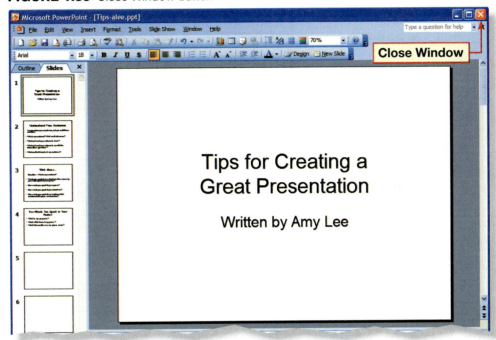

FIGURE 1.34 PowerPoint screen with presentation closed

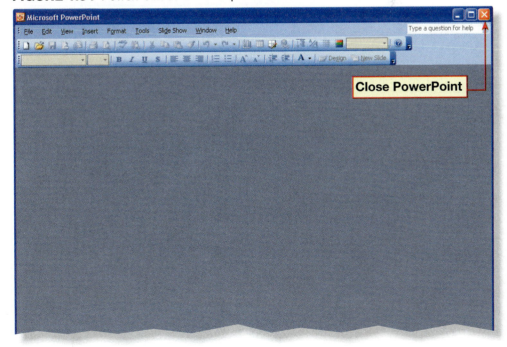

Lesson 1: Exercise 1-18

PowerPoint 24

Step-By-Step

1. In your **Music** file, click **Slide Sorter View**.

2. Select **Slide 5**. Choose **Slide Show>Animation Schemes**.

3. In the **Slide Design** task pane, under **Apply to Selected Slides**, under **Subtle**, click **Faded zoom**.

4. (CHECK) Your screen should look like Figure 3.33.

5. Click **Normal View**. In the task pane, click **Play** to replay the effect.

6. (CHECK) Your screen should look like Figure 3.34. Close the task pane.

7. Save your file. Continue to the next exercise.

You Should Know

Be careful when adding animation to a slide or presentation. Too much animation may distract your audience from the information you are trying to present.

EXERCISE 3-15:
Apply an Animation Scheme

An **animation scheme** adds movement to individual slides or to an entire presentation. PowerPoint provides Subtle, Moderate, and Exciting animation schemes. Use a Subtle scheme when you want to gently emphasize important content. Use a Moderate or Exciting scheme when you want to add a lot of movement to a slide. Select No Animation when you want to remove an animation scheme that you have applied.

FIGURE 3.33 Slide Sorter View

FIGURE 3.34 Animation scheme applied to slide

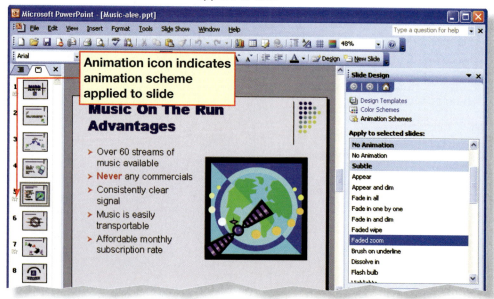

Lesson 3: Exercise 3-15

Writing MATTERS

Know Your Audience

You have been invited to give a presentation about your prized comic book collection to an art class at the local community college. You are excited to share your love of comics, but you are not sure how to do it.

Evaluate Your Audience's Needs

No matter what you are writing—a presentation, a report, a letter, a memo—it is always important to understand the needs of your particular audience. Ask yourself:

1. Who will read or see this piece of writing?
2. What do I want them to know?
3. What background do they bring?
4. What do I want this piece of writing or presentation to accomplish?

Focus on the Audience

PowerPoint is an excellent tool for customizing presentations, such as the comic book presentation described here.

You call the community college and learn that the class is a beginning art class on creating comics. Most of the students have little experience in art, and may know nothing about comic books. The class is made up of adults, ranging in age from 19 to 25. You decide to bring several examples of good comic books. You make sure to leave time for plenty of questions. You even try to predict a few of the questions audience members may ask, so that you can be prepared with good answers.

SKILLBUILDER

1. **List** What are three questions to ask yourself about your audience?

2. **Explain** Why is it a good idea to understand your audience?

3. **Apply** You are invited to give your presentation again. This time, however, your audience is fifth and sixth graders. Key a paragraph that introduces your comic book collection. Make sure your paragraph is appropriate for your new, younger audience.

Lesson 1: Writing Matters

PowerPoint 25

Step-By-Step

1. In your **Music** file, select **Slide 8**.

2. Click **100% Customer Satisfaction**.

3. Place the pointer over the green dot that appears.

4. Click the green dot. Hold the mouse button down and rotate to the left until the green dot is at the top of the slide (see Figure 3.31). Release the mouse.

5. With the text still selected, press SHIFT. Click the Clip Art and the **Guaranteed** banner so all three items are selected.

6. Choose **Draw>Align or Distribute>Align Center** to center the objects. Deselect the three images.

7. CHECK Your screen should look like Figure 3.32.

8. Save your file.

9. Continue to the next exercise.

EXERCISE 3-14:
Rotate and Align Shapes and Other Graphics

As with pictures, you can rotate shapes and graphics to turn them 90 degrees to the right or left. You can also align shapes and graphics so they are correctly grouped together on a slide.

FIGURE 3.31 Rotated WordArt

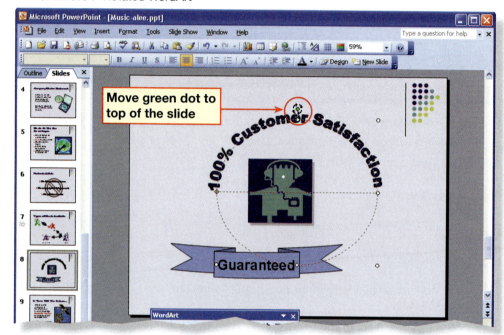

FIGURE 3.32 Images center aligned

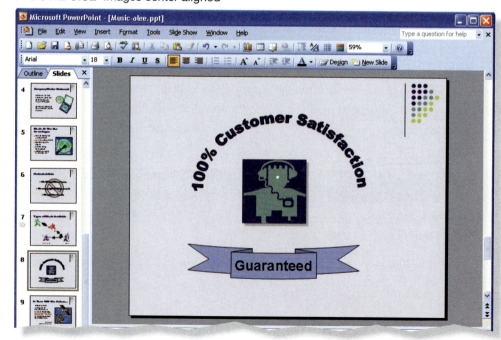

LESSON 1 Quick Reference

The following main commands were covered in the lesson. See Appendix A on page 151 for a listing of all the commands used in this book.

Function	Button	Menu	Keyboard	Speech
Close a presentation	✕	File>Close	CTRL + F4	☑
Create a new presentation	🗋	File>New	CTRL + N	☑
Exit PowerPoint	✕	File>Exit	ALT + F4	☑
Exit a slide show			ESC	☑
Open a presentation	📂	File>Open	CTRL + O	☑
Print	🖨	File>Print	CTRL + P	☑
Print Preview	🔍	File>Print Preview	CTRL + ALT + I	☑
Run a slide show		Slide Show>View Show	F5	☑
Save As		File>Save As	F12	☑
Save a presentation	💾	File>Save	CTRL + S	☑
Slide Sorter View		View>Slide Sorter	ALT + V / D	☑
Use the Help feature	❓	Help>Microsoft Office PowerPoint Help	F1	☑

Tech Tip

If the picture on a button is light gray, or dimmed, the button is not available.

Step-By-Step

1. In your **Music** file, select **Slide 7**.

2. Right-click the connector between **Classical** and **Rock/Alternative**. Click **Custom Animation**.

3. Choose **Add Effect > Entrance > Wipe**. Under **Modify: Wipe**, click the **Direction** drop-down arrow. Click **From Right**.

4. Click the **Rock/Alternative** image. Choose **Add Effect > Entrance > Fly In**.

5. **CHECK** Your screen should look like Figure 3.29. Click **Play** to preview the slide. Close the task pane.

6. Move to **Slide 8**. Click the central image. On the **Drawing** toolbar click the **Fill Color** drop-down arrow. Under **Automatic**, click the fourth box from the left.

7. With the image still selected, click **Shadow Style**. Choose **Shadow Style 6**. Deselect the image.

8. **CHECK** Your screen should look like Figure 3.30. Save your file. Continue to the next exercise.

EXERCISE 3-13:
Add Effects to Connectors and Pictures

You can add effects to connectors and pictures. For example, you can add animation effects to make the connectors and pictures move on the slide. As with other graphics, you can also add fill and shadow effects to pictures to make them more visually interesting.

FIGURE 3.29 Animation added to connector and picture

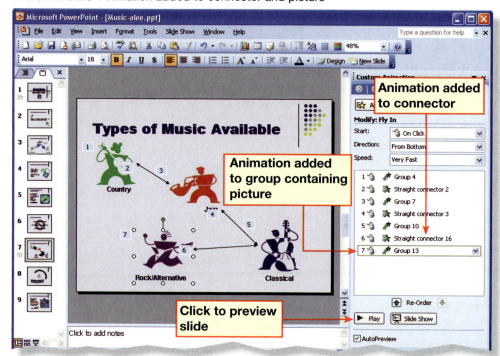

FIGURE 3.30 Picture with fill and shadow effect

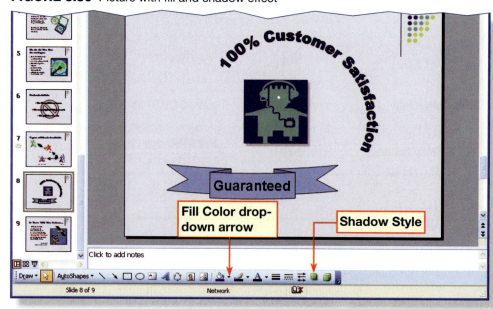

Lesson 1: Concept Review

Key Terms

Button
Cursor
Dialog box
Folder
Insertion point
Key
Menu
Menu bar
Menu command
Outline pane
Pointer
ScreenTip
Scroll bar
Slide icon
Slide pane
Slide Sorter View
Slides pane
Status bar
Task pane
Title bar
Toolbar

Reviewing Key Terms

Complete the following statements on a separate piece of paper. Choose from the Key Terms list on the left to complete the statements.

1. The _____ displays the text in the presentation as an outline. (p. 13)
2. The _____ at the top of the screen displays the name of the current presentation. (p. 7)
3. The _____ is an optional part of the PowerPoint screen that lets you perform tasks quickly. (p. 9)
4. The _____ at the bottom of the screen shows you the total number of slides in the presentation. (p. 7)
5. A(n) _____ is a description of an object that appears when you point to the object. (p. 8)

Key Term Activity

6. Key a paragraph that describes one skill you learned in this lesson. (For example, explain how to run a slide show manually.)
   A. Decide what topic you are going to write about.
   B. List five Key Terms that relate to the topic.
   C. Key a paragraph that explains your topic. Include all five Key Terms.
   D. Exchange your paragraph with a classmate. Use your classmate's feedback to revise your paragraph.

Reviewing Key Facts

Answer the following questions on a separate piece of paper.

7. Which of the following is a task pane? (p. 9)
   A. Drawing
   B. Formatting
   C. Getting Started
   D. Slide Show

8. The New button is located on which toolbar? (p. 7)
   A. Formatting
   B. Standard
   C. Tools
   D. Drawing

9. Which menu would you use to set up a slide show? (p. 18)
   A. File
   B. View
   C. Slide Show
   D. Tools

10. How can you see what a slide looks like before you print it? (p. 21)
    A. Choose **File>Print**
    B. Choose **File>Print Preview**
    C. Choose **View>Task pane**
    D. Choose **File>Open**

Step-By-Step

EXERCISE 3-12: (Continued)
Align and Connect Pictures

9. Hold the left mouse button down and draw a connector line to the **Rock/Alternative** image.

10. Place the mouse over the blue box to the right of the **Rock/Alternative** image. Release the mouse.

11. **CHECK** Your screen should look like Figure 3.27.

12. Click the **Classical** image. With the image still selected, press SHIFT. Click the **Rock/Alternative** image.

13. With the two objects selected, choose **Draw > Align or Distribute > Align Bottom**. Deselect the images.

14. **CHECK** Your screen should look like Figure 3.28.

15. Save your file.

16. Continue to the next exercise.

FIGURE 3.27 Two images connected with a connector

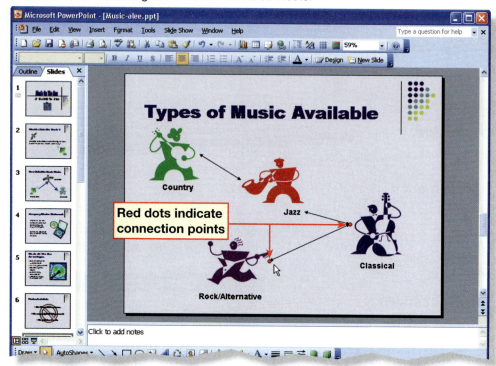

FIGURE 3.28 Connected images aligned

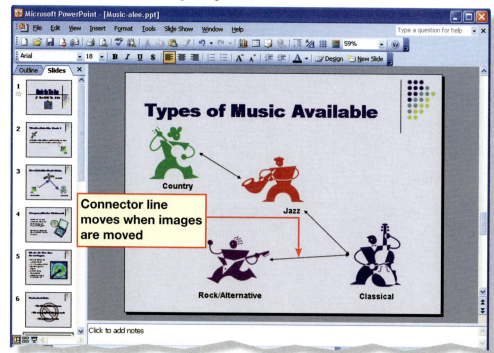

Lesson 3: Exercise 3-12

PowerPoint **88**

LESSON 1 Practice It Activities

1 Explore the PowerPoint Screen

Follow the steps to complete the activity.

Step-By-Step

1. Choose **Start>Programs>Microsoft PowerPoint**. Close the task pane, if necessary.

2. Choose **File>Open**. Locate the data file **Pizza**. Click **Open**.

3. (CHECK) Your screen should look like Figure 1.35.

4. Save the file as: Pizza-[your first initial and last name]1.

5. On the **Slides** pane, click **Slide 2**. In the third bullet, double-click **baking**. Key: pizza.

6. Click the **Outline** tab. Click the slide icon next to **Slide 1**.

7. (CHECK) Your screen should look like Figure 1.36. Click the **Slides** tab.

8. (CHECK) Your screen should again look like Figure 1.35.

9. Save and close your file.

FIGURE 1.35 Pizza presentation

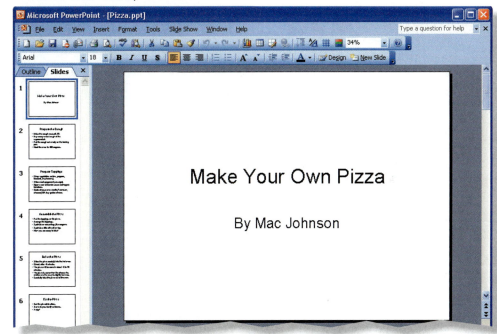

FIGURE 1.36 Using the Outline pane

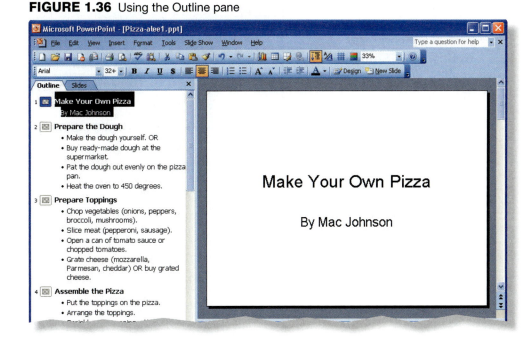

Lesson 1: Practice It Activities

PowerPoint 28

Step-By-Step

1. In your **Music** file, select **Slide 7**. Click the **Rock/Alternative** image.

2. With the image still selected, press SHIFT. Click the text **Rock/Alternative**.

3. With the two objects selected, choose **Draw>Align or Distribute>Align Right**.

4. With the objects still selected, choose **Draw>Group**.

5. **CHECK** Your screen should look like Figure 3.25.

6. Click the connector line between **Classical** and **Rock/Alternative**. Press DELETE.

7. Choose **AutoShapes>Connectors>Straight Double-Arrow Connector**. The pointer becomes a plus-sign.

8. Move the pointer over the **Classical** image. Place the pointer over the left blue box (see Figure 3.26).

Continued on the next page.

EXERCISE 3-12:
Align and Connect Pictures

As with text, you can align objects such as pictures on a slide. Once you have objects aligned correctly, you can group them so they will always stay together. You can also join objects by using connectors. When objects are joined by a connector, the connecting line moves when you move either object.

FIGURE 3.25 Aligned and grouped images

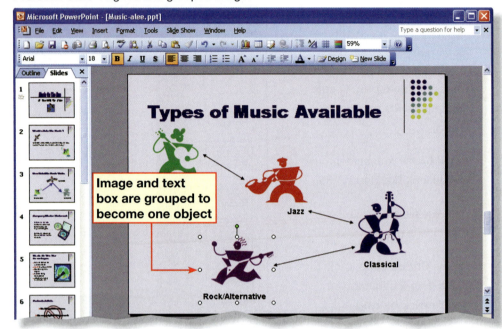

FIGURE 3.26 Classical image connector box

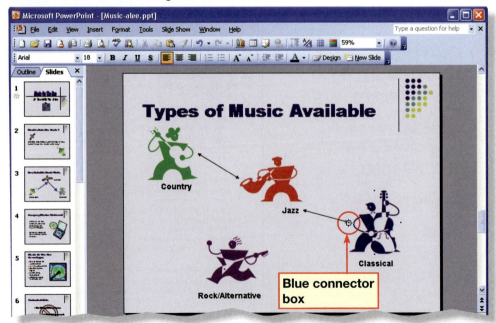

Lesson 3: Exercise 3-12

PowerPoint 87

LESSON 1: Practice It Activities

2 Edit Text and Use Slide Sorter View

Follow the steps to complete the activity. You must complete Practice It Activity 1 before doing this activity.

FIGURE 1.37 Editing text

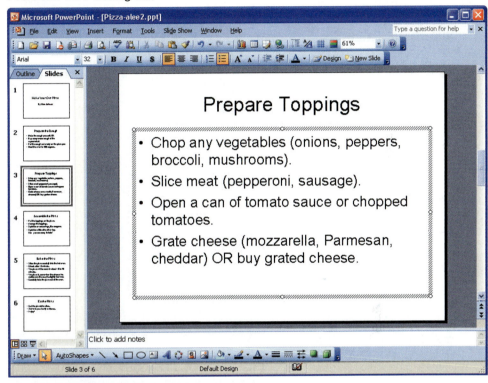

Step-By-Step

1. Open your **Pizza-1** file. Save as: Pizza-[your first initial and last name]2. Close the task pane, if necessary.

2. On the **Slides** pane, select **Slide 3**.

3. In the **Slide** pane, click before the word **vegetables**.

4. Key: any. Press the **spacebar** once.

5. **CHECK** Your screen should look like Figure 1.37.

6. Click **Slide Sorter View**.

7. Drag **Slide 2** after **Slide 3**.

8. **CHECK** Your screen should look like Figure 1.38.

9. Click **Normal View**. Save and close your file.

FIGURE 1.38 Rearranged slides

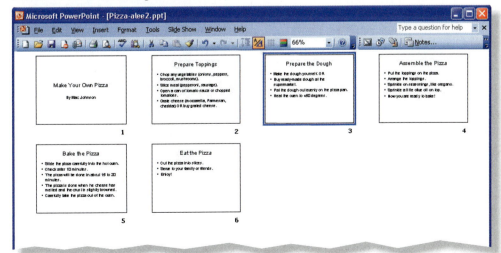

Lesson 1: Practice It Activities

Step-By-Step

1. In your **Music** file, select **Slide 7**. Click the **Rock/Alternative** image.

2. On the **Drawing** toolbar, choose **Draw>Rotate or Flip>Rotate Right 90°**.

3. **CHECK** Your screen should look like Figure 3.23.

4. Right-click the image. Select **Format Picture**.

5. In the **Format Picture** dialog box, on the **Size** tab, change the **Height** to **1.5"**. Press TAB.

6. On the **Picture** tab, click **Recolor**.

7. In the **Recolor Picture** dialog box, click the **New** drop-down arrow.

8. In the second row, select the sixth color. Click **OK** twice. Deselect the image.

9. **CHECK** Your screen should look like Figure 3.24.

10. Save your file.

11. Continue to the next exercise.

EXERCISE 3-11:
Rotate, Resize, and Recolor a Picture

Using Clip Art is an easy way to add visual interest to a presentation. When you select a piece of Clip Art, you usually have to modify it to fit your presentation. For example, you can rotate an object to turn it 90 degrees to the right or left. As with other graphics, you can resize Clip Art to better fit your slides. You can also recolor Clip Art so it better suits the design and needs of your presentation.

FIGURE 3.23 Rotated picture

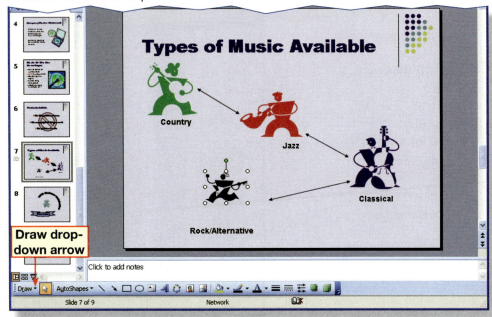

FIGURE 3.24 Picture resized and recolored

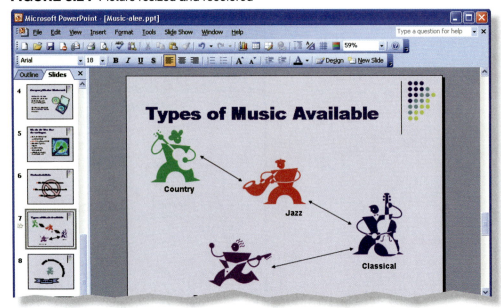

Lesson 3: Exercise 3-11

LESSON 1 Practice It Activities

3 Run a Slide Show and Print

Follow the steps to complete the activity. You must complete Practice It Activity 2 before doing this activity.

Step-By-Step

1. Open your **Pizza-2** file. Save as: Pizza-[your first initial and last name]3.

2. Choose **Slide Show>Set Up Show**. Under **Show type**, make sure **Presented by a speaker (full screen)** is selected.

3. Under **Show slides**, make sure **All** is selected. Under **Advance slides**, click **Manually**.

4. **CHECK** Your dialog box should look like Figure 1.39. Click **OK**.

5. Choose **File>Print**. In the **Name** box, click the drop-down arrow. Ask your teacher which printer you should use.

6. In the **Print what** box, click the drop-down arrow. Click **Handouts**. In the **Slides per page** box, click the drop-down arrow. Click **6**.

7. **CHECK** Your dialog box should look similar to Figure 1.40.

8. With your teacher's permission, click **OK** to print the slides. Save and close your file.

FIGURE 1.39 Set Up Show dialog box

FIGURE 1.40 Print dialog box

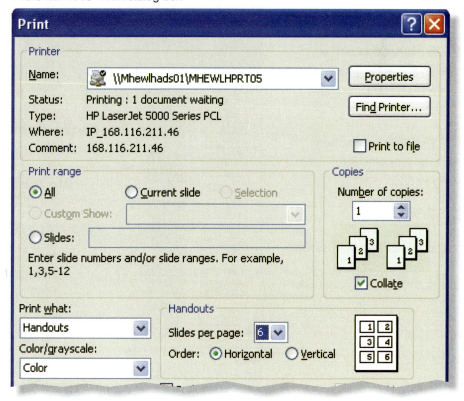

Lesson 1: Practice It Activities

PowerPoint 30

EXERCISE 3-10: (Continued)
Format and Add an Effect to a Shape

Step-By-Step

9. In the **Fill Effects** dialog box, on the **Gradient** tab, under **Colors**, click **Two colors**.

10. Click the **Color 1** drop-down arrow. In the second row, click the fifth box from the left.

11. Click the **Color 2** drop-down arrow. In the second row, click the first box.

12. Under **Transparency**, change **From** to **80%**. Change **To** to **85%**.

13. **CHECK** Your dialog box should look like Figure 3.21. Click **OK** twice.

14. Select the shape and position it in the center of the bulleted list. Deselect the shape.

15. **CHECK** Your screen should look similar to Figure 3.22.

16. Save your file.

17. Continue to the next exercise.

FIGURE 3.21 Fill Effects dialog box

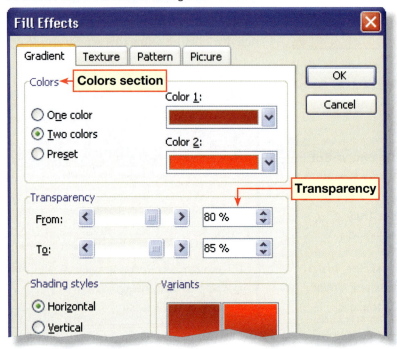

FIGURE 3.22 Modified shape with gradient effect and transparency applied

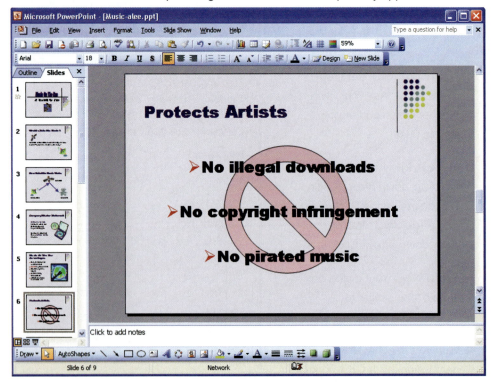

LESSON 1 You Try It Activities

4 Peer Teaching

Your classmate missed the first lesson of your PowerPoint class. Your teacher asked you to use an existing PowerPoint presentation to teach her some basic skills.

Step-By-Step

1. Open your saved **Tips** presentation. Save as: Tips-[your first initial and last name]4.

2. Move to **Slide 2**. Switch to the **Outline** pane.

3. **CHECK** Your screen should look like Figure 1.41.

4. Switch to **Slide Sorter View**. Change the order of the third and fourth slides.

5. Double-click the third slide.

6. **CHECK** Your screen should look like Figure 1.42.

7. With your teacher's permission, print the third slide in the presentation.

8. Save and close your file.

FIGURE 1.41 Outline pane

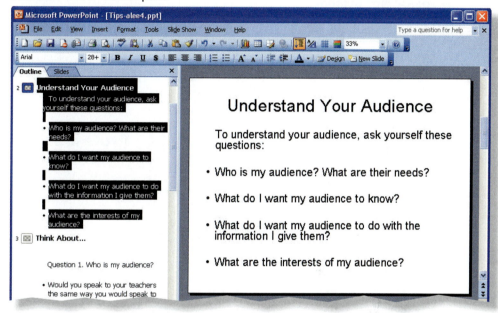

FIGURE 1.42 The third slide

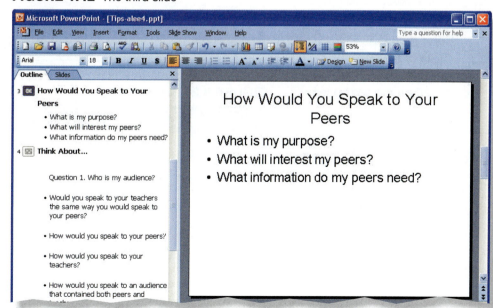

Lesson 1: You Try It Activities

PowerPoint 31

Step-By-Step

1. In your **Music** file, select **Slide 6**.

2. On the **Drawing** toolbar, select **AutoShapes>Basic Shapes>"No" Symbol**.

3. Click in the middle of the bulleted list on the slide.

4. **CHECK** Your screen should look similar to Figure 3.19.

5. Right-click the AutoShape. Select **Format AutoShape**.

6. In the **Format AutoShape** dialog box, on the **Size** tab, under **Size and rotate**, change the **Height** to **4"** and the **Width** to **4"** (see Figure 3.20).

7. On the **Colors and Lines** tab, under **Fill** click the **Color** drop-down arrow. Click **Fill Effects**.

Continued on the next page.

You Should Know

You can also access the **Fill Effects** dialog box by clicking the **Fill Color** button on the **Drawing** toolbar.

EXERCISE 3-10:
Format and Add an Effect to a Shape

As with graphics, you can resize and add color and effects to shapes. For example, you can use the Fill Effects dialog box to apply a ==gradient== effect. This effect gives an object gradual shading from one side or corner to the other. You can also use the Fill Effects dialog box to add texture, patterns, or pictures to shapes and other objects. If you want to place a shape behind text, use the Transparency settings so viewers can read the text over the shape.

FIGURE 3.19 Shape inserted into slide

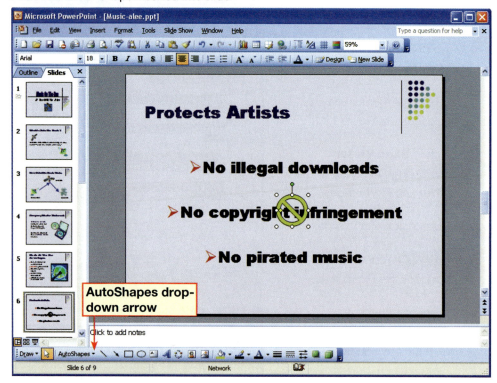

FIGURE 3.20 Size tab

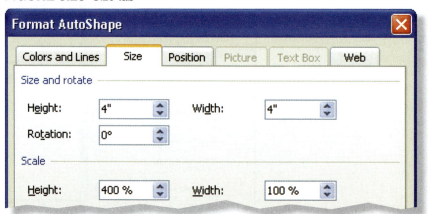

Lesson 3: Exercise 3-10

PowerPoint 84

LESSON 1 You Try It Activities

5 Create Folders for PowerPoint Presentations

You are a summer intern at a high-tech sales organization. The sales team creates customized presentations for their clients all over the world. You need to create three new folders to organize their presentations.

FIGURE 1.43 New folder

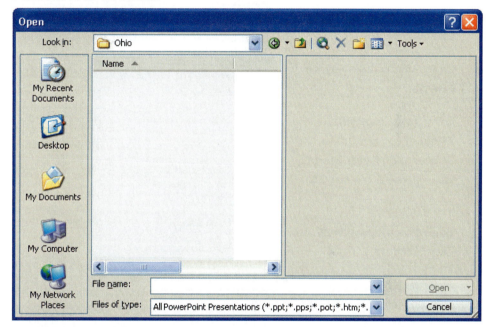

FIGURE 1.44 New title slide

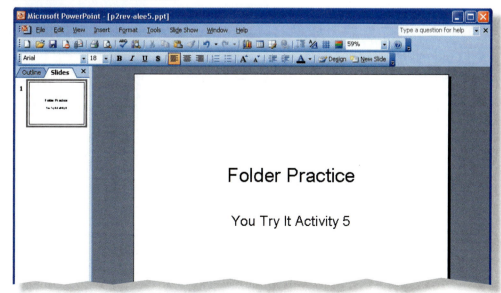

Step-By-Step

1. Start PowerPoint. Choose **File>Open**.

2. Change the **Look in** location to **Desktop**.

3. Create a folder called **Ohio**. Click **Open**.

4. **CHECK** Your screen should look like Figure 1.43.

5. Change the location back to **Desktop**.

6. Create two more folders for two other states. Put all three folders on the Desktop.

7. Create a new presentation named: p2rev-[your first initial and last name]5. Save it in one of the new folders.

8. In the new presentation, key: Folder Practice in the title box.

9. Key: You Try It Activity 5 in the subtitle box.

10. **CHECK** Your screen should look like Figure 1.44. Save and close your file.

EXERCISE 3-9:
Add an Effect to a Graphic

There are many different effects you can add to a slide to make objects such as graphics more visually interesting. You can, for example, add an animated effect to make a graphic move or transform itself in a particular way. Adding such an effect can help you emphasize important content. You can modify an effect by choosing the animation's speed, appearance, and other features. An animation icon appears in the Slides pane next to slides that have an effect applied to them.

FIGURE 3.17 Add Emphasis Effect dialog box

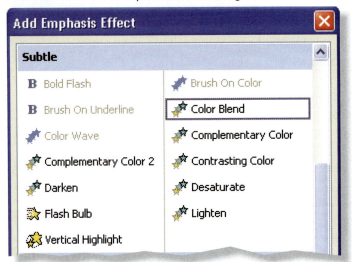

FIGURE 3.18 Graphic with custom animation applied

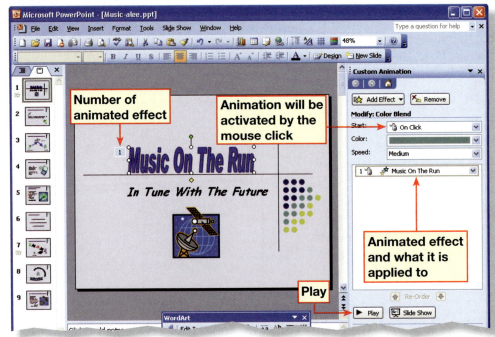

Step-By-Step

1. In your **Music** file, select **Slide 1**.

2. Right-click the WordArt. Click **Custom Animation**.

3. In the **Custom Animation** task pane, click the **Add Effect** drop-down arrow.

4. Choose **Emphasis>More Effects**.

5. In the **Add Emphasis Effect** dialog box, under **Subtle**, click **Color Blend** (see Figure 3.17). Click **OK**.

6. In the task pane, click the **Speed** drop-down arrow. Click **Medium**.

7. **CHECK** Your screen should look like Figure 3.18.

8. Click **Play** to preview the effect.

9. Close the **Custom Animation** task pane. Save your file.

10. Continue to the next exercise.

Lesson 3: Exercise 3-9   PowerPoint 83

LESSON 1 Critical Thinking Activities

6 Beyond the Classroom Activity

Revise a Slide Presentation You are the director of sales in a large company. It is your responsibility to forecast next year's sales. You need to update the presentation that you gave last year. The forecast for each quarter was written as a separate report. Each report is contained in a separate slide. To prepare your new presentation, you need to:

- Switch your forecasts for the first and third quarters. This means that the first slide in last year's presentation (Report 1) will become the third slide (Report 3), and the third slide (Report 3) will become the first slide (Report 1).
- Edit the sales numbers for Reports 2 and 4.
- Print a new presentation handout.

Key a paragraph that explains how the skills that you learned in this lesson will help you prepare your revised presentation. Save your work as: p2rev-[your first initial and last name]6.

7 Standards at Work Activity

 Microsoft Office Specialist Correlation PP03S-1-2
Insert and edit text-based content

Identify Oral Presentation Skills PowerPoint presentations are often used as part of an oral presentation. Evaluate an oral presentation that you gave for school or some other occasion. Then, open your saved **Tips-4** presentation and perform the following tasks:

- Select Slide 5. Key a bulleted list of three skills that an individual should develop to give a great presentation (for example, speak clearly).
- Give the slide an appropriate title.

Save your work as: Tips-[your first initial and last name]7.

8 21st Century Skills Activity

Evaluate a Presentation Think about a time when you were listening to a classmate's report. Then, key a paragraph about your experience. Did the presentation keep your attention? Why or why not? How can evaluating your classmate's presentation make you a better presenter? Save your work as: p2rev-[your first initial and last name]8.

Student Online Learning Center

Go to the book Web site to complete the following review activities.

Interactive Review
To review the main points of this lesson, choose **Interactive Review> PowerPoint Lesson 1.**

Online Self Check
Test your knowledge of the material in this lesson by choosing **Self Checks> PowerPoint Lesson 1.**

iCheckExpress.glencoe.com

Step-By-Step

1. In your **Music** file, select **Slide 1**.

2. Right-click the text **Music On The Run**. In the shortcut menu, click **Format WordArt**.

3. In the **Format WordArt** dialog box, on the **Colors and Lines** tab, under **Fill**, click the **Color** drop-down arrow.

4. Click the blue shown in Figure 3.15.

5. Under **Line**, click the **Color** drop-down arrow.

6. In the row under **Automatic**, select the fourth box from the left.

7. Click the **Size** tab. Under **Size and rotate**, in the **Height** box, key: 1".

8. Click **OK**. Deselect the WordArt.

9. **CHECK** Your screen should look like Figure 3.16.

10. Save your file.

11. Continue to the next exercise.

EXERCISE 3-8: Change the Size and Color of a Graphic

When you resize a graphic, you make it larger or smaller so it fits better on a slide. In Lesson 2, you learned how to use sizing handles to resize graphics. If you want a graphic to be a specific height or width, you can key the exact measurement you need into the formatting dialog box. You can also use the dialog box to change the **fill color** inside the graphic and the **line color** of the graphic's outside edge.

FIGURE 3.15 Format WordArt dialog box

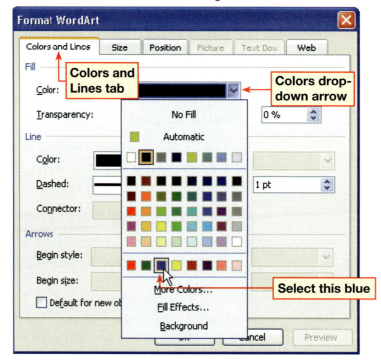

FIGURE 3.16 Graphic with modified size and color

Lesson 3: Exercise 3-8

PowerPoint 82

LESSON 1 Challenge Yourself Projects

9 Fine-Tune Your Presentation

Key Text From what you know so far about PowerPoint, what steps do you think might be necessary to "fine-tune" a presentation? For example, when you are finished with a presentation, you need to check for spelling errors. What other examples can you think of?

- Key a paragraph that lists at least three steps. Explain why you think your three steps are important.

Save as: Tips-p1rev-[your first initial last name]9. Then share your steps with your class.

10 Research a Topic

Create a Slide Use the Internet or another method of research (such as your school library) to find information about creating a presentation. What suggestions can you find that are not covered in the short **Tips** presentation? What suggestions do you think that you might add?

- Open your saved **Tips-7** presentation.
- Save as: Tips-[your first initial and last name]10.
- Use your research to create your own text for the sixth slide.
- Add a title and three bullet points to the slide.
- When finished, print all six slides as a handout.
- Print the entire presentation and save your work.

11 Write Instructions

Create a Presentation Use the **HowTo** data file to create a short presentation that outlines how to do something you enjoy. For example, you may want to tell people how to:

- Plan a prom
- Play a sport (for example, list three key rules of basketball)
- Make brownies or another favorite dish

Add text to all four slides. Make sure the slides progress in a logical order (use the **Pizza** presentation as a model, if necessary). Save your presentation as: HowTo-[your first initial and last name]11. With your teacher's permission, present your presentation to the class.

Step-By-Step

1. In your **Music** file, select **Slide 6**.
2. Select the three bulleted points.
3. Choose **Format > Bullets and Numbering**.
4. In the **Bullets and Numbering** dialog box, on the **Bulleted** tab, in the second row, click the third box from the left.
5. In the **Size** box, increase the size to **110%** of text.
6. Click the **Color** drop-down arrow. In the second row, select the fifth color from the left.
7. **CHECK** Your dialog box should look like Figure 3.13.
8. Click **OK**. Click outside the text box to deselect it.
9. **CHECK** Your screen should look like Figure 3.14.
10. Save your file.
11. Continue to the next exercise.

EXERCISE 3-7: Modify Bulleted Lists

Bulleted lists are common in PowerPoint presentations since they allow you to present information in short, readable sections. As with other text, you can modify the appearance of a bulleted list. Use the Bullets and Numbering dialog box to change the type, size, and color of the bullets used on a slide.

FIGURE 3.13 Bullets and Numbering dialog box

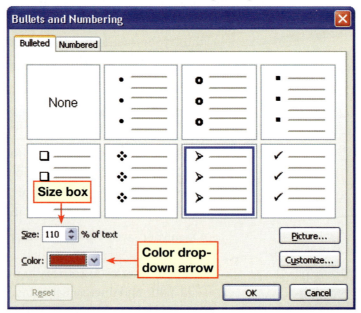

FIGURE 3.14 Modified bullets

Lesson 3: Exercise 3-7

LESSON 2: Create Content and Collaborate

You Will Learn To:

- Use templates
- Promote and demote text
- Create diagrams, tables, and charts
- Insert Clip Art, pictures, shapes, and WordArt
- Use Spelling Checker and Thesaurus
- Compare, merge, and track changes
- Use AutoContent wizard

Standards

The following standards are covered in this lesson. Refer to pages xvii and 156 for a description of the standards listed here.

ISTE Standards Correlation

NETS•S	Performance Indicator
1, 3, 4	5, 9

Microsoft Office Specialist Correlation

PP03S

1-1, 1-2, 1-3, 1-4, 1-5, 3-1, 3-2, 3-3

Study Skill

Find a Study Buddy Studying with a friend can make your study time more productive and enjoyable. Together you can compare classroom notes, and quiz each other.

You have already learned how to insert and edit text in PowerPoint slides. In this lesson, you will learn how to add your own content to PowerPoint presentations. Using ready-made design templates and creating visuals such as tables and shapes will make your presentation attractive. You will also learn how to merge two presentations and track changes made by someone else to a presentation.

21st CENTURY SKILLS

Get Involved Think of someone you know who spends time helping people in need. This person might promote local charities, visit with senior citizens, or help organize pledge drives. When you volunteer, either on your own or through an organization, you are helping people and helping to build a stronger community. In fact, people who volunteer often say that they receive as much or more from their efforts as the people they are helping. *What are a few ways you can get involved?*

Step-By-Step

1. In your **Music** file, select **Slide 9**.
2. Select the paragraph under the title **In Tune With The Future**.
3. Click **Align Left**.
4. Deselect the text.
5. **CHECK** Your screen should look like Figure 3.11.
6. Select the name and title at the bottom of the slide.
7. Click **Align Right**.
8. **CHECK** Your screen should look like Figure 3.12. Deselect the text.
9. Save your file.
10. Continue to the next exercise.

Tips and Tricks

Triple-click a paragraph to select it.

EXERCISE 3-6:
Align Text

A text's **alignment** refers to where the text lines up in relation to a text box's margins. Left-aligned text lines up along a text box's left side. Right-aligned text lines up along a text box's right side. Centered text is positioned in the middle of a text box. You can also justify text so it lines up with both the left and right sides of the text box. Justify text if you do not want your text to have any jagged-looking edges.

FIGURE 3.11 Left-aligned text

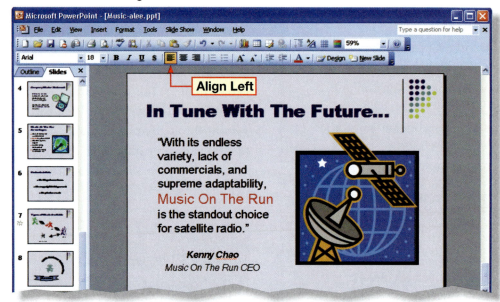

FIGURE 3.12 Right-aligned text

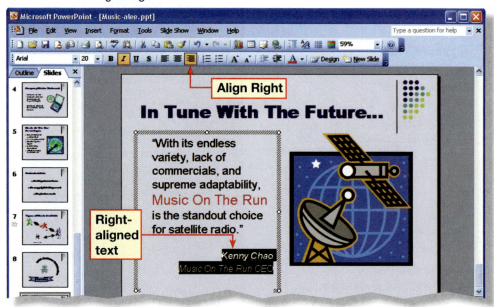

Lesson 3: Exercise 3-6 — PowerPoint 80

LESSON 2: Key Terms

Knowing these terms will help you complete the exercises in this lesson. Use this chart as a study guide when you review the lesson.

Key Term	Definition	Page Number
AutoContent wizard	A tool that helps you put content together into a professional presentation.	60
Chart	A graph created from the data entered into a datasheet.	48
Clip Art	Premade graphics that can be inserted into a presentation.	46
Comments	Notes that can be added to a presentation without appearing as actual changes to the presentation.	57
Compare and Merge	A tool for combining the comments and edits made to multiple copies of the same presentation into one presentation.	58
Content	The text and graphics included on a slide.	38
Datasheet	Holds information in cells. Similar to a worksheet.	48
Demote	In outlines, changes selected text to the next-lower heading level (down one level, to the right).	42
Diagram	A graphic that you use to organize and present information visually in a slide.	43
Markups	Call-out boxes containing a reviewer's name, date, and details of the comments and changes made.	58
Object	A document, picture, worksheet, presentation, or other item that can be inserted into an open file in another application.	53
Promote	In outlines, changes selected text to the next-higher heading level (up one level, to the left).	42
Revisions task pane	Allows you to quickly and easily view a list of suggested changes to a presentation.	59
Table	A device used to organize information into rows and columns.	45
Template	A guide that contains the formatting for a particular type of document or presentation.	38
Thesaurus	A research tool that allows you to find synonyms for words and replace them in the text.	55
Tracking	A feature that shows all changes made to a presentation by a reviewer. Changes by different people are indicated by different colors.	59
WordArt	Decorative text that is shadowed, rotated, stretched, or fitted to predefined shapes.	52

Step-By-Step

1. In your **Music** file, select **Slide 9**.
2. In the main paragraph, select the text **Music On The Run**.
3. On the **Formatting** toolbar, click the **Font Size** drop-down arrow. Click **32**.
4. Deselect the text.
5. **CHECK** Your screen should look like Figure 3.9.
6. Reselect **Music On The Run**.
7. Click the **Font Color** drop-down arrow.
8. In the menu, in the second row, select the fifth color from the left. Deselect the text.
9. **CHECK** Your screen should look like Figure 3.10.
10. Save your file.
11. Continue to the next exercise.

EXERCISE 3-5:
Modify Font Size and Color

Font size refers to how large or small characters are. Consider the text's importance when choosing its font size. For example, Title text is generally large so the title is highly visible. Adding color to a font can also bring attention to a key point. When using different colored fonts, make sure the colors you select contrast with the slide background. Light fonts work best on a dark background, while dark fonts are more readable against a light background.

FIGURE 3.9 Text with increased font size

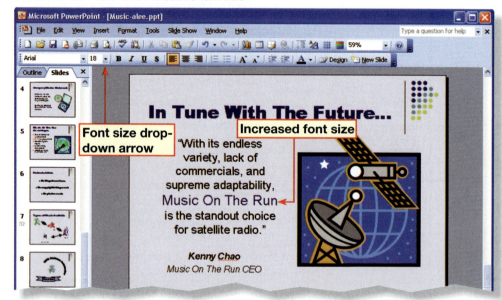

FIGURE 3.10 Text with modified color

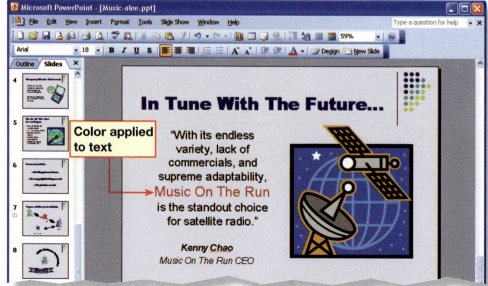

Lesson 3: Exercise 3-5

PowerPoint 79

LESSON 2 — Key Concepts

Now you are ready to start building your own slide show. Fortunately, PowerPoint has many features to help you along the way.

Using Templates

You may already be familiar with templates from other applications such as Microsoft Word. PowerPoint templates are an easy way of setting up your presentation's framework. In one easy step, they establish color schemes, font styles, and background art.

Working with Text, Charts, and Tables

You can edit, delete, and reorganize text in PowerPoint just as you would in other Office applications. In addition, you can import text from other documents. For example, if you have used Word to create a bulleted list of a school club's goals, you can easily import this list into a slide.

If you need to create an organizational chart for your club, PowerPoint helps you by providing the chart's basic structure. All you need to do is modify it as necessary and key the text. Tables can be created just as easily to organize information visually in a presentation.

Adding Clip Art and Shapes

The right art can make your slides more effective when combined with text. Clip Art and basic shapes such as stars and arrows make presentations visually appealing and can make a point without using words.

Polishing Your Presentation

The words we choose are important—they have power to create mental images and affect people's thoughts. The Thesaurus can help you pick the right word. Likewise, Spelling Checker can aid in achieving your goal of a polished, error-free presentation.

In today's business world, working as a team strengthens us all. Encouraging classmates, and eventually coworkers, to review your presentations sends the message that you want them to be as good as possible. PowerPoint contains special tools to let others provide input by adding comments and changes to your presentation. You can then review these suggestions and decide whether you wish to incorporate them. Using these tools effectively is vital in today's business world. As you work through Lesson 2, keep the big picture in mind: how can I use the tools offered here to create presentations that will help me achieve my goals?

Reading Skill

Find Your Study Method Consider your reading weaknesses and strengths. Think about recurring problems you have when you study and take a test. Then go back over the Reading Skills at the beginning of each lesson in this book. Determine which suggestions would be most useful to you. Try using one or more Reading Skills when you read through this lesson and review the material.

Step-By-Step

1. In your **Music** file, select **Slide 1**.
2. Select the text **In Tune With The Future**.
3. Select **Format>Font**.
4. In the **Font** dialog box, under **Font**, select **Comic Sans MS**.
5. Under **Font** style, click **Bold**. Click **OK**.
6. Click anywhere in the slide to deselect the text.
7. **CHECK** Your screen should look like Figure 3.7.
8. Reselect the text **In Tune With The Future**.
9. Click **Italic**. Deselect the text.
10. **CHECK** Your screen should look like Figure 3.8.
11. Save your file.
12. Continue to the next exercise.

EXERCISE 3-4:
Modify Fonts and Font Styles

Characters are individual letters, numbers, symbols, and punctuation marks. A **font** (also called **typeface**) is the unique design of a set of characters. Some fonts are more serious (Times New Roman), while others are more fun (Comic Sans MS). Choose fonts that match the tone of your presentation. The **font style** refers to effects such as bold, italic, underline, and shadow. To preserve consistency, try not to use too many different fonts and styles when creating slides.

FIGURE 3.7 Text with new font and style applied

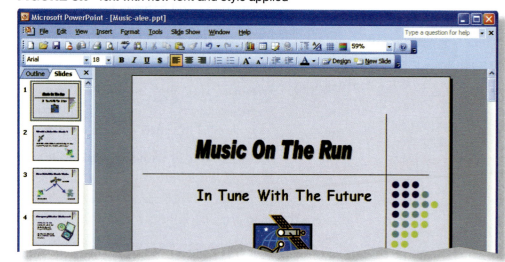

FIGURE 3.8 Text with Italic style applied

Step-By-Step

1. Start **PowerPoint**. Choose **File > New**.

2. Click the **Other Task Panes** drop-down arrow. Click **New Presentation**.

3. Under **Templates**, click **On my computer**.

4. In the **New Presentation** dialog box, click the **Design Templates** tab.

5. Click **Glass Layers** (see Figure 2.1). Click **OK**.

6. Save your file as: Garden-[your first initial and last name]. (For example, *Garden-alee*).

7. **CHECK** Your screen should look like Figure 2.2. Continue to the next exercise.

You Should Know

You can find more templates online if you have Internet access. Select **Additional Design Templates** or **Design Templates on Microsoft Office Online**.

EXERCISE 2-1:
Create a Presentation Using a Template

Using templates makes it easy to create professional-looking presentations. A **template** is pre-designed for a model presentation. Each PowerPoint template provides a layout with selected colors and backgrounds. Placeholder text indicates where to place your **content** (the text and graphics included on a slide).

FIGURE 2.1 New Presentation dialog box

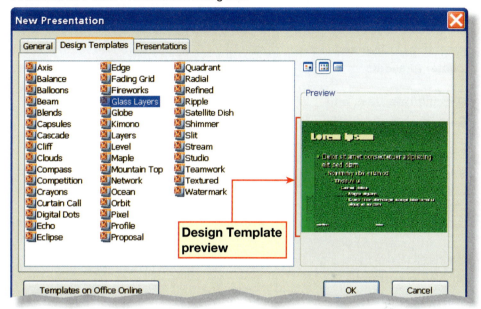

FIGURE 2.2 Glass Layers design template

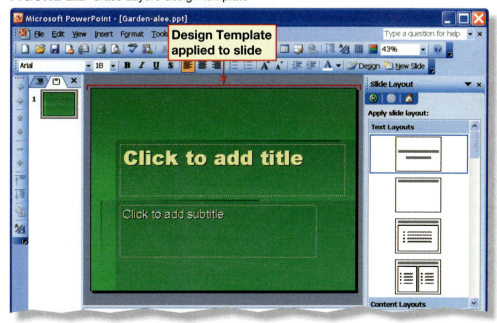

Lesson 2: Exercise 2-1

Step-By-Step

1. In your **Music** file, select **Slide 5**.
2. Choose **Format>Slide Layout**.
3. In the **Slide Layout** task pane, scroll to **Text and Content Layouts**.
4. Click the **Title, Text, and Content** drop-down arrow.
5. Click **Apply to Selected Slides** (see Figure 3.5).
6. Close the **Slide Layout** task pane.
7. On the slide, use the sizing handles to enlarge the Clip Art.
8. **CHECK** Your screen should look similar to Figure 3.6.
9. Save your file.
10. Continue to the next exercise.

EXERCISE 3-3:
Modify Slide Layout

Slide layout refers to how text, graphics, and other content are arranged on a slide. PowerPoint has two main slide layouts—Title and Title and Text. You can use the Slide Layout task pane to change a slide's layout to better fit the content you want to include. You can apply a new layout before you add content to a slide, or you can change the layout of a slide you have already created.

FIGURE 3.5 Slide Layout task pane

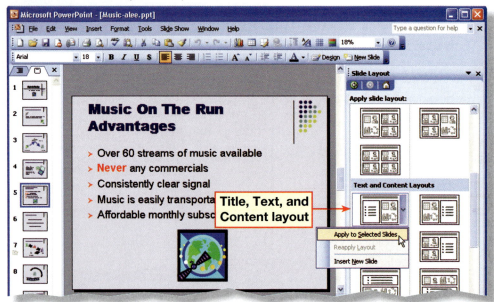

FIGURE 3.6 Slide with new layout

Lesson 3: Exercise 3-3

PowerPoint 77

Step-By-Step

1. In your **Garden** file, click in the title text box. Key: **Corporate Volunteer Opportunities**.

2. Click in the subtitle text box and key: **Community Garden Project**. Click outside the text box.

3. **CHECK** Your screen should look like Figure 2.3.

4. Choose **Insert > New Slide**. In the title box, key: **Get Involved Now!**.

5. Click in the bulleted text box and key: **Meet New People**.

6. Press ENTER.

7. Key the remaining four bulleted points shown in Figure 2.4.

8. **CHECK** Your screen should look like Figure 2.4.

9. Save your file.

10. Continue to the next exercise.

EXERCISE 2-2: Add Text to Slides

PowerPoint provides text boxes to make it easy to enter text. Use the title text box, at the top of each slide, for the slide titles. The first slide of a presentation also has a subtitle text box. Other slides in a presentation have text boxes where you can key bulleted lists or insert other content.

FIGURE 2.3 Slide with title and subtitle

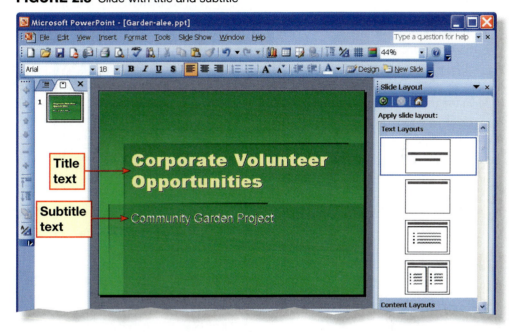

FIGURE 2.4 Bulleted text

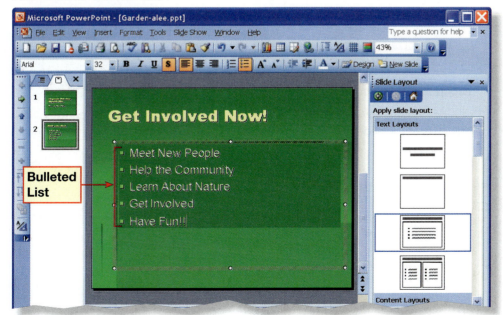

Step-By-Step

1. In your **Music** file, select **Slide 1**.
2. Choose **Format > Background**.
3. In the **Background** dialog box, click the **Background fill** drop-down arrow.
4. In the menu, select the last box in the top row (see Figure 3.3).
5. Click **Apply to All**.
6. **CHECK** Your screen should look like Figure 3.4.
7. Save your file.
8. Continue to the next exercise.

Tips and Tricks

To open the **Background** dialog box, right-click a blank area of the slide and click **Background**.

EXERCISE 3-2:
Customize Slide Backgrounds

A **background** is a solid color, pattern, or picture that appears behind content on a slide. You can add a background to a single slide, or add the same background to an entire presentation. Every design template has a specific background color as part of its **color scheme**. You can change this color to suit your particular needs. When changing colors, try to use a color from the template's color scheme to make sure your presentation is as consistent as possible.

FIGURE 3.3 Background dialog box

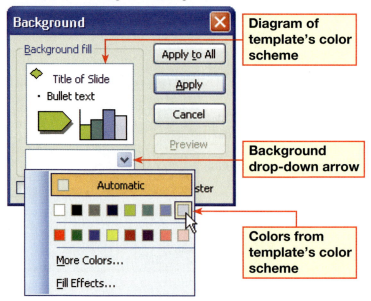

- Diagram of template's color scheme
- Background drop-down arrow
- Colors from template's color scheme

FIGURE 3.4 New background applied to slides

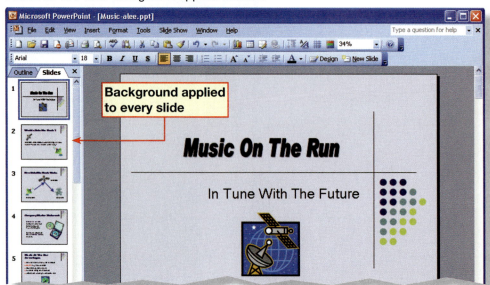

- Background applied to every slide

Step-By-Step

1. In your **Garden** file, close the **Slide Layout** task pane.
2. Click the **Outline** tab. If necessary, select **Slide 2**.
3. Click inside the title text box.
4. Double-click the word **Now** to select it.
5. Press [←BACKSPACE].
6. **CHECK** Your screen should look like Figure 2.5.
7. Click inside the bulleted list placeholder.
8. Select the fourth bulleted item.
9. Press [←BACKSPACE].
10. **CHECK** Your screen should look like Figure 2.6.
11. Save your file.
12. Continue to the next exercise.

EXERCISE 2-3:
Delete Text from Slides

You can copy, delete, or replace existing text in a slide. To delete text, you must first select the text within a text box. When you click inside a text box, a gray box appears around the text. You can then edit the text.

FIGURE 2.5 Modified title

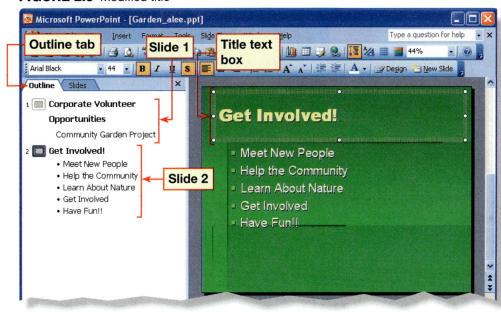

FIGURE 2.6 Bulleted list with bullet deleted

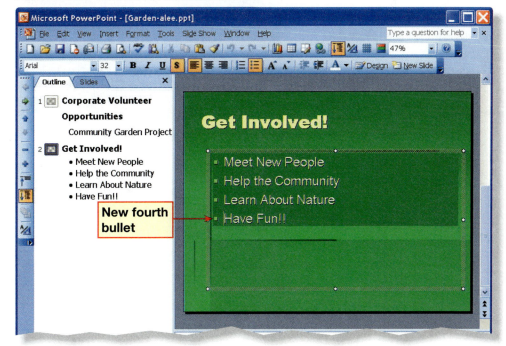

EXERCISE 3-1:
Apply Design Templates

A design template adds visual interest to a presentation, and helps give it a consistent look or **formatting**. When selecting a template, think about what you want the tone of your presentation to be. Some combinations of colors and fonts set a serious tone, while other combinations create a fun look. Know your audience, and select a template that supports or matches the purpose of your presentation.

FIGURE 3.1 Slide Design task pane

FIGURE 3.2 Design applied to slide

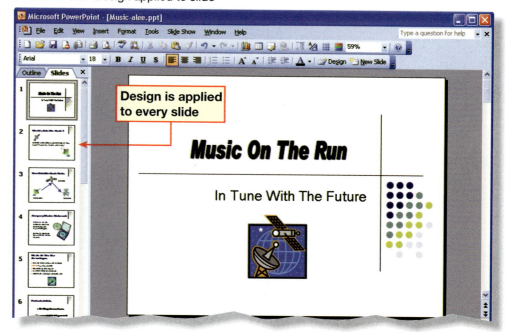

Step-By-Step

1. Locate and open the data file **Music.ppt**. Save as: Music-[your first initial and last name]. (For example, *Music-alee*).

2. In the **Slides** pane, select **Slide 1**.

3. Choose **Format > Slide Design**.

4. In the **Slide Design** task pane, locate **Network.pot**.

5. Click the **Network** drop-down arrow. Select **Apply to All Slides** (see Figure 3.1).

6. Close the **Slide Design** task pane.

7. **CHECK** Your screen should look like Figure 3.2.

8. Save your file.

9. Continue to the next exercise.

EXERCISE 2-4:
Import Text from Other Sources

PowerPoint allows you to import, or bring in, text from different sources into your presentation. For example, you can import a Word outline. When you insert the outline, PowerPoint automatically creates slide titles, subtitles, and bulleted lists.

FIGURE 2.7 Insert Outline dialog box

FIGURE 2.8 Slide created from Word outline

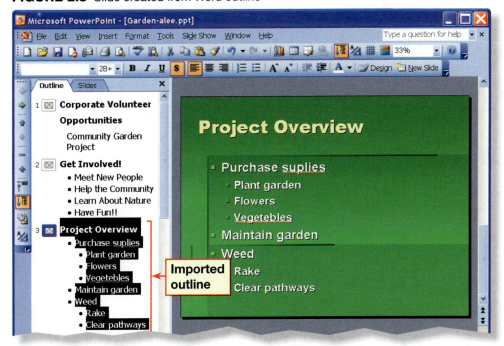

Step-By-Step

1. In your **Garden** file, choose **Insert > Slides from Outline**.

2. In the **Insert Outline** dialog box, browse to the data file **Outline.doc** (see Figure 2.7).

3. Select **Outline.doc**. Click **Insert**.

4. **CHECK** Your screen should look like Figure 2.8. Notice the outline was inserted on Slide 3.

5. Save your file.

6. Continue to the next exercise.

You Should Know

Use heading styles to create an outline in Word if you plan to import it into PowerPoint.

Lesson 2: Exercise 2-4 — PowerPoint 41

LESSON 3: Key Concepts

Templates, premade graphics, and WordArt can help you create a good presentation. However, creating the most effective presentation requires that you customize the presentation to your purpose. A template gives you a starting point, just as the outline for a report guides you toward your target. Customizing the template helps you hit the bull's eye.

Laying It Out

Just as a blueprint guides workers in creating a building, slide layouts guide you through positioning items such as text, charts, and pictures. The Slide Layout task pane lets you select from over 20 premade slide layouts, or templates. You can also customize these templates to reflect the exact color scheme and layout that will match the tone of your presentation.

Formatting Text

The appearance of your text should match the goals of your presentation. For example, a quarterly business report will probably call for a more formal-looking font than a presentation on kite-building. Likewise, you may want to make major points stand out by using a large font or boldfacing. You can also choose different colors and effects, such as shadowing and italicization for your text. Be careful not to overdo it, though, as your slides may become too busy and hard to read.

Modifying Graphics

Modifying a graphic, such as a piece of Clip Art, lets you customize it to the available space and the style of your presentation. For example, you may want to attract viewer attention by enlarging and slightly rotating a picture of your company's logo. In addition, you can animate objects. In the case of the logo, you could have it spin around and "grow" as it appears on screen.

Transitions and Masters

Transitions alter the way the show moves from one slide to another. You will want to experiment with different transitions to see which ones best meet your needs. Once you have chosen all of your transitions, be sure to view the entire presentation so that you can see how it looks as a whole.

Using master slides is another way to put PowerPoint to work for you. Each slide has a master slide that determines things like fonts, bullet styles, and background colors. Properly using master slides is one of the most important concepts you will learn in this lesson.

Reading Skill

Read in Short, Frequent Sessions It has been proven that short bursts of concentration repeated frequently are much more effective than one long session. So, even if you only have 10 minutes, DO IT. Take a break. Then read another 10 minutes.

EXERCISE 2-5:
Promote and Demote Text

In Outline View, text is organized in levels. Slide titles are on the first level, subtitles on the second level, and bulleted text on the third level. Use the Outlining toolbar to change the level of text. For example, you can **promote** bulleted text and make it a subtitle. You can also **demote** title text and make it bulleted text.

Step-By-Step

1. In your **Garden** file, click the **Outline** tab, if necessary.
2. Choose **View > Toolbars > Outlining**.
3. On the **Outline** pane, select the text **Plant garden**.
4. Click **Promote**.
5. (CHECK) Your screen should look like Figure 2.9.
6. On **Slide 3**, select the word **Weed**.
7. Click **Demote**.
8. (CHECK) Your screen should look like Figure 2.10.
9. Save your file.
10. Continue to the next exercise.

FIGURE 2.9 Promoted text

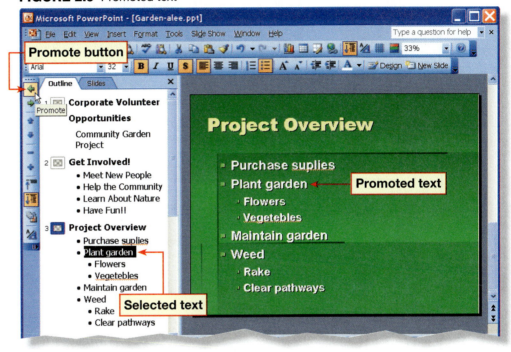

FIGURE 2.10 Demoted text

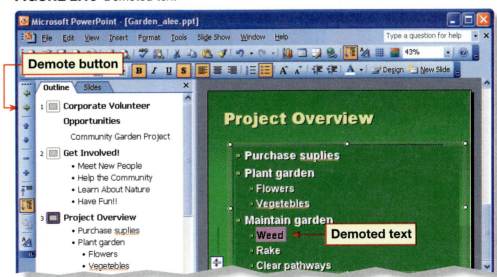

You Should Know

When text has been promoted, it shifts to the left. When it has been demoted, it shifts to the right.

Lesson 2: Exercise 2-5

PowerPoint 42

LESSON 3 — Key Terms

Knowing these terms will help you complete the exercises in this lesson. Use this chart as a study guide when you review the lesson.

Key Term	Definition	Page Number
Alignment	The position of text and graphics in relation to a text box's margins and to other text and graphics on a slide.	80
Animation scheme	An effect that, when applied, causes text and graphics to move and display on screen in specific ways. Animation schemes can be Subtle, Moderate, or Exciting.	91
Background	Solid colors, patterns, or pictures that fill the entire slide and appear behind the slide's content.	76
Color scheme	The eight colors used in a slide's design. Each design template has a specific color scheme that is used for the presentation's background, text and lines, shadows, title text, fills, accents, and hyperlinks.	76
Fill color	The color applied to the interior of a shape.	82
Font	The unique design of a set of characters. Also referred to as typeface.	78
Font style	Effects such as bold, italic, underline, and shadow that are applied to text.	78
Footer	One or more text boxes at the bottom of every slide, handout, or notes page. May contain the date, presentation title, or slide number.	98
Formatting	The appearance of content on a slide.	75
Gradient	The gradual shading of a graphic from one side or corner to the other.	84
Header	Information that appears at the top of every notes page or presentation handout.	98
Landscape	The orientation of a slide that is wider than it is tall.	93
Line color	The color applied to a line or to the border of a shape.	82
Portrait	The orientation of a slide that is taller than it is wide.	93
Rotate	To turn an object, usually 90° to the left or right.	86
Slide layout	The arrangement of text and graphics on a slide.	77
Slide master	A slide that serves as a model for every slide in a presentation except the Title slide.	96
Title master	A slide that serves as a model for the Title slide.	95
Transition	An effect that occurs between slides during a slide show.	92
Typeface	The unique design of a set of characters. Also referred to as font.	78

EXERCISE 2-6: Create a Diagram

A **diagram** is a graphic that organizes information visually in a slide. PowerPoint provides many different types of diagrams that can be easily inserted into a presentation.

FIGURE 2.11 Diagram inserted into slide

FIGURE 2.12 Text keyed into top box

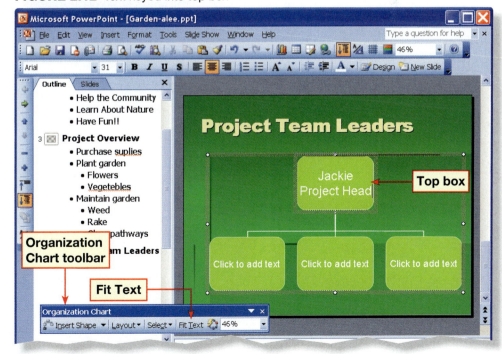

Step-By-Step

1. In your **Garden** file, select **Slide 3**.

2. Choose **Insert > New Slide**. Close the task pane.

3. In the title box, key: Project Team Leaders.

4. Choose **Insert > Diagram**.

5. In the **Diagram Gallery** dialog box, click **Organization Chart**. Click **OK**.

6. **CHECK** Your screen should look like Figure 2.11.

7. Click in the diagram's top box. Key: Jackie.

8. Press ENTER. Key: Project Head.

9. On the **Organization Chart** toolbar, click **Fit Text**.

10. **CHECK** Your screen should look like Figure 2.12.

Continued on the next page.

Lesson 2: Exercise 2-6

LESSON 3 Formatting Content

Professional-looking presentations start with consistent formatting. In a consistently formatted presentation, the contents of all slides work together to give the entire presentation a specific look. In this lesson, you will learn how using tools such as templates and slide masters can help you create consistent presentations. You will also learn how to add animations and effects to highlight your message and to keep your audience interested.

You Will Learn To:

- Customize slide backgrounds
- Modify slide layouts, fonts, and text
- Modify and add effects to pictures, shapes, and graphics
- Apply animation and transition effects
- Modify page setup
- Work with multiple masters
- Use headers and footers

21st CENTURY SKILLS

Practice Ethical Behavior Ethics are the principles of conduct that govern a group or society. Practicing ethical behavior is an important part of a successful future. An ethical code of behavior is one where you behave in a way you feel is just and fair. For instance, if you took credit for a friend's hard work, that would be unethical. Employees who behave ethically do not lie, cheat, or steal. *What ethical behaviors should you practice at school?*

Standards

The following standards are covered in this lesson. Refer to pages xvii and 156 for a description of the standards listed here.

ISTE Standards Correlation

NETS•S	Performance Indicator
1, 2, 3, 4	4, 5, 9, 10

Microsoft Office Specialist Correlation

PP03S-2

2-1, 2-2, 2-3, 2-4, 2-5, 2-6, 2-7

Study Skill

Routine Break Taking regular study breaks can actually help you get your work done faster. When you feel your attention drifting, take a few minutes to change your environment.

Lesson 3: Formatting Content

Step-By-Step

11. Click in the left subordinate box. Key: Rhonda. Press ENTER. Key: Team A.

12. **CHECK** Your screen should look like Figure 2.13.

13. Click in the middle subordinate box. Key: Miguel. Press ENTER. Key: Team B.

14. Click in the right subordinate box. Key: Aaron. Press ENTER. Key: Team C.

15. Click anywhere outside the diagram box.

16. **CHECK** Your screen should look like Figure 2.14.

17. Save your file.

18. Continue to the next exercise.

Troubleshooter

If you delete something by mistake, press CTRL + Z to undo.

EXERCISE 2-6: (Continued)
Create a Diagram

FIGURE 2.13 Text keyed into subordinate box

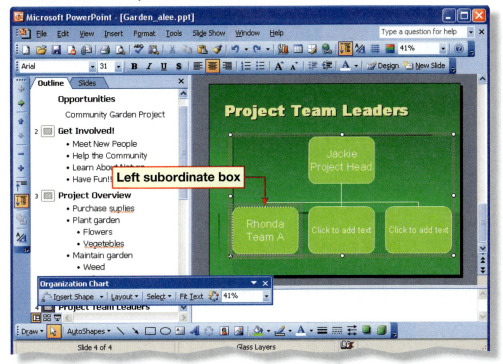

FIGURE 2.14 Final diagram

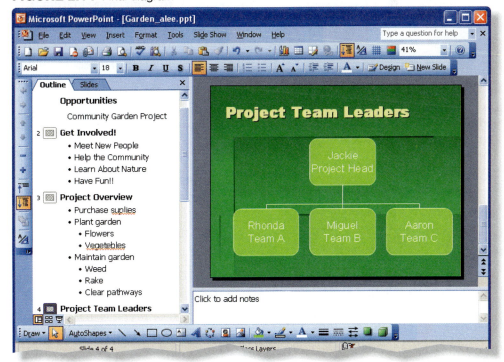

LESSON 2: Challenge Yourself Projects

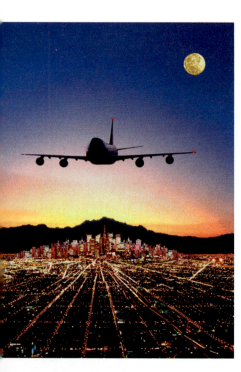

9 Create a Presentation

Write Text for Slides   You have a client who is coming to town for an important meeting. Your client has never been to your town. Use a design template to create a presentation that will prepare your client for her visit. In your presentation:

- Identify where your client is staying.
- Identify where the meeting is being held.
- Identify two sites that your client should know about (e.g., places to eat, where the local movie theater is, etc.).
- Provide a brief schedule for your client. Include dates and times in a table. Include when the client will arrive in town, when the meeting is being held, and when the client will leave town.

Your presentation should include at least five slides. Save your presentation as: p2rev-[your first initial and last name]9.

10 Add Content to Slides

Insert Visuals   Visuals make a presentation more interesting. Open the presentation you created in Project 9. Add at least one piece of Clip Art or a photo and at least one piece of WordArt or an AutoShape.

Add a table to your presentation that provides important contact information for your client (e.g., the hotel's telephone number, your telephone number, etc.). Add a second slide that uses an organizational chart to give your client an overview of your company's structure. Save your presentation as: p2rev-[your first initial and last name]10.

11 Review a Presentation

Edit Content   With your teacher's permission, team up with another member of your class. Exchange the presentations that you each created in Projects 9 and 10. Review your classmate's presentation. As you review:

- Correct any misspellings or other errors you might find.
- Use the Thesaurus to suggest a change of wording on one slide.
- Insert comments with constructive suggestions.

When finished, compare and merge your presentation with the reviewed presentation. Read his or her suggestions. Accept or reject changes as appropriate. Make any edits that you think will improve your presentation. Save your presentation as: p2rev-[your first initial and last name]11.

Step-By-Step

1. In your **Garden** file, select **Slide 4**.

2. Choose **Insert>New Slide**. Close the task pane.

3. In the title box, key: Team Tasks.

4. Click in the text box. Click **Insert Table**.

5. Drag to select 3 columns across and 3 rows down (see Figure 2.15).

6. Release the mouse button to insert the table.

7. In the first cell of the first row, key: Team A. Press TAB.

8. Key the text shown in Figure 2.16 into the table. Press TAB to move between cells.

9. **CHECK** Your screen should look like Figure 2.16. Save your file.

10. Continue to the next exercise.

EXERCISE 2-7:
Create a Table

A **table** organizes your information into rows and columns. PowerPoint tables work like Word tables. The area where a row and a column intersect is called a cell. Enter text into cells like you do into a text box. Press Tab to move from cell to cell.

FIGURE 2.15 Select columns and rows

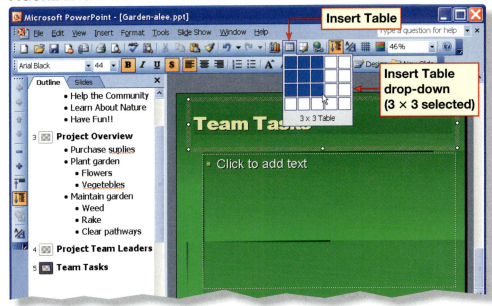

FIGURE 2.16 Finished table

Lesson 2: Exercise 2-7

PowerPoint 45

LESSON 2 Critical Thinking Activities

6 Beyond the Classroom Activity

Review a Presentation You are reviewing a coworker's presentation. Open the data file **Sales.ppt**. Save as: Sales-[your first initial and last name]6. Use what you learned in this lesson to edit the presentation and suggest changes. You should:

- Check spelling.
- Add comments.
- Use the Thesaurus to change at least one word.

7 Standards at Work Activity

 Microsoft Office Specialist Correlation PP03S-1-1
Create new presentations from templates

You decide to create an employee orientation for your company. First, identify your company (e.g., a surf shop, a graphics firm, a pet store, etc.). Then, use the AutoContent Wizard training template to create a short presentation that covers the following topics:

- The company's name and purpose.
- The company's main services and/or products.
- What you (the employer) expect from your employees.
- What your employees should expect from their employer.

Include at least one piece of Clip Art in your presentation. Use AutoShapes and WordArt to create a logo for your company. Save your file as: p2rev-[your first initial and last name]7.

8 21st Century Skills Activity

Promote Getting Involved A local charity is planning a walkathon to raise money for cancer research. As a member of the charity, you want to encourage people to participate in the event. Use a design template to create a brief presentation that encourages people to get involved with the walkathon. In your presentation, state what the issue is, why the issue is important, and what people can do to get involved.

Add Clip Art, photos, AutoShapes, and WordArt to your presentation as needed (include at least two visuals in your presentation). Your presentation should also include at least one of the following: a table, a diagram, or a chart. Save your file as: p2rev-[your first initial and last name]8.

Student Online Learning Center

Go to the book Web site to complete the following review activities.

Interactive Review
To review the main points of this lesson, choose **Interactive Review> PowerPoint Lesson 2**.

Online Self Check
Test your knowledge of the material in this lesson by choosing **Self Checks> PowerPoint Lesson 2**.

iCheckExpress.glencoe.com

Step-By-Step

1. In your **Garden** file, select **Slide 5**. Choose **Insert>New Slide**. Close the task pane.

2. In the title box, key: Supplies Needed.

3. In the text box, key the three bullet points shown in Figure 2.17.

4. Choose **Insert>Picture> Clip Art**.

5. In the **Clip Art** task pane, under **Search for**, key: garden.

6. Under **Search in**, make sure **All collections** is selected.

7. Click the **Results should be** drop-down arrow. Make sure only **Clip Art** is selected. Click **Go**.

8. **CHECK** Your screen should look similar to Figure 2.18.

9. Click the image (or a similar image) shown in Figure 2.18.

Continued on the next page.

EXERCISE 2-8:
Add Clip Art to a Slide

Images help make your presentation visually interesting. You can use PowerPoint to locate premade graphics known as **Clip Art**. The Clip Art task pane helps you search for the image that best fits your presentation.

FIGURE 2.17 Slide 6 text

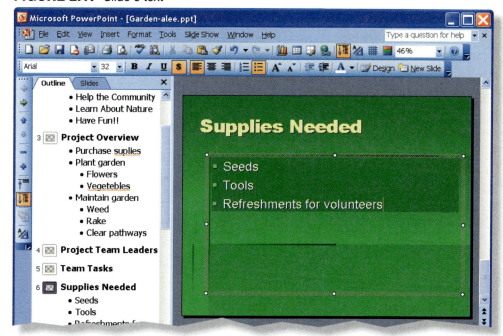

FIGURE 2.18 Clip Art task pane

LESSON 2 You Try It Activities

5 Review and Edit a Presentation

Your manager reviewed your employee orientation and suggested some changes. You need to review her suggestions and edit your presentation. You must complete You Try It Activity 4 before doing this activity.

Step-By-Step

1. Open your **Theater-4** file. Save as: Theater-[your first initial and last name]5. Close the task pane.

2. Compare and merge with the data file **Theater_reviewed.ppt**.

3. Select **Slide 2**. Apply the suggested changes. Close the **Revisions** task pane.

4. Check spelling. Make any needed corrections to Slide 2.

5. **CHECK** Your screen should look like Figure 2.57.

6. Read the comment on Slide 7. Delete the comment.

7. Add a new Slide 8. Close the task pane. Add the text shown in Figure 2.58 to the slide.

8. Choose **AutoShapes > Stars and Banners** to add a star to Slide 8.

9. Use WordArt to add the word **Welcome!** to Slide 8.

10. **CHECK** Your screen should look like Figure 2.58. Save and close the file.

FIGURE 2.57 Slide 2 edited

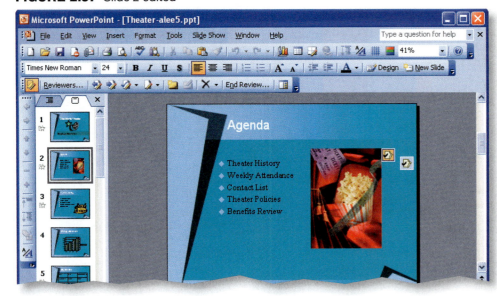

FIGURE 2.58 New Slide 8

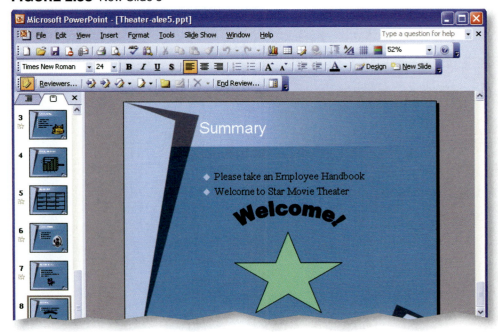

Lesson 2: You Try It Activities

PowerPoint 69

Step-By-Step

EXERCISE 2-8: (Continued)
Add Clip Art to a Slide

10. Close the **Clip Art** task pane.

11. Click the image and drag it under the bulleted text.

12. Press SHIFT and drag the sizing handle in the lower right corner down to enlarge the image (see Figure 2.19).

13. Release the mouse button. Click anywhere in the slide.

14. **iCHECK** Your screen should look similar to Figure 2.20.

15. Save your file.

16. Continue to the next exercise.

FIGURE 2.19 Enlarging the image

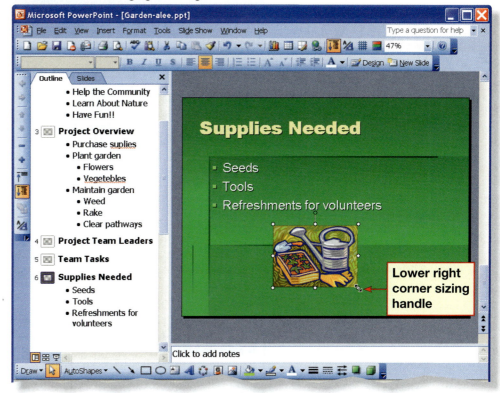

FIGURE 2.20 Slide with Clip Art inserted

Tips and Tricks

Another way to insert Clip Art is to drag an image from the **Clip Art** task pane to your slide.

Lesson 2: Exercise 2-8

PowerPoint 47

LESSON 2 You Try It Activities

4 Add Content to Slides

You are an assistant manager for the Star Movie Theater. Your manager asked you to develop a PowerPoint presentation to help orient new employees.

Step-By-Step

1. Open the data file **Theater.ppt**. Save as: Theater-[your first initial and last name]4. Close the task pane.

2. Select **Slide 2**. Add the data file **Theater.jpg** to the slide. Resize the photo as necessary.

3. Select **Slide 4**. Add a chart to the slide.

4. Fill in the chart datasheet using the information shown in Figure 2.55.

5. **CHECK** Your screen should look like Figure 2.55.

6. Select **Slide 5**. Insert a table with 3 columns and 4 rows into the slide.

7. Fill the table in using the information shown in Figure 2.56.

8. **CHECK** Your screen should look like Figure 2.56.

9. Save and close the file.

FIGURE 2.55 Chart added to Slide 4

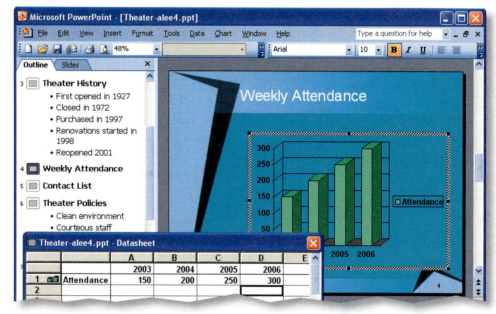

FIGURE 2.56 Table added to Slide 5

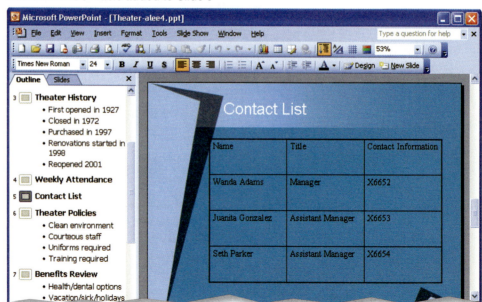

Step-By-Step

1. In your **Garden** file, select **Slide 6**.

2. Choose **Insert>New Slide**. Close the task pane.

3. In the title box, key: Supply Breakdown.

4. Choose **Insert>Chart**. A datasheet opens that contains sample data (see Figure 2.21).

5. Choose **Chart>Chart Type**. In the **Chart Type** dialog box, under **Chart type**, click **Pie**.

6. **CHECK** Your dialog box should look like Figure 2.22.

7. Click **OK**.

Continued on the next page.

Tips and Tricks

Right-click on the chart to select a different chart type.

EXERCISE 2-9:
Create a Chart

Like a diagram, a **chart** displays information in a visually interesting way. Enter your information into a **datasheet**, which displays your information like a worksheet. Your data is then shown in the form of a chart, such as a bar chart or a line chart.

FIGURE 2.21 Sample chart inserted

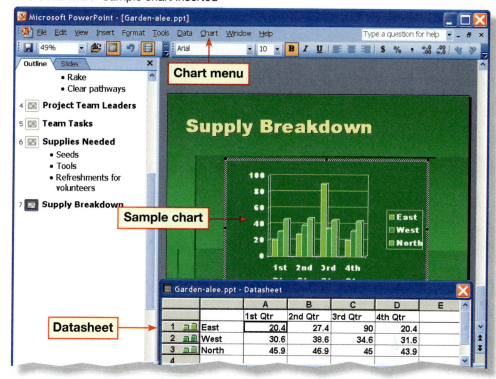

FIGURE 2.22 Chart Type dialog box

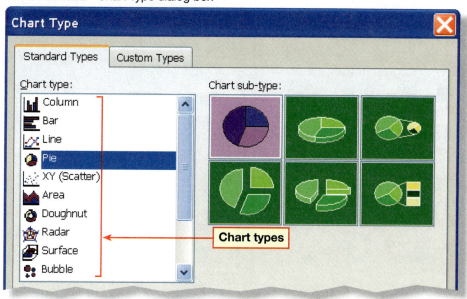

Lesson 2: Exercise 2-9

LESSON 2 Practice It Activities

3 Review a Presentation

Follow the steps to complete the activity. You must complete Practice It Activity 2 before doing this activity.

Step-By-Step

1. Open your **Fundraiser-2** file. Save as: **Fundraiser-[your first initial and last name]3**. Close the task pane.

2. Choose **Tools > Compare and Merge Presentations**.

3. Locate and select the data file **Fundraiser_reviewed**. Click **Merge**. Click **Continue**.

4. Select **Slide 2**. Select the first markup. Click **Unapply**.

5. Click **Next Item**. Click **Apply**. Click **End Review...**. Click **Yes**.

6. **CHECK** Your screen should look like Figure 2.53.

7. Click **Spelling**.

8. Under **Suggestions**, click **Restoration**. Click **Change**. Click **OK**. Click anywhere outside of the text area.

9. **CHECK** Your screen should look like Figure 2.54. Save and close your file.

FIGURE 2.53 Slide 2 with changes applied

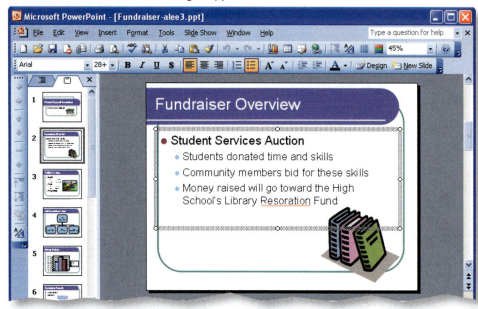

FIGURE 2.54 Final Slide 2

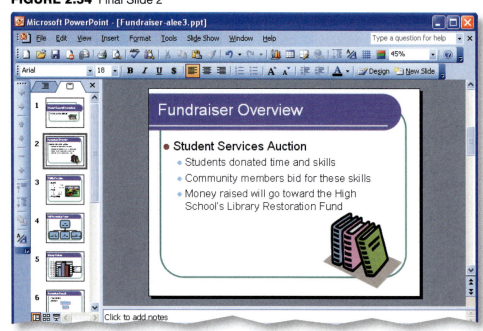

Step-By-Step

EXERCISE 2-9: (Continued)
Create a Chart

8. In the **Datasheet**, right-click **Select All** (see Figure 2.23).

9. Click **Clear Contents**.

10. Under Column A, key: **Food**. Press TAB.

11. Fill in the rest of the datasheet as shown in Figure 2.23.

12. Close the **Datasheet** box.

13. Choose **Chart > Chart Options**.

14. On the **Data Labels** tab, click **Percentage**. Click **OK**.

15. Use the sizing handles to enlarge the chart. Click twice outside the chart.

16. **CHECK** Your screen should look like Figure 2.24.

17. Save your file.

18. Continue to the next exercise.

FIGURE 2.23 Information entered into Datasheet box

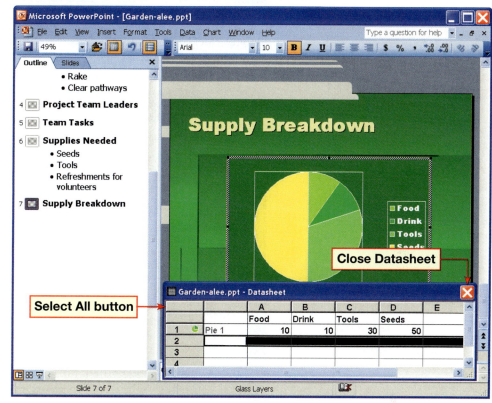

FIGURE 2.24 Finished pie chart

LESSON 2 Practice It Activities

2 Insert Diagrams and WordArt

Follow the steps to complete the activity. You must complete Practice It Activity 1 before doing this activity.

Step-By-Step

1. Open your **Fundraiser-1** file. Save as: Fundraiser-[your first initial and last name]2. Close the task pane.

2. Click **Slide 4**. Choose **Insert > Diagram**. Click **Organization Chart**. Click **OK**.

3. In the top box, key: Paul. Press ENTER. Key: Team Leader. Fill in the bottom three boxes (see Figure 2.51). Click **Fit Text**.

4. CHECK Your screen should look like Figure 2.51.

5. Select **Slide 5**. Insert a New Slide. Close the task pane. Key the title: Fundraiser Results.

6. Click on the text area border and press DELETE to remove the text placeholder. Click **Insert WordArt**.

7. Select the fifth box in the second row. Click **OK**. Key: Total Raised. Press ENTER. Key: $375.00. Click **OK**. Resize the WordArt.

8. CHECK Your screen should look like Figure 2.52. Save and close your file.

FIGURE 2.51 Organization chart added to slide

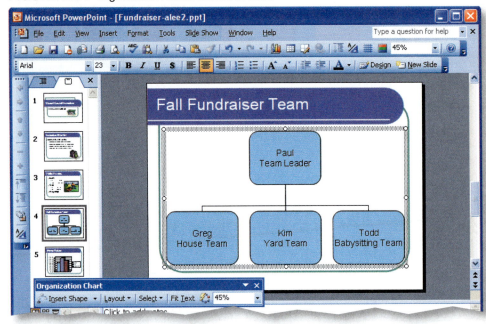

FIGURE 2.52 WordArt added to slide

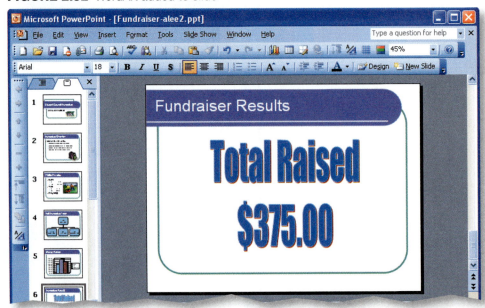

Step-By-Step

1. In your **Garden** file, select **Slide 7**.

2. Choose **Insert>New Slide**. Close the task pane.

3. In the title box, key: Thank You!

4. Choose **Insert>Picture> From File**.

5. In the **Insert Picture** dialog box, locate the data file **Flowers.jpg** (see Figure 2.25).

6. Click the file. Click **Insert**.

7. In the slide, use the sizing handles to enlarge the photo.

8. **CHECK** Your screen should look similar to Figure 2.26.

9. Save your file.

10. Continue to the next exercise.

EXERCISE 2-10:
Add a Picture to a Slide

Pictures are images that are made up of small dots. A typical picture would be a photograph or artwork created in a software program like Microsoft Paint. You can insert pictures from your own scanned images, digital camera, or picture CD-ROM.

FIGURE 2.25 Insert Picture dialog box

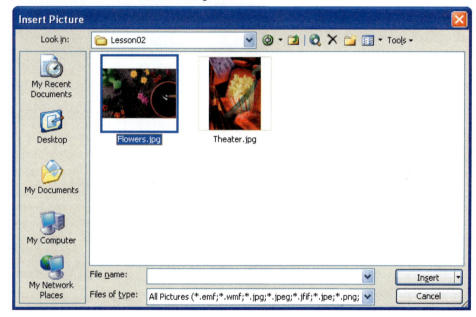

FIGURE 2.26 Inserted picture

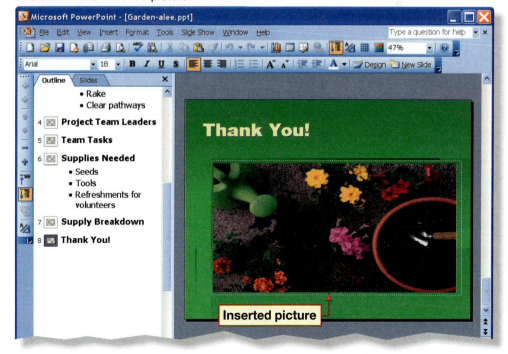

Lesson 2: Exercise 2-10

PowerPoint 50

LESSON 2 Practice It Activities

1 Create a Slide

Follow the steps to complete the activity.

FIGURE 2.49 Slide 3

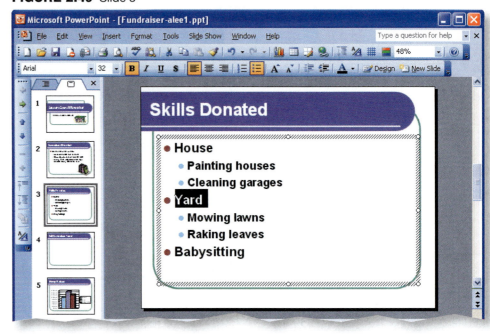

FIGURE 2.50 Clip Art added to Slide 3

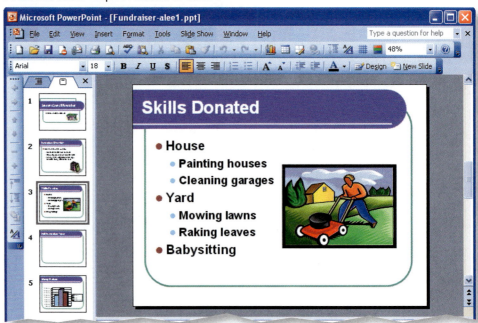

Step-By-Step

1. Start PowerPoint. Open the data file **Fundraiser.ppt**. Save as: Fundraiser-[your first initial and last name]1. Close the task pane.

2. Click **Slide 2**. Choose **Insert > Slides from Outline**. Locate and select the data file **PI_Outline.doc**. Click **Insert**.

3. Select the word **Yard**. Click **Promote**.

4. **CHECK** Your screen should look like Figure 2.49.

5. Choose **Insert > Picture > Clip Art**. Search for: mowing lawns.

6. Select an image similar to that shown in Figure 2.50. Close the task pane.

7. Position the clip as shown in Figure 2.50. Resize as necessary.

8. **CHECK** Your screen should look similar to Figure 2.50.

9. Save and close the file.

Lesson 2: Practice It Activities

Step-By-Step

1. In your **Garden** file, select **Slide 2**.

2. On the **Drawing** toolbar, click the **AutoShapes** drop-down arrow.

3. Choose **Basic Shapes**.

4. Click **Sun** (see Figure 2.27).

5. Click in the lower right corner of Slide 2.

6. Click and drag the pointer to create a sun. Release your mouse button to finish.

7. **✓CHECK** Your screen should look similar to Figure 2.28.

8. Save your file.

9. Continue to the next exercise.

EXERCISE 2-11:
Add Shapes to Slides

Adding Clip Art and pictures is not the only way you can add interest to your presentation. You can also use PowerPoint's AutoShapes, which are pre-designed shapes such as rectangles, ovals, and stars.

FIGURE 2.27 Select the Sun shape

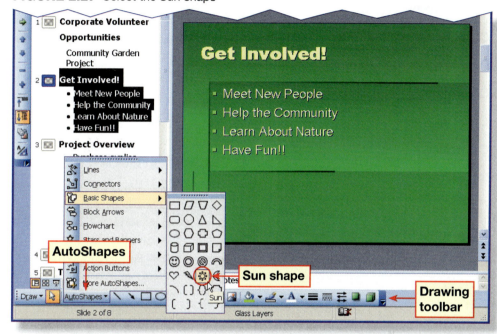

FIGURE 2.28 Sun shape added to slide

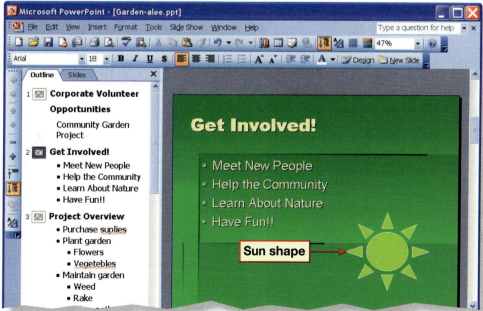

Lesson 2: Exercise 2-11

PowerPoint 51

LESSON 2 Concept Review

Key Terms

AutoContent Wizard

Chart

Clip Art

Comments

Compare and Merge

Content

Datasheet

Demote

Diagram

Markups

Object

Promote

Revisions task pane

Table

Template

Thesaurus

Tracking

WordArt

Reviewing Key Terms

Complete the following statements on a separate piece of paper. Choose from the Key Terms list on the left to complete the statements.

1. The _____ button changes text to the next higher level. (p. 42)
2. Use _____ to combine and identify comments and changes made to multiple copies of the same presentation into one presentation. (p. 58)
3. The PowerPoint _____ feature uses different colors to show the changes made to a presentation by different people. (p. 59)
4. The _____ allows you to quickly and easily view a list of suggested changes to a presentation. (p. 59)
5. Decorative text such as shadowed, rotated, and stretched text is called _____. (p. 52)

Key Term Activity

6. Create a five-question quiz in the form of a PowerPoint presentation based on this lesson's Key Terms and their definitions.
    A. Choose five Key Terms. Describe each Key Term in your own words.
    B. Create a 10-slide presentation. On the first slide, display one Key Term. On the second slide, display the Term's definition.
    C. Create slides for the remaining four Key Terms.
    D. Present your quiz to a classmate or to the entire class.

Reviewing Key Facts

Answer the following questions on a separate sheet of paper.

7. Where can you find a list of templates to use when creating a new presentation? (p. 38)
    A. Revisions task pane
    B. Drawing toolbar
    C. New Presentation task pane
    D. Thesaurus

8. What appears as small yellow boxes on a slide? (p. 57)
    A. Pictures
    B. WordArt
    C. Clip Art
    D. Comments

9. Which button would you use to decrease the level of selected text? (p. 42)
    A. Lower
    B. Demote
    C. Decrease
    D. Delete

10. You use which feature to give a presentation a consistent look and feel? (p. 38)
    A. Template
    B. Comments
    C. Compare and Merge
    D. Demote

Lesson 2: Concept Review

EXERCISE 2-12: Add WordArt to a Slide

WordArt allows you to turn text into artwork. As with any graphic, WordArt can make your presentation more effective. Too much WordArt will distract your audience.

FIGURE 2.29 WordArt Gallery dialog box

FIGURE 2.30 Inserted WordArt

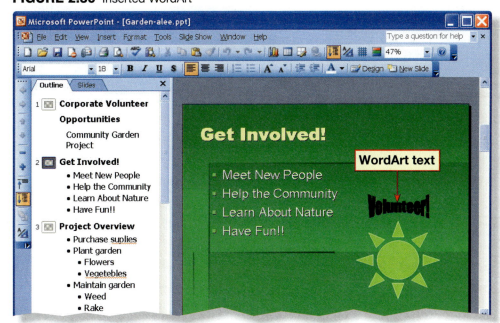

Step-By-Step

1. In your **Garden** file, select **Slide 2**.
2. On the **Drawing** toolbar, click **Insert WordArt**.
3. Click the WordArt style box shown in Figure 2.29. Click **OK**.
4. In the **Edit WordArt Text** dialog box, key: Volunteer!
5. Click **OK**.
6. Position the WordArt so it is above the sun shape. Deselect the text.
7. **CHECK** Your screen should look similar to Figure 2.30.
8. Save your file.
9. Continue to the next exercise.

You Should Know

To edit WordArt, double-click the WordArt text to open the **Edit WordArt Text** dialog box.

LESSON 2 Quick Reference

The following main commands were covered in the lesson. See Appendix A on page 151 for a listing of all the commands used in this book.

Function	Button	Menu	Keyboard	Speech
Choose a design template	Design	Format>Slide Design	ALT + O / D	✓
Compare or merge multiple presentations		Tools>Compare and Merge Presentations	ALT + T / P	✓
Create a shape	AutoShapes	Insert>Picture>AutoShapes	ALT + I / P / A	✓
Create slides based on an outline		Insert>Slides From Outlines	ALT + I / F	✓
Find a synonym		Tools>Thesaurus	SHIFT + F7	✓
Insert a chart		Insert>Chart	ALT + I / H	✓
Insert a comment		Insert>Comment	ALT + I / M	✓
Insert a diagram		Insert>Diagram...	ALT + I / G	✓
Insert an object		Insert>Object...	ALT + I / O	✓
Insert a picture		Insert>Picture>From File	ALT + I / P / F	✓
Insert a table		Insert>Table	ALT + I / B	✓
Insert Clip Art		Insert>Picture>Clip Art...	ALT + I / P / C	✓
Insert WordArt		Insert>Picture>WordArt...	ALT + I / P / W	✓
Spell check a presentation		Tools>Spelling	F7	✓
View markup comments		View>Markup	ALT + V / A	✓

Lesson 2: Quick Reference

EXERCISE 2-13:
Insert an Object into a Presentation

You can easily insert files from other Microsoft applications into a presentation. The inserted item is called an **object**. Word documents, Excel spreadsheets, and Access databases are treated as objects by PowerPoint once they are inserted into a presentation.

Step-By-Step

1. In your **Garden** file, select **Slide 5**.

2. Choose **Insert>New Slide**. Close the task pane.

3. In the title box, key: **Team Time Commitments**.

4. Choose **Insert>Object**. Click **Create new**.

5. Under **Object type**, click **Microsoft Excel Chart** (see Figure 2.31). Click **OK**.

6. Click the **Sheet1** tab. In the worksheet, right-click **1** (Row 1). Click **Clear Contents**.

7. Click cell **B1**. Key: **Team A**. Press TAB.

8. Key: **Team B**. Press TAB. Key: **Team C**.

9. **CHECK** Your worksheet should look like Figure 2.32.

Continued on the next page.

FIGURE 2.31 Insert Object dialog box

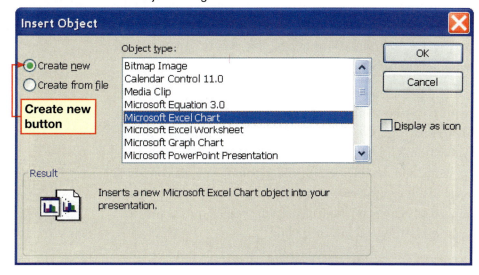

FIGURE 2.32 Excel worksheet inserted into slide

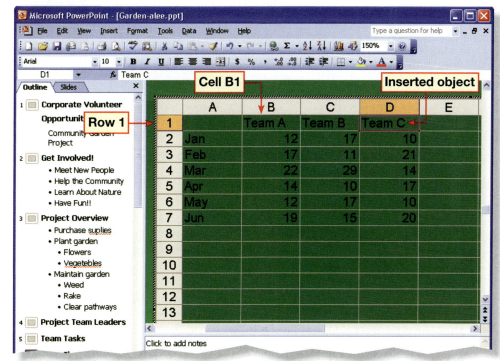

Lesson 2: Exercise 2-13   PowerPoint 53

21st Century LEARNER

Develop Media Literacy

Two rival baseball teams play a major game. In the winning team's hometown, the local newspaper tells one story. In the losing team's hometown, the local newspaper tells a different story. You ask yourself, "Why might the two newspapers have different perspectives on the same game?"

When people use the term "literacy," they are usually referring to the ability to read and write. "Media literacy" means having the ability to analyze and evaluate the hundreds of messages you get every day from all types of media. These media can include print, video, radio, and the Internet. Anything from the media contains a message that is created for a purpose. Being "media literate" means learning to recognize and evaluate the purposes behind the messages that you are hearing, seeing, or reading.

MEET THE MANAGER

Media literacy is important because the media can have a tremendous influence on how you see your world and your community. "We are the eyes, ears, and voice of the community," says Susan Tordella, editor of the weekly community newspaper the *Littleton Independent*, in Littleton, Massachusetts. "We collect information and we share it. I judge our success when I see our stories and photos tacked to refrigerators and bulletin boards at schools and businesses." Ms. Tordella believes community newspapers are like the hub of a wheel, keeping the community connected.

Being media literate means being critical of everything you read, hear, or see.

SKILLBUILDER

1. **Define** In your own words, explain what it means to be "media literate."

2. **Compile** Keep a one-day media journal. Record every type of media you encounter during the day. Which type of media did you encounter the most throughout the day?

3. **Compare** Locate one local newspaper and one national newspaper. Compare the first pages of each newspaper. How are they different, and how are they similar? Does the local newspaper seem to have a different perspective from the national newspaper? Why or why not?

EXERCISE 2-13: (Continued)
Insert an Object into a Presentation

Step-By-Step

10. Click cell **B2**.
11. Key: 20. Press TAB.
12. Key: 10. Press TAB. Key: 10.
13. Click cell **B3**.
14. Complete the worksheet using the information shown in Figure 2.33.
15. Click the **Chart 1** tab. Click off the chart to deselect the object.
16. **CHECK** Your screen should look like Figure 2.34.
17. Save your file.
18. Continue to the next exercise.

FIGURE 2.33 Completed Excel worksheet

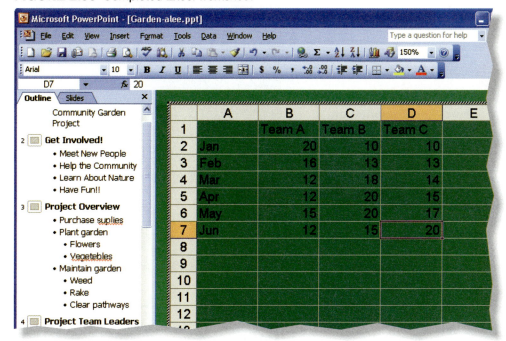

FIGURE 2.34 Final Excel chart

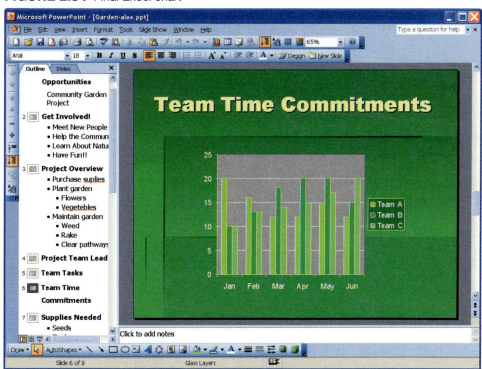

You Should Know

You can also create a worksheet in Excel and import it into your PowerPoint presentation by choosing **Create from file** in the **Insert Object** dialog box.

Lesson 2: Exercise 2-13   PowerPoint 54

Step-By-Step

EXERCISE 2-19: (Continued)
Create a Presentation with the AutoContent Wizard

7 Click **Next**. The **Presentation style** page appears.

8 Select **On-screen presentation** button. Click **Next**. The **Presentation options** page appears.

9 In the **Presentation title** box, key: Study Strategies (see Figure 2.47).

10 Click **Next** to continue to the **Finish** page.

11 Read the last **AutoContent Wizard** dialog box. Click **Finish**.

12 Choose **File > Save**. Ask your teacher where you should save your file.

13 Name your new file: AutoContent-[your first initial and last name]. Click **Save**.

14 **✓CHECK** Your screen should look like Figure 2.48.

15 Close your file. Close PowerPoint.

FIGURE 2.47 Presentation title

FIGURE 2.48 New presentation

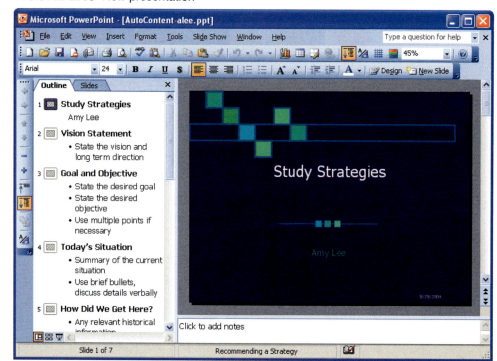

Lesson 2: Exercise 2-19   PowerPoint   61

EXERCISE 2-14:
Use the Thesaurus

Slides that contain many words are difficult to read. Your text has to say exactly what you want to say in as few words as possible. The **Thesaurus** contains groups of words with similar meanings, allowing you to pick the exact word you need.

FIGURE 2.35 Thesaurus

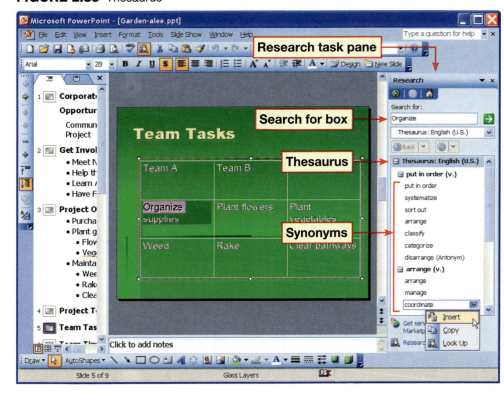

FIGURE 2.36 Replaced word

Step-By-Step

1. In your **Garden** file, select **Slide 5**.

2. In the table, select the word **Organize**.

3. Choose **Tools > Thesaurus**.

4. In the **Research** task pane, move your pointer over **coordinate**. Click the drop-down arrow (see Figure 2.35).

5. Click **Insert**. Close the **Research** task pane.

6. **CHECK** Your screen should look like Figure 2.36.

7. Save your file.

8. Continue to the next exercise.

Tips and Tricks

You can hold down **Alt** and click on a word to view the definition and open the Thesaurus.

Step-By-Step

1. In PowerPoint, select **View>Task Pane** to open the task pane.

2. Click the **Other Task Panes** drop-down arrow. Select **New Presentation**.

3. In the **New Presentation** task pane, click **From AutoContent wizard** (see Figure 2.45).

4. Read the **Start** page of the **AutoContent Wizard** dialog box. Click **Next** to continue.

5. One the **Presentation type** page, click **General**. Select **Recommending a Strategy**.

6. **CHECK** Your dialog box should look like Figure 2.46.

Continued on the next page.

Tips and Tricks

Press ENTER to advance quickly through the steps in the **AutoContent** wizard.

EXERCISE 2-19:
Create a Presentation with the AutoContent Wizard

An **AutoContent wizard** presentation is a collection of slides that work together to create a particular type of presentation. Available presentation types include Recommending a Strategy, Business Plan, Employee Orientation, and Marketing Plan. Each slide in the presentation is a template in which you can add your own content. These templates make it easier to create professional presentations quickly.

FIGURE 2.45 New Presentation task pane

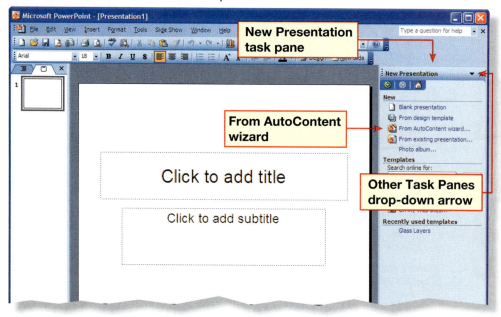

FIGURE 2.46 AutoContent Wizard Presentation Type page

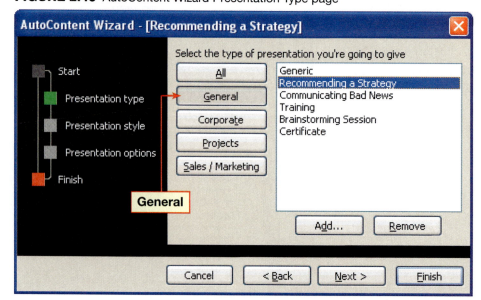

Lesson 2: Exercise 2-19

PowerPoint 60

Step-By-Step

1. In your **Garden** file, select **Slide 3**.
2. Click **Spelling**.
3. In the **Spelling** dialog box, under **Suggestions**, click **supplies** (see Figure 2.37). Click **Change**.
4. The Spelling Checker locates **Vegetebles**. Under **Suggestions**, click **Vegetables**. Click **Change**.
5. When the spelling check is complete, click **OK**.
6. **CHECK** Your screen should look like Figure 2.38.
7. Save your file.
8. Continue to the next exercise.

Tips and Tricks

When you see a misspelled word, you can right-click the word and choose the correct spelling from the list that appears.

EXERCISE 2-15: Use the Spelling Checker

You should always use the Spelling Checker to make sure every word in your presentation is spelled correctly. PowerPoint also checks words against its built-in dictionary as you create each slide. A wavy red line appears under any words that the dictionary does not recognize.

FIGURE 2.37 Spelling dialog box

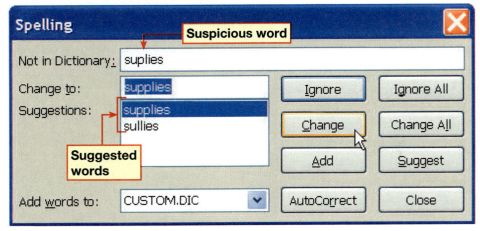

FIGURE 2.38 Spelling check is complete

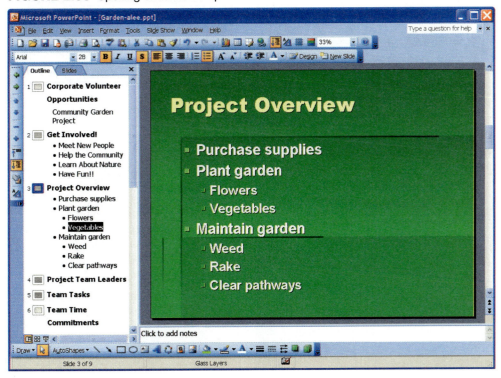

Lesson 2: Exercise 2-15

PowerPoint 56

Step-By-Step

1. In your **Garden2** file, select **Slide 3**.

2. On the **Revisions** task pane, click the first markup.

3. Click in the box next to **Inserted "Garden"** to accept the change.

4. **✓CHECK** Your screen should look like Figure 2.43.

5. On the **Reviewing** toolbar, click **Unapply** to reject the change.

6. Click **Next Item**.

7. Click **Apply** to accept the change.

8. **✓CHECK** Your screen should look like Figure 2.44.

9. Click **End Review...**. Click **Yes**.

10. With your teacher's permission, print your presentation. Save and close your file. Continue to the next exercise.

EXERCISE 2-18:
Track, Accept, and Reject Changes

PowerPoint provides markups by **tracking**, or recording the changes made by the reviewer to your document. The **Revisions task pane** allows you to view a list of changes made by each reviewer.

FIGURE 2.43 Reviewer markup

FIGURE 2.44 Accepted and rejected changes

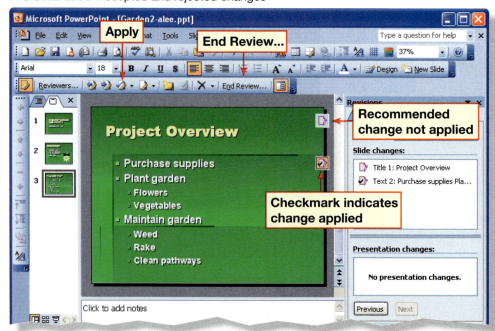

Lesson 2: Exercise 2-18

PowerPoint 59

EXERCISE 2-16:
Add, Edit, and Delete Comments

Before you deliver a presentation, you might want to have coworkers review it and suggest improvements. Or, you might review a co-worker's presentation. You can add **comments** to the presentation so he or she can see what your suggestions are. Comments are like sticky notes that appear as small boxes on the slide.

FIGURE 2.39 Comment added to slide

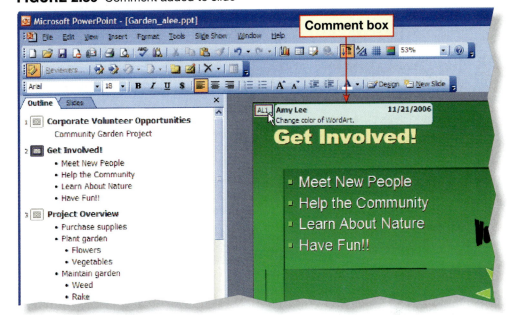

FIGURE 2.40 Slide with edited comment

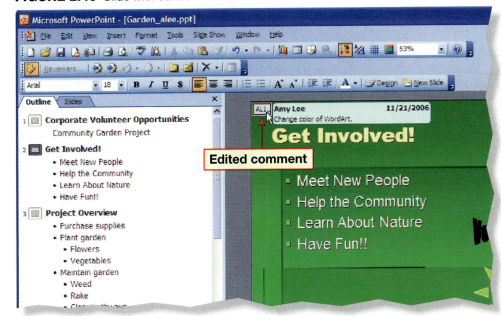

Step-By-Step

1. In your **Garden** file, select **Slide 2**.

2. Choose **Insert > Comment**. In the comment box, key: Change color of WordArt.

3. Click outside the comment box. Place your pointer over the comment.

4. **CHECK** Your screen should look like Figure 2.39.

5. Right-click the comment box. Click **Edit Comment**.

6. Replace the text with: Add effect to WordArt. Click outside the comment box.

7. Right-click the comment box. Click **Delete Comment**.

8. Press CTRL + Z. Place your pointer over the comment.

9. **CHECK** Your screen should look like Figure 2.40.

10. With your teacher's permission, print the document. Save and close the file. Continue to the next exercise.

EXERCISE 2-17:
Compare and Merge Presentations

Your coworker reviewed your presentation, added changes, and returned her edited file to you. To see her comments and changes, you must **compare and merge** her document with your original document. When you merge the presentations, PowerPoint shows you all of the reviewer's **markups**. Each markup is presented in a call-out box with the reviewer's initials or name and change or comment details.

FIGURE 2.41 Original presentation

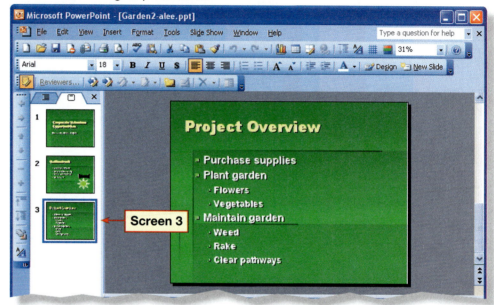

FIGURE 2.42 Merged presentation

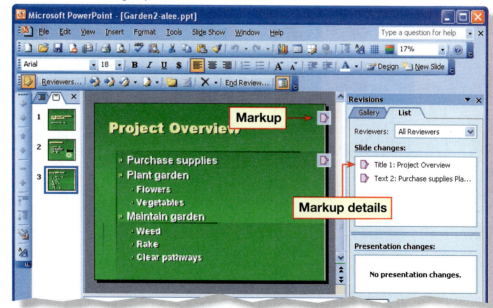

Step-By-Step

1. Open the data file **Garden2**. Save your file as: Garden2-[your first initial and last name]. Select **Slide 3**.

2. **CHECK** Your screen should look like Figure 2.41.

3. Choose **Tools > Compare and Merge Presentations**.

4. Locate and select the data file **Garden_reviewed**.

5. Click **Merge**. Click **Continue**.

6. **CHECK** Your screen should look like Figure 2.42.

7. Choose **View > Markup**. The markups are hidden.

8. Choose **View > Markup**.

9. **CHECK** Your screen should once again look like Figure 2.42.

10. Save your file.

11. Continue to the next exercise.

Lesson 2: Exercise 2-17

PowerPoint 58